MINDLESS BODY, ENDLESS SOUL 1

Amar J. Singh, MD, DFAPA
and Danvir Singh

MINDLESS BODY, ENDLESS SOUL 1

iUniverse books may be ordered through booksellers or by contacting:

iUniverse
1663 Liberty Drive
Bloomington, IN 47403
www.iuniverse.com
1-800-Authors (1-800-288-4677)

ISBN: 978-1-5320-4007-8 (sc)
ISBN: 978-1-5320-4006-1 (hc)
ISBN: 978-1-5320-4005-4 (e)

Library of Congress Control Number: 2018901135

Print information available on the last page.

iUniverse rev. date: 02/15/2018

PREFACE AND INTRODUCTION

This book was inspired by the great wise people of the world who have hunted for the soul, from ancient humans to philosophers, neuroscientists, religious sages, atheists, and common people. This journey has been arduous and difficult to get a handle on. Everyone has the desire to find the answer to this myth or reality including me. Mystics tried their best to explain it through their experience and imaginations, lacking scientific tools, which fortunately we have now. Humans had a long, evolutionary transformation, which they followed regularly with the development of the brain (especially the frontal lobe).As philosophies evolved, so did religions. Science took a leap but remained unable to explain the nature of the soul. Descartes did try to explain it in scientific terms with the knowledge he had at the time, but he fell short of explaining the true nature of the soul. I was highly moved by Dr. Penfield, who, during his experiments mapping the functions of various parts of the brain to connect them with various functions of the body explained that there is something higher than the function of the neurons of the brain. He called it higher neuronal "functions." Neuroscientists were and are still trying to understand how the brain combines all the actions, thoughts, and results. We have billions of neurons acting at the same time. They concluded that because of the connections between various parts of the brain, we are able to coordinate all these function in fractions of seconds. John Dylan has postulated that a decision is made seven seconds before an action is taken. To this question, my exclusive view is that it is the magnetic soul that acts as an additional mechanism to coordinate multiple tasks and decisions made in the fraction of a second. Neuroscientists call it combining theory, which is fully explained in this book. I learned about the action potential of the neurons. Physiologists found that there is an electric current that controls all bodily functions. When I learned that all electric currents produce electromagnetic fields, it gave me insight to carry on this scientific research. My own conclusion was that it is the electromagnetic field that controls not only bodily functions but our behaviors, emotions, feelings, thoughts, and actions. In order to pay my respects to those who dedicated their lives in search of the soul, I decided to name this magnetic energy "soul." Readers and researchers have an open-ended wish to call this form of energy of the brain whatever they wish to, but I am going to stick to the soul. My gratitude goes to Richard Swinburne, who, without any hesitation, stood by his belief in the existence of the human soul. He argues that there really are mental events and states that are different from brain processes and observable public behaviors, and they really do make a difference to the organism's public behaviors. We can only make sense of the continuity of this conscious life by supposing that there are two parts to a person. The body is the ordinary material object, and the brain is an essential part of it and is connected to the soul. This book explains in depth the statement of Richard Swinburne, who predicted that someday, we will have a scientific answer to the burning question of *soul* in his YouTube interview. This book is not a text but a simplified version of neurology and neuroscience. I have made a sincere effort to simplify the neurology part of the chapter, but names of the parts are unchangeable, so I could not be helpful to my readers in that. If you feel the need to learn and understand neuroscience to integrate the scientific concept of the soul, then please feel free to read the chapter. If not, you can skip that chapter. Putting it all together will allow you to make full sense and achieve understanding of the concept of the soul. Our thoughts and feeling do not exist in thin air or a vacuum.

There is an appropriate energy and existence somewhere, which was ignored and taken over by mystics, who used their imagination and wisdom to explain human actions and thinking. Human brain science is a fast-moving field with new inventions and tools to acquire knowledge of how the brain works. These laboratory studies educate us and give us information about how the human body and brain work. Based on such scientific studies, I have made an effort to explain the anatomy and physiology of the soul. The brain is the ultimate organ. It sits in the dark box of our skull, and by it, we navigate through this world throughout our entire life. Though we humans have tried to search for our soul, now, in these modern scientific times, we do not have to search because it resides within us and in all living creatures. Countless philosophers, religious sages, and neuroscientists have dedicated their lives to understanding the mechanisms by which we think and have emotions, desires, beliefs, wisdom, and spirituality. We operate as an automatic machine day in and day out. Though we have many questions remaining, I am sure as our knowledge about neuroscience grows, we will be able to find more answers to our questions, especially in the chapter of neuroscientific investigations to support my hypotheses of the magnetic soul.

The goal of writing this book is not only to elucidate current scientific explanations of how our brain works in day-to-day life events but also to create an interest in neuroscience, psychiatry, and psychology, so researchers conduct further studies in this field of science and probe further to seek answers for our lives. They may someday find answers for the mental illnesses and behavioral problems we face in this world. Our consciousness, thoughts, and feelings have a neurological basis. They all are based on the principle of energy use, so I have made an effort to explain to every human being so he or she can understand how humans function and how they can apply their knowledge to gain wisdom and spirituality and live a healthy and happy life. Sharon Beagle, in her book *Train Your Mind and Change Your Brain*, writes that one of the questions raised by his holiness Dalai Lama was particularly provocative: can the mind change the brain? He had raised this question with scientists many times over the years; he usually received a dismissive answer. After all, one of the cardinal assumptions of neuroscience is that our mental process stems from brain activity: the brain creates and shapes the mind, not the other way around. But the data reported suggests there may be a two-way street of causality, with symptomatic mental activity resulting in the very structure of the brain. I concur with this scientific fact. In this book, you will find that many neuroscientists have produced studies with scientific data that meditation can cause neurogenesis and neuroplasticity throughout our entire life regardless of our age. Neurogenesis occurs in the dentate nucleus of the brain. How we train our brain to achieve that goal has been answered by Jon Kabata-Zinn, PhD, in his book *Full Catastrophe Living*. He has cited many studies to prove the neuroanatomical changes in our brain. His program is the mindfulness-based reduction program of stressful reduction (MBSR) clinic at the University of Massachusetts

Medical Center. For enthusiasts, I strongly recommend the book and the program at the clinic. My theory enhances the concept based on energy generated by our nervous system and the rest of the body. There is an enormous amount of electric current generated in our body and brain; all the functions of our brain and body are based on this electric current, which generates an electromagnetic field. I call this electromagnetic field the soul. Our soul interacts with our neurons, and this form of energy generates thoughts, consciousness, emotions, feelings, love, and all aspects of our behaviors and actions through a two-way mechanism. Our soul and neurons have a symbiotic relationship. One cannot survive without the other. Both work together to promote wisdom, spirituality, beliefs, and the way of life we choose to live. I have explained all in this book.

Physiologists and neuroscientists have studied action potential and mechanisms of electrical activity and conduction to and from the brain in various parts of the body extensively. As a matter of fact, some neuroscientists (Penfield) have suggested that physicists may have learned how to produce and distribute electricity from human physiology. The evolutionary physiologists have studied genetic makeup, the structure of the human cells, and functioning of the cells, but seldom have these scientists given any account of important aspects and characteristics of humans, like feelings, desires, hope, beliefs, and emotions. Orthodox neuroscience has basically abandoned the centuries-old concept of the soul and focused on the mind. There are many explanations of the mind in philosophy. I do not believe or buy the concept of the mind. Is it energy or a composite of energies? Does it exist in imagination or in a vacuum. Is the mind a material, or is it a functional unit of the brain? In either case, what exactly is it—air, metal, or cell bodies? Is it attached to something? Is it the sum total description of the functioning of the brain or body or both? Is it a mystery invented by mystics? Is it a physical property of living beings? Then why don't neuroscientists, neurophysiologists, or some other kind of scientists explain it? I propose you read the "Structure of the Soul" chapter in this book to replace the concept of the unknown mind. The new science will start explaining the body-soul interaction so we are able to understand and investigate the mechanisms involved in human and animal behavior. My view of the soul is clear; every living creature has a soul, including trees and shrubs.

Love is a higher neuronal function. Our love is felt and initiated in our soul in a magnetic form of energy. A mother's love has additional mechanisms; it is not only nine months of pregnancy, where the fetus gets all the nutrition, neurotransmitters, hormones, and various chemicals through the placenta and umbilical cord. Besides rearing and protecting the baby, mothers love their babies. There is an unconditional truth of a mother's love. The truth is that all the mitochondria in the fetus come from the mother's egg. After fertilization, the tail of the sperm, which has small percentage of mitochondria, is shed, and fetus has all the mitochondria in each cell of the body. Mitochondria are the soul of the cell and provide oxygen and nutrition to each cell of our body regardless of the sex of the fetus. My hypothesis is that we all have soul energy from our mother's cells in the cells of our body; therefore, love for our mothers and the love of our mothers is unconditional and everlasting in our lives. Without mitochondria, a cell cannot survive. I have explained in a later chapter that the soul is the seat of our love for our mothers and vice versa.

The anatomy and physiology of consciousness and unconsciousness is very well defined in this book; as we understand very well that neurons and synapses grow at a fast pace in young children. At or around age twenty-five, there is a pruning of our dendrites and synapses. This process of neurogenesis and neuroplasticity continues throughout our entire lives as our learning process continues. My hypothesis is that some of our neurons, dendrites, and synapses die forever, and memory of our experiences disappears forever because there is no magnetic energy generated. This file disappears from the soul's cloud computing system. Some of the neurons, dendrites, and synapses remain dormant and still store the memory and experiences of our lives. They produce some magnetic energy, and at times, these dormant connections become an unconscious part of our lives, which could be stimulated during sleep, hypnosis, and therapy sessions by analysts or professional psychiatrists and therapists. At times, even a symbolic representation of past experiences that remain dormant can be stimulated, and such thoughts or events can become activated and become conscious events or thoughts. Dreams could be explained on such anatomical and physiological bases. Activation of such neurons and synapses produces bizarre and sometimes real events of our life in our dreams. Neurons, dendrites, and synapses that remain active and continue to form new connections become the conscious parts of our lives. This process continues throughout our entire lives, and our brain becomes the site of our consciousness. The brain never stops producing electromagnetic energy even while we are asleep. This is how our magnetic soul keeps storing memories and experiences. For example, if you get bitten by a snake in your dream, you will feel the same pain and fear as if you were awake. This pain goes away when we wake up from our dream. In a nutshell, the neurons, dendrites, and synapses that remain activated give rise to our consciousness, and those neurons, dendrites, and synapses that remain dormant give rise to unconsciousness. Wisdom is an evolutionary process; though our brain is the primary organ for storing the knowledge and experience gained in our lifetimes, higher neuronal mechanisms are the function by which our wisdom is demonstrated. It is the magnetic energy of our soul that hosts our wisdom and makes it available to us on demand when needed. It starts with Amar's six A's, which are the primary ingredients to attain wisdom:

1. Accumulation of information
2. Assimilation and processing of information
3. Association of information
4. Authorization of the information to be dispersed
5. Availability
6. Addition

All of these are explained in the chapter "Wisdom and the Soul." The frontal lobe and all sensory apparatuses are involved in attaining a state of wisdom. Spirituality is the final stage of wisdom. To attain this state in one's life, each step of wisdom has to be attained. Meditation and yoga practice are major factors in reaching such a state of mind, which is the goal of those humans who wish to have such a blessing.

CHAPTER 1

HISTORY OF THE SOUL

A s human beings, we have an ultimate desire to search for the "soul" and to understand the origin and existence of the soul. Philosophers, religious sages, neuroscientists, psychologists, doctors, and intellectuals have made numerous efforts to explain the soul. Some have rejected the notion of the existence of the soul. Some have given it a different name and tried to explain what it is. Is it material or nonmaterial? Mortal or immortal? Functional or nonfunctional? Is it relevant or irrelevant? Inside or outside of the body? Is it part of God or independent of any supernatural being? The soul has the goal of joining God. Is it different from animals and plants and nonliving objects? Many opinions and beliefs have been expressed about the existence or nonexistence of the soul. Some have asserted that it is a part of the body; some have argued it is independent of the body. Some claim there are multiple souls, and some say that there is but a single soul. Some have related it to spirits, some to "jeeva-atman," according to Vedic Hindus (1:36). According to Abrahamic religions, only humans have souls. Jainism believes that even nonliving objects have souls, like a flower that has a bulb underground.

The English word *soul* originated from the old English word *sawal*. In the eighth century, Old High German called it *Seual Sela*. Old Franconians called it *sela*. Lithuanians called it *siela*. It meant "coming from the sea."

1

Koine Greek used the word *psyche* (life, spirit, consciousness). It was derived from a verb that means "to cool," "to blow" (related to breathing). Hebrews called it NEPHEH, which means "vital breath of life." Ancient Greeks created the concept of being "ensouled."

Erwin Rohde refers to the soul as lifeless when it departs the body and with no hope to return to the body. According to Christianity, each individual soul is created by God either at the moment of conception or at some later time. The soul comes from natural generation.

Hinduism started with the Vedas, the Bhagavad Gita and the Upanishads. The Vedas were recorded around 4000 BC. (2, 19) According to Eknath, the Upanishads existed before or around 6000 BC. Around 2000 BC, Indo-Europeans, called Aryans, entered India through the Hindu Kush in the Indus Valley (2'16, 17).

According to the Bhagavad Gita, Krishna is a symbol of *atman* (soul), and Arjuna is the symbol of the deepest self (3, 84). They found a civilization thousands of years old with advanced technology. They worshiped natural forces and the elemental power of life: sun and wind, storm and rain; dawn and night, earth, heaven, and fire. Hindus refer to the soul as the *jiva*, with *atman* meaning the individual self. According to Advita, those who are advanced and have realized the truth are considered to have energy (*sakti*), knowledge, or consciousness. Jiva atman, or the soul, stands as a symbol of cognizance (1'100). Paranas were described as life energy in the Upanishads (2'123), which explains life and death. When the soul attains illuminations, it goes beyond the confines of Parakriti into the spiritual realms of Purusha. Until then, the soul must learn to deal with these powerful forces (3'221). *Sattva* means "goodness, purity, light, harmony, and balance." It is at the highest level of being human. *Rajas* means "anger, hatred, greed, and motivation to act." Rajas provide motivation, which is not a bad thing in the evolution of the soul. *Gunas* and *tams* mean "inertia, darkness, ignorance, and insensitivity"; in any given personality, all three gunas are likely to be present. All these explain experiences. Any one of these gunas could be dominant or weak and balanced (3).

In Hinduism, the Sanskrit word *soul* means 1) jiva, 2) atman, and 3) purusha, meaning individual selves. Hindus emphasize the individual self and mental faculties of the self to deal with desires, thinking, understanding, reasoning, and self-image (ego). All sects of Hinduism agree that the soul is related and controlled by Brahman (Paramatman). The atman, "the soul," involves the process of reincarnation (the life-and-death cycle).

Consciousness is common between soul and Paramatma. The spiritual path consists of self-realization, which turns to Brahman. According to the Bhagavad Gita, there is no birth or death of the soul; it is eternal and cannot be destroyed or slain. It is part of the soul god. When the soul leaves the body, it is called death, and it transmigrates from one body to another body based on the law of karma. If you do good deeds, you transform it into a good body. You will reap the reward of your actions. A super soul exists in every soul. The individual soul is engulfed with material energy; it tries to enjoy the pleasures of life. The Upanishads compare the soul and super soul to two friendly birds sitting on a tree. One of them is eating the fruit (individual soul), and the other bird is watching (super soul) the friendly bird. All of the birds are similar in nature; one is captivated by the fruit of the material tree, while the other is self-satisfied, simply watching the activities of its friend.

The living soul can live in material energy or spiritual energy. The super soul is always eager to take it to spiritual energy. Thus, an intelligent soul who understands the difference between the self soul and super soul can advance toward a blissful eternal life of knowledge. As per Deepak Chopra, the soul is as mysterious as God. The soul is really not personal. The soul does not feel or move. It does not travel with you as you go on in your life. It has no shape. It is impossible to understand. It is a junction between time and the timeless, though we feel it is somewhere. So, it is a mistake to think that soul and personal souls are the same (6'275). According to Chopra, the soul begins at the quantum level and has two parts: jiva, which is life and journey and tells us what type of person you are, and atman, which does not accompany us in the journey of life. It is stagnant. The worst criminal and the holiest saint have the same soul. According to Deepak Chopra, You need jiva to remember who you are personally. You need atman to remember yourself as pure spirit. You need jiva to have reason to act, think, and dream. You need atman for the peace beyond all the actions. You need jiva for the journey through time and space and atman to live in timelessness. Jiva preserves the personality. Atman allows you to become universal beyond identity. The soul is a connection between the five senses and inconceivable things like eternity, infinity, omniscience, grace, and so on. The mind leads to a soul, which leads to God.

Mayans believe in the existence within each individual of various souls, such as shadows, breath, blood, and bones. Loss or death of any one of these souls leads to a specific disease called *susto* in classic Mayan. The Soul is connected with souls who protect them like animals. One can change into coessences, acting like werewolves. Mayans had a whole array of soul companions, which were called *wayob*. After life, Yucatee Mayans believe they descend into an underworld to be restful there, while some go to Flower Mountain, a special aquatic and solar paradise. Pre-Hispanic Mayans commonly buried their loved ones under their houses or in their property, mainly because of their belief in the reincarnation of their ancestors and property being acquired by their ancestors. Thus, they were carefully guarded and considered to be in a place of curation, transformation, and regeneration. Mayans' placement of the dead is not only the disposition of the body but also disposition of the soul and other metaphysical components of the deceased. There is considerable, historic archeological evidence of belief in a "soul"; this links to the belief that there is a link between the mortal body and the immortal soul. Early (1200–900 BC) graves at Ceullo Velize were constructed while the houses were occupied. Both sexes and bodies of all ages were found after the houses were abandoned. They were believed to represent the entire family. This practice is still continued in the highlands of Guatemala. Bloom and Lafarge (1926–1927) reported that in the Chiapas highlands, the dead were buried under their own beds in their houses.

Kings and elders of higher status were worshiped and honored. Some historians indicate that burial of the dead was due to the belief in the transformation of the dead into ancestral spirits, who in modern practice can be used as guides to past souls and mediators between living human beings and powerful cosmic forces. People of higher status were cremated, and their ashes were put in a jar and placed in temples. Rituals were performed, and food was offered on occasion to the souls of the dead. Among the people of some Guatemalan regions, deceased kings were cremated, and from the ashes and bones, artificial body parts were bound with thick gold thread. Even houses were built on the graves of the deceased. Like Hindus, Mayans believed in the immortality of the soul and afterlife possibilities.

Precious stones were placed in the mouths of the dying in order to catch their souls on their departure from their bodies. Some scholars noted the existence of the soul, "the white flowering thing." After death, the soul might go on a journey or remain around the grave and eventually would enter the body of a newborn, usually a grandchild. In some segments of

Mayan culture, the same name was not given to the child because the child would fully acquire the soul, and the deceased one then would not exist.

Native Americans arrived in America in 12,000 BC. Their migration route was from eastern Siberia across the land bridge. Claims were made that they came as early as 25,000 years ago and spread throughout America as time passed (8'11). They believed in a supernatural realm (8'25). They believed in spirits, which were present in animals, streams, trees, and even rocks. Hunters believed that animals would listen to their prayers and accept their sacrifices, and those who didn't listen to their prayers would not be killed.

Shamans or medicine men were believed to manipulate the spirits for the benefit of the community. Shamans also had magical power. The gods they worshipped were sun and fire. Spiritual rituals were performed in a sweat lodge, where people gathered and poured water on hot rocks in a small shed, and heat caused sweating. Tobacco was smoked as a spiritual ritual. Dancing was a ritual, like the snake dance for sufficient rainfall and the corn dance for good production of corn. Plains Indians believed in harmony between humans, animals, and the environment. They accepted the connection between visible and invisible. Theirs was a holistic view of the universe. They understood conscious life, a soul that existed in humans, animals, and plants (9'111). Plains Indians recognized the existence of a powerful spirit being, a holy one above. Many Plains Indians had the concept of three parallel worlds: the sky, the earth, and the underworld. Beneath the surface of lakes and rivers existed a powerful force that controlled animals, plants, and underworld spirits. The sky above was the upper world, dominated by spirits, such as thunder and lightning, which matched the underworld.

SHAMANISM

The word *shaman* possibly originates from Tungusic Evenki, a language of northern Asia. The Evenki word is from the Pali Sanskrit *Sramana*, meaning "ascetic monk, devotee." Shamanism is a practice leading to an altered state of consciousness in order to perceive and interact with the spirit world and direct these transcendental energies into the world. A shaman can enter into a trance-like state during rituals and practices of healing. The term *shamanism* was used by Western anthropologists to refer to the ancient religion of Turks and Mongols. Shamans were thought to heal ailments and illnesses by affecting the soul or spirit, thus restoring the physical body to wholeness. Shamans invoke supernatural powers to obtain solutions to the problems of the community. Shamans may enter the other world to bring guidance to misguided souls and to cure illnesses of the human soul caused by foreign, unknown elements. There is a worldwide movement by scholars to learn and practice shamanism, called "neoshamanism," which claims to gain knowledge via the spirit world. They have dreams or visions that convey certain messages. They may have gained many spirit guides, which guide them into the spirit world. Shamans heal within the spiritual power by returning lost parts of the human "soul." Shamans also cleanse excessive negative energy, which confuses or pollutes the "soul." Shamans can retrieve the soul since they believe that part of the human soul is free to leave the body. It will leave to avoid any damage in case of trauma, and a soul piece may not return to the body on its own. Shamans perform a variety of functions and rituals, depending upon the culture, like storytelling, singing, and fortune-telling to "guide the soul." Shamans may guide the soul of the deceased and cure illnesses. Shamans have long known what neuroscientists are now confirming: there is a power designed to change the brain by lifting up its higher-order neural connections to neurons (9, 122).

Shamanists believe that spirits exist and that they play an important role in human society. Shamanists can foretell the future by their cultural rituals. They create animal images and use them in ritualistic ways to guide humans. Shamans believe that spirits can leave the human body and can find answers using supernatural powers. They have the knowhow and the knowledge to communicate with other spirits and the souls of humans or animals. They can heal the sick spirits (souls) and guide them to follow the path of healing by special rituals designed by a particular culture or cultures, depending upon the belief system of their leaders or the followers of their leaders. Shamans were very well trained to create a state of trance or hypnotism in the masses, thus enriching their beliefs and evoking ecstasy to create a vision of well-being and the future. They would use dance or chants or even hallucinogens, LSD-like substances. Shamans in ancient times used the power of suggestion on their followers—no other force or forces could change the belief or beliefs of the followers. Usually, they used hallucinogens, like mushrooms and alcohol.

Shamanism in Soviet Russia was destroyed by the government.

They were persecuted and accused of being frauds and illogical with their religious beliefs. Islam and Christianity were blamed for eradicating shamanism. Though in literature, Nikolai Gogol, Leo Tolstoy in 1840, and Fyodor Dostoyevsky have contributed a lot to descriptions of the word "*soul*" (colusa). It is based on cultural, life events from a religious and philosophical symbolic perspective. Dusha was a belief in personal identity, behavior, cultural understanding, intellectual depth, compassion, and strength. It is the Russian "soul." According to Dostoevsky, the Russian soul has the power to suffer for others, the will to die for others, and humility for others. In Gogol's writing in 1842, *Dead Souls*, landowners referred to serfs as "souls." Landowner Vissarion Belinskii came up with the term *national soul*, which existed apart from government and was founded in the lives of the lower class. German philosophers had a great influence on the concept of the Russian soul. Friedrich Wilhelm, Joseph Schelling, George Wilhelm, and Friedrich Hegel introduced the concept of the "world soul," a creative connection between humanity and the divine. Hegel developed the concept of a "national spirit." The Slavophil used Hegel's concept of the Russian spirit embodied by the peasantry. Russian soul was an expression of optimism, historical youth, and the ability and wisdom of the peasants to become saviors of the world.

According to the Hindu Vedas, there is nothing absolutely stable, nothing permanent in the whole universe, a system of ceaseless "going on" (*jagati*, collective movement) with everything in it continually moving and changing. Hindus attained and formed their own rituals, which in my opinion they learned from the shamans, who knew they were shamans by themselves. Vedic literature came into writing existence about 6000 BCE, so who is to say Hindus did not practice ancient shamanistic rituals, because shamanism existed since 65,000 BCE. It is the duty of a Brahmin to chant the mantras repeatedly so that necessary vibrations are created again and again for one's own well-being. The power so created can cause the general well-being of the world. Yajna (rituals in Hindu philosophy) has a threefold advantages: 1) well-being through the devas, 2) living happily after death in the world of Devas, and 3) attainment of *moksha*, which means release from the cycle of birth and death.

When I attend any ceremony in a Hindu temple, I watch the Hindu priest performing a ceremony by putting lights (devas) in a metal plate, reciting mantras, and throwing butter (ghee) into them to keep the lights burning repeatedly, which explains the three reasons why they do it. To me, it is a ritual that preexisted Hindu rituals, a shamanic ritual, but was modified as the time passed and thus philosophy and intellectual explanations were developed. An article in the *Times of India* was titled "Rise of the Shamans in India." They believed that all illnesses have spiritual causes, which manifest in the physical body. Hence, healing the spiritual causes healing in the body (18).

Islam means "surrender or submission to the will of God." Muslims have tended to place primary emphasis on obeying or following God's will as set forth in Islamic law. Muslim philosophers agreed with Greek philosophers that the soul has one nonrational and two rational parts. The nonrational was for plant and animal souls. It was considered separate from the body by nature. The rational part of the soul is in the body, and its function is to manage the body, like practical intellect, to manage worldly affairs, and to know eternal aspects of the universe. They thought that the ultimate end or happiness of the soul depended on its ability to separate itself from the demands of the body and to focus on grasping the eternal aspect of the universe. Ibn Sina believed in the "soul," because bodies perform actions with the "will," like seeking nourishment, growing, reproducing, moving, and having perceptions. These functions also belong to entities other than bodies, which he called "souls." According to him, animals and plants have souls because they nourish and grow. The rational soul is defined as primary perfection for the body to act rationally and understand universal facts. The practical soul deals with intellect and gains knowledge to act rationally and properly in the family and in the environment. It must manage its body, family, surroundings, ethics, home, political issues, and others, acknowledging their existence. It manages the realities of natural things, like nature, God, and metaphysical events. The theoretical intellect is the "rational soul" with its face upward. Practical intellect is similar to a "celestial soul." Islam asserts that man was created by Allah, providing him or her an outer structure and inner hidden aspects like the mind, emotions, and soul. The uniqueness of the human's nature lies in the fact that he or she has been endowed with freedom of choice and judgment between right and wrong—the capacity to think, transmit knowledge, feel, and act. It is an immortal soul, which lives on after the death of the physical body and has not been given to other creatures. Although the human body dies, the soul, the personality, has an existence extending beyond the present life; it is a continuous entity whose inner state will accompany it into the hereafter. Thus, the human is a composite of many aspects, levels, and functions, the totality of which represents the reality of human nature (418).

In the Zoroastrian concept of soul, the human is, by origin, a spiritual being, and the soul, in the shape of what Zoroastrians call the *favahr* preexists his body and has five constituents. The first is the body (*abu*), which means the life of human begins implied as earthly existence of the person. According to their belief, the soul was created first and then came the body, which acquired the soul for the function of the body, which has the responsibility to create the material world. It is the duty of the human to nurture and nourish the physical body in order that the "abode of the soul" may be in harmony with other creations. Second is the breath of life, which maintains the natural functions of the body. When it weakens and vanishes, death is the result in the physical world. Third is the soul, *urvana*. It consists of wishes, which may either be good or bad, according to the goodness and badness of the objects wished for. The urvana of a person can be good or evil, depending upon the inner desires and outwardly speech and activity of that person. It is essential therefore that the soul should be in perfect harmony and have control over the body in order that it may direct the person to make the right choices. The soul is the instrument that directs the body, the breath of life, the prototype image, and the guardian spirit (419). The soul fulfils its role through the agency of a number of discernible qualities that an individual is latently deemed to possess. The soul receives its input primarily from its wisdom, innate reason, and intellect, which stimulates the faculty of knowing and will to act in the soul. Enemies of the soul are lies, anger, vengefulness, excessive desire, disrepute, envy, and any attribute that is in excess or deficit in a person. The lie, when it attacks the person, pollutes his or her essence and defiles his or her body by attempting to annihilate the soul. Evil tries to tempt the soul into generating wicked thoughts, uttering wicked words, and performing wicked deeds. If the soul is vanquished, it will find itself in hell upon death, where it will remain until the end of time. Zoroastrianism defines the concept of *khawarr*. Although the soul is the motivating force and the prime mover within the person, khawarr is the god-given talent within the person. He or she must cultivate it to its full capacity, because growth, fulfillment, and prosperity are integral parts of Zoroastrianism. Khwarr is said to have preexisted the person's physical birth; therefore, it should be cultivated and nurtured to its fullest capability and existing potential. (418).

I believe shamans were the first human beings to create the concept of the soul spirit since evolution from unicellular organisms to the multicellular organisms, which were to have multitasked functions. A fish is more complex than a sponge. A bear is more complicated than a snake, and monkey is more complicated and task-oriented than lower animals. In the same way, humans are more multitask-oriented than apes, the closest relatives of humans. Thus we humans are a highly evolved animal species. We can create, invent, write, and store the material as we wish. Thus, we can control all other organisms by using our intellect and multisensory mechanisms. In the survival of the fittest, not only will the strongest survive but the most intelligent will also outsmart the strongest. In my research, I came to believe we humans have a sixth sensory organ that we cannot see. It is the "soul," which has the power of intuition, anticipation, and wisdom and enormous power over other subsouls. Shamans were the first social human beings who created the group system and worked in a cohesive manner, thus following the leader of the group. There were territorial wars and bloodshed for survival, using tools of the time invented by the shamans. We experienced our ability to process knowledge. We can see a stick and find numerous uses for it, not only for fighting, but for staking in the ground and creating a shelter. We can sharpen it and use it as a spear to fish and kill other animals for food. We can burn the same stick and create fire. Early shamans created the valuable and useful food for humans, either through their own experiences or by learning from animals, like monkeys and apes. Thus, our physical arena became a magnificent learning environment. We were able to differentiate between cause and effect, thus learning to avoid causes with harmful effects and seek causes with beneficial effects. Though shamans had their territorial and survival issues, they developed the means of civility and relationship with other groups of Shamans for trade and to exchange goods necessary for day-to-day survival. They developed social, economic, political, and cultural norms of patriarchal and matriarchal family values.

CHINESE PHILOSOPHY OF THE SOUL

The Chinese have given names to the soul in their own language and according to cultural norms and beliefs—Hun po. Hun (2'17) means "cloud soul" and po means "white soul." According to ancient traditions, every human living has "hun," a spiritual yang soul that leaves the body after death and "po," a substantive "yin soul" that remains with corpse of the deceased. According to Daoism, soul stricture has three hun and seven po. According to Yu Ying Shih, current concepts support "hun and po." Hun and po were first recorded during 475–721 BCE. Later historians write "hun" as the "spiritual soul," which makes the personality. "Po" was identified as the vegetative or animal "soul," which signifies physiological growth. More than 2,500 years ago, the Chinese developed hun and po. The ancient Chinese believed that the human body has physical parts and a spiritual part, the "soul." The Body part survives through food and drink and prevails on the earth. The spiritual part depends on chi energy, which comes to the body from heaven. Breathing air is an integral part of survival. But the body and spirit are controlled by the soul, po and hun. The yin, po, and the yang, hun, are Chinese spiritual and medical beliefs in Zang Fu, or "organs." The hun soul is associated with the liver, and po is associated with blood, lungs, and breath. The liver stores blood, hence, "hun" is in the liver. If energy is depleted in the liver, it results in fear and anger. When lung energy is depleted, there is fast breathing to restore the po energy. Hun and po weakness can cause confusion. Some ancient Chinese would put jade stone in the mouth of the deceased in burial ceremonies in the belief it would delay decaying of the body. This all happened during the Hun Dynasty. During this dynasty, the Chinese believed in "hun" as the heavenly soul and po as the earthly soul. During the Dao Dynasty, hun and po were accepted, but they added that the hun wanders about, leaving the body during sleep. They devised methods to restrain hun by keeping humans constantly awake. Daoism developed the methods and rituals to summon the hun and po back into a person's body. Sme minerals were used to perform such a ritual—cinnabar, arsenide, malachite, and magnetite. Mixtures of these metals were put into the mouth of the deceased person and washed with sulfur into the gut, with a belief that the body would rise and be able to live.

BUDDHISM

Buddha grew up in a wealthy family with princely status. While he was a young man, he chose to experience suffering in order to learn about the difference between the luxury of life and suffering. Once he went to a nearby town and met a sick man. On his second trip, he met an old man. On his third trip, he saw people carrying a corpse to its resting place. He learned from this that wealth and privilege offered little protection from suffering. Around the age of twenty-nine, he left his house and began the life of a religious wanderer. For six years, he learned from his spiritual master how to deal with suffering. Around the age of thirty-five, he sat quietly and learned about human conditions. While sitting under a tree, he was enlightened. He foresaw a life of discipline without extremes of self-indulgence or self-modification. According to him, there are basic three things for existence: 1) everything is not permanent, which is the core of existence; 2) there is no self or immortal soul; and 3) suffering and dissatisfaction are the core of existence. He proclaimed we must learn noble truth to overcome sufferings. The first truth is that suffering exists. Second, desires are the root cause of suffering, and third if we get rid of desires, we can end suffering. Fourth is that there is path to enlightenment. Meditation and mindfulness are the path to happiness. According to Buddha, insight, personal transformation, and deep awareness of reality lead to personal and social liberation (22'24).

Scientist and artist Leonardo da Vinci (1452–1519) sought to understand the physical basis of how the body and the mind function. In his earliest anatomical drawings of brain structures, he learned that sensory input comes together; "the sense commune" was the seat of the "soul" in the brain. He injected wax into ventricles of the brain to obtain an accurate model for his drawings. He described how fantasy, imagination, and cognition were related to specific brain sites. He described how the light enters through eyes, which are the windows to the "soul." He was among the first to argue that vision was a matter of light entering the eyes and then being transmitted to the brain. He studied smell and touch. The picture of the enigmatic Mona Lisa show he was a careful observer of the world, the body, and the human "soul"; some thinkers describe the soul as whiskey mixed with water, which means it is part of the body (23'75). This mixture produces an individual. A group of scientists performed an experiment in which they weighed the living body and the dead body and found that a body with life weighed more than its corpse. They attributed the difference to the presence of the "soul" in the body. Many thinkers discarded this hypothesis.

According to Harold Waldwin, the soul is a real, literal fact and is indestructible. Consciousness is the senior element unit in the body, which progresses after experiences and growth of the body. I believe he meant that the "soul" is like the president of a country, which is organized by cabinet members. We have different divisions of government; we have defense, central intelligence, education, health, foreign policy, and numerous other departments with specific functions to create healthy functioning in the country. Our brain has similar departments, which explain and report to the soul their duties and future growth. Our soul, like the president, has the final authority to make decisions that are in the best interests of the individual. The "soul" is the head of the institution, a dean or headmaster of a school who has professors and teachers in different faculties with the specific functions to teach the students. They teach math, science, English, and medicine, but all of this is under the guidance of a dean or headmaster. Without students, teachers, and professors, the institution does not exist. The same holds true for the soul. Without bodily functions, like those performed by the brain, heart, lungs, and other body parts, the soul cannot exist. The soul carries the involuntary and voluntary functions of the body. It interacts between the inside of the body and the external environment by thinking, feeling, and desiring. It reflects the healthy and unhealthy aspects of our body. The soul represents our thinking and various functions of the body. The soul is the seat for attaining perfection and imperfections of the body. The body is subject to death. Scientists have long been trying to extend the life span of the body, but they have not been able to control death. Science has been able to develop stem-cell technology and has mapped out the human genome. We have been able to clone and grow cells to replace organs and some parts of the body. People who hear the word *soul* think it is a religious and cultural belief. When asked how you define it or explain it, no philosophy or religion has been able to describe how it works or what it is made of. So it is a mystery for some.

Some neuroscientists, doctors, and psychologists have abandoned or rejected the existence of a soul, but some avid scientists are still working on it to find an answer. The soul may be a mystery for some, but it is indispensable for living creatures.

GREEK PHILOSOPHY OF SOUL

There were many philosophers in Greek history who talked about the soul. Plato and Aristotle were very well respected and accepted philosophers during their times and even now are held in high esteem. Socrates accepted death and left his legacy for Plato (429–348) BCE. Plato wrote in the form of dialogues in which Socrates was a spokesperson for Plato's own view. Socrates was the first secular saint. In Plato's meeting with Socrates in jail, he claimed the immortality of each person's "soul." Plato's concept was that the human is a soul, by which he meant that there was survival of bodily death by reincarnation from a previous body. This was a very eastern Hindu belief. The soul enters into the new body, and depending upon law of Karma continues and remains immortal till it joins the godly super-soul. Prior to Socrates, Greeks believed that soul leaves the body in the last breath of the person. Plato emphasized that the soul is immortal and is without parts. Plato's view was that the soul detached from the body, remembers past lives, and has the knowledge of necessary truth, or the form that is acquired when released from the body. He added that some are divided into rational spirits and "appetitive" parts. It is the interaction of these parts that explains how people behave. Plato stressed that only the rational part of the soul is immortal; the other perishes with the body. There is a harmony of the soul and reasoning. Thus, it is in one's self-interest for reason to rule; reason dictates whether that person acts selfishly or for the welfare of others. Plato proposed that the soul is made of air, earth, fire, and water (51). According to Plato, the soul is attracted by pleasures of the body, such as food, drink, and sexual satisfaction (Phaedo Gud). These pleasures distract the soul, whose true purpose of being is to reason about and know what is true. Plato describes the immortal part of the human to be situated above the neck and the mortal part to be below the neck. The inferior part of the soul is related to courage, passion, and love. It is situated between the head and the middle of the neck and has functions to control and limit desires (51). Well, it seems to me that he somehow refers to "*chakras*," specifically the seventh and sixth chakras, as per the Hindu philosophy of chakras (20, 315).

THE ARISTOTELIAN PHILOSOPHY

Aristotle (384–322 BCE) suggested that the soul and the body react sympathetically to each other. A change in the state of the soul produces a change in the shape of the body, and conversely, a change in the shape of the body produces a change in the state of the soul. His concern was the relationship of the soul to the body. Aristotle's view was that except for inorganic matter, everything has a psyche or soul, which is significant for life. Most of the soul is inseparable from the body and psyche; at the bottom scale is the nutritive or vegetative soul. This is important for nutrition and reproduction. The sensitive soul accounts for perceptions in the form of touch, sight, taste, smell, and hearing (the five senses). This is the distinction between the plant and animal soul. The core thinking of Aristotle is that the soul is the form or first actuality that potentially has life (*De Anima* 412, 53). The soul is the form of the body and an active and vital principle that informs its body and gives to it its life and configuration. Aristotle clarifies that soul is not, as Plato claims, to be primary substance that either does not exist or could have on its own before it entered the body or could exist independently (once again). According to Aristotle, the soul cannot do these things because it is not a thing or entity that exists on its own, distinct from its body. Aristotle made it clear that the soul could not survive the death of the body. Aristotle maintained the notion that the existence of the soul is the "individual soul-body composite." Thus, it is not the soul but the body that experiences pain, pleasure, desires, and so on. The soul is a subject called "psychological existence" and is aware of the consciousness perception of white color and a sweet taste. In addition to consciousness, attention is what we see and hear; we are aware of both. The same holds true of thinking, hearing, and walking or any other movement in the body. Aristotle also stated that each sense is responsible for the distinction of each one, like the color we see, the sound we hear, the sweetness we taste, the air we smell, and the touch we feel. According to Aristotle, the rational soul can sense and think. Since everything is a potential object of thought, thought is not material. This part of the soul is called intellectual. It can think about something without the actual existence of the object. Thus, it is not to be quantified. Aristotle was not a dualist and maintains that the soul is a substance in its own right, which is separate from its body (26' 27). As described by Aristotle, the soul has the capacity for desire (*De Anima*, 433), which is directed at what is good or believed to be good. Thus, human beings have the power of reasoning and the means to reach the goal. The desires and reasoning process produce the individual's choice to act and initiate bodily movement to achieve the purpose. There is mental and physical causation. Aristotle expanded on the notion of fetal conception and development. He noted that the "vegetative soul" existed potentially in semen and matter supplied by the mother (the egg). Thus, the sensitive soul existed potentially in the vegetative soul and came into being in a similar way. He claimed that the intellectual or rational soul cannot have been generated internally. Intellect comes from without. In the rational soul, there is the power of acting and of being acted upon.

JUDAISM

The Mihnah (Talmud) included a discussion of some topics, such as the immortality of the soul and its superiority to the body, which received little attention. There were many commentators in Jewish holy scriptures. The first Jewish philosopher was Philo (20–40 CE). He more or less followed Plato's concept that God existed from eternity as an immaterial being without the world and then brought the world into existence. God then continued to exist as an immaterial being over and above a material world. Philo accepted Plato's distinction between rational and irrational souls, which were created at the beginning of the world (23'43). The Hebrew Bible (or Christian Old Testament) and the New Testament believe that the soul is trapped inside the human body. After life, they believe in the resurrection of the body. At death and before death, the soul is with God. After death, the spirit will rise and join God. Augustine, who converted into Christianity at the age of thirty-three, maintained the notion that the soul is the principle of life, so everything that is ennobled with a soul is alive, and all those who are not alive are without soul. The view held by Augustine was that the soul by its presence gives life to this earth and the death-bound body. It makes a unified body and maintains it as such, keeping it from disintegrating and wasting away. It balances distribution of nourishment to the body's parts. It preserves the body's harmony, beauty, growth, and reproduction. These faculties are common with plants, since they are alive. Plants preserve their generic being, nourishment, growth, and reproduction. It is God who made the soul for everyone. Animals have all five senses but lack intellect. Augustine believed that each one of us is aware of the soul since we are souls. Reasoning is a strong characteristic of the soul, and it may be a special substance, joined with the body. Since we exist, the external world exists around us. Augustine asked how the soul did not know it is the body by itself. No, it is not the body because it can turn away to God from the body. When the soul knows it is a soul, then nothing is hidden from it. Augustine stated God, the highest substance, existed, while the other substances, including the human soul derived their existence from him. The human soul, which was the vital principle of life, was immaterial, but subject to time, it occupied a midpoint. The divine the corporeal had the capacity to move upward or downward in accordance with its desires, joy, fear, and sorrow. As a principle of motion in bodies, the soul was the source of its own movement, and the knowledge of its ability to displace itself was the motivation behind its will to bring about the motion. Augustine's confession is unique in the ancient literature of the soul, rather than the doctrine that the inner self is veiled, mysterious, or inaccessible. His story hovers between thought and the world before it enters the world (31'10, 11, 15, 16).

According to Augustine, a human is not a body alone, nor a soul alone, but was composed of both. The soul is the better part of a human. When they join, they create a human. When a person is alive, the body and soul are united. The body is the outward person, and the soul is the inward person. In Augustine's view, the dogma of a body's resurrection requires a more intimate relationship between the soul and the body. In sensation, the soul uses the body as an instrument. Inner is our soul, so are our will and reason. Common with the animals are the senses and memory and images of outer things. Memory is a great faculty and an awesome mystery. There is more to the self or person than the mind and memory. Augustine justifies that the human soul is immaterial and immortal by appealing both to Christian scriptures and human psychology. Since humans are made in the image of God, whom he described as immaterial, humans must be immaterial, at least in part. That we can feel pain indicates that the soul permeates the body, which it could not do if it was material, nor could it think. Nobody hates the body; thus, it should be considered as a "temple." Thus, the soul rules the body, and the body acts as a subordinate. He claimed that after death, when the soul is separated from the body, the soul yearns to reunite with the body. His concept was that each person's soul existed before it became associated with the body, but he refused to accept that the soul was put in the body as a punishment for sin. God handed over the soul through the parents. He claimed that the same body that existed on earth goes to heaven, but in the case of people who are deformed, with some exceptions, their deformities would be removed. The exception included the martyrs, whose scars were a badge of honor. After life, those who never grew to maturity, such as aborted fetuses, and those who grew up to maturity but were always deformed, while composed of the same bits as their earthly bodies, would be beautifully formed and mature. Augustine held that there would still be a distinction of the sexes in heaven. Both sexes would retain whatever contributed to their physical beauty. He suggested that, since nothing is hidden in heaven, heavenly bodies would be transparent, inner organs exposed to view.

Bonaventure stated that resurrection is reuniting the body and soul according to nature and hence is a natural event. The corruptible body becomes incorruptible when it joins the soul. God acts like a craftsman in creating a supernatural union of body and soul. If an "ark" is dismantled and then remade from the same planks, according to the same order, we do not say it is another ark but the same. Like Bonaventure, Aquinas was an Italian but a Dominican who spent the important part of his career at the University of Paris. He held the opinion that the human soul is a unity in which there are faculties of power of acting. These faculties are arranged as vegetative, sensitive, and then rational. The passive intellect, a power neither wholly sensitive nor wholly rational, is at the lowest level of the rational faculty. It deals with particular knowledge, not with universals. Above the passive intellect are the active and possible other potential intellects, including intellectual memory.

Grosseteste maintained that the rational soul is infused at conception but uses its lower vegetative and sensitive power until the body develops. Aquinas's view was that prior to the arrival of the rational soul, the growth and organization of the embryo is directed first by the vegetative soul and then subsequently by the sensitive soul, upon whose arrival the vegetative soul is obligated. Both of these souls are biologically transmitted. It is created by God at the end of human generation. Aquinas's view was what we call conception, which is a fertilized egg that eventually develops into an embryo. It is after a while when an immortal soul emerges. In fact, it is not even human. Sensitive and vegetative parts perish with the body, along with other parts. The intellect must remain in the soul after the destruction of the body. The whole body and soul play a part in producing sensations, which belong to both while in union and then to either separately. Some parts of the soul are capable of existing independently of matter and some are not. Those that are capable are spirits or intelligible substances. Some of these, as angles, are capable of spiritual or intelligible substances. What makes them substances? Bonaventure held on to the view that there are two substances. Aquinas maintained the view that immortal matter is the principle of individuation. Thus, there is one angle or separate angles that are assigned to their own species, of which each is the only member. These drastic solutions might have been required for humans as well, if the human rational soul had never joined with matter in the first place to form a human being. Thus, Aquinas held the notion that there is one form of body and soul, which at the time of resurrection is the same one. Human knowledge of particulars requires the sensation or imagination, and this power of the rational soul requires a living body. This knowledge perishes with the body at death. Thus, the separate soul has only abstract, not concrete, knowledge of its previous activities and of the life of the individual. Instead, perhaps in compensation during this phase of its existence, the soul acquires better knowledge of the universe, and other intelligences acquire a deeper understanding of God. Only when it returns with a body at resurrection does the soul acquire concrete knowledge of the whole person's life. But at resurrection, the soul requires power that it had during the separation from the body. Aquinas rejects Plato's notion that the soul is the "pilot of the ship" (104, *Brief History of the Soul*). To him, souls uniting with the body are natural and appropriate. According to Thomas Aquinas, the soul is part of human nature. It can exist apart from the body; it can even be united with the body; thus, it cannot be called an "individual substance." Henceforth, we cannot speak about it as a "person." While the human being is alive, its soul is distinct from the soul of another human being because of the difference of the matter. It is due to the rational account of the soul's individuation. It is due to the relation to the matter in which it exists. Aquinas held the notion that God created the soul and infused it into matter to produce a soul-body complex or a human being. God's creation of the soul is the end of a process that includes the arising and passing away of the vegetative and sensitive soul.

Paracelsus (1493–1541) viewed humans as consisting of three parts—an "elemental body," which is corporeal; an "astral" body, which is not included within the organism but sends out signals to and receives them from the whole universe; and the soul, which is the seat of a human's highest spiritual activity (54). The combination of all three leads to mystical experiences, thereby overcoming illusions of separation. According to him, the human body consists of two kinds of flesh. One of these has the "origin of Adam" and is "coarse," "earthly," and nothing but flesh. It is inherited biologically and may be compared to wood and stone. It is mortal. The other flesh, the astral body, is not from Adam. It is "subtle" and not capable of being bound because it is not made of earth. It is what makes a person of spiritual activities, but it is not human from the beginning. This flesh is "eternal." As per Paracelsus, the human is a divinity making, maturing, and completing the process of life (alchemy), which includes cooking, weaving clothes, inventing medicines and art—because art cannot be completed without blessings and because nature cannot be put to use without art. According to him, God did not create the planets and stars with the intention that they should dominate humans. He gives the example if a weed being swayed back and forth in the water. An animal is swayed the same way. Henceforth, humans are not swayed like animals but can get power over the stars; animals failed to achieve what the human mind has achieved. This would not be possible if humans, like animals, had only elemental and astral bodies. Because humans have a soul, they can rise above the stars and free themselves from them by understanding the natural laws and using them to their advantages and by cultivating spiritual power that goes beyond the natural laws.

A bodily death, a microcosm, is separated from the macrocosm. The elemental body decays and becomes consumed or disintegrated in the ground or burned to ashes. The astral body does not occupy space and has no element of time. It is spaceless and timeless in where it started and where it will end. The astral body is naturally eternal. It will arise from death at resurrection to join the spirit or soul, which has already returned to the "aerial chaos"—God. Paracelsus emphasized that medicine should be learned by one's own experience. As a matter of fact, he threw the book of Galen and Avicenna in the fire in front of his students. He meant medicine is for practicing, which is more important than reading books. As an intellectual and revolutionary man, he became known as "Luther of Medicine." He addressed the issues related to plague and venereal diseases. He wrote a lot about chemistry. Many of his admirers consider him as the father of the medical chemistry. He attributed some forms of mental disturbance to the disruption of the power of attraction from the moon. Some claim that he may have used the word *unconscious* for the first time.

In *De Berub Natura*, Bernardino Telesis (1509–1588) wrote that in humans, there is a biological, inherited material, the "soul," made of the subtlest form of matter, which is located in the brain and is diffused throughout the body. This is the material soul, which slightly differs from the animal soul. This human soul has psychological functions and activities like perceptions, emotions, and memory. In addition, humans are divine and noncorporeal, and the soul is implanted directly by God. This soul functions as a thinker and has desires. Humans have a nonmaterial soul, which makes them have free will. Giordano Bruno's (1548–1600) basic idea was that God is not only transcendent but immanent, above nature but also in nature, as the world soul. He believed that the universe is an animated whole, permeated throughout by the infinite power of God. He thought that all matter, even stones, was infused with a living soul. He called it *monads*, and it appeared to animate everything. At the same time, each monad will come to express itself in an overtly animated being, sometimes playing a minor role and other times becoming the soul of living beings. It is in the intellectual soul infusing matter as a seminal seed that a human body is formed and maintained (54). He added that the human organism is formed by atomic material (atoms) and is constantly changing. The formative soul, which uses replacement atoms, remains the same. He believed that center of the soul is formed and is present in the heart of humans. Thus, upon the death of a human, the governing soul leaves the heart. Having left the human body, it moves to other forms of existence with which it combines, depending on how it lived in its human reincarnation. Bruno felt that the unity of the whole universe comes from the immanent power of God. Monads act through the atoms to energize and construct all possibilities of nature. The goal of human existence is knowledge and to know God through this knowledge, understand nature, and thus get beneath the surface of things to their physical and metaphysical cores. This applies to self-understanding too. Bruno's radical idea did not sit well with the church authorities, and he fled Italy. He was sentenced to death by burning. Since he refused to retract his philosophy, including that Jesus was no bigger God than every human being, he was burned at the stake on February 17, 1600.

In modern science, we understand how we feel, what the blue sky looks like, how the red flames of fire look, how hot and cold are felt, and how taste and smell are processed in our brains. A blind man can understand the physics of blue color, though only the sighted man can understand what it is like to experience blue color. Galileo Galilee (1564–1642) explained that primary qualities (e.g., weight and texture) are inherent in bodies, while secondary qualities (e.g., taste, perceptions, and colors) are not in the external world but in the minds of observers. He described it as primary qualities are objective and secondary ones are subjective. Galileo emphasized the concept of objective and subjective. He pointed out that while we can conceive a material object that has no secondary qualities, for example taste or color, we cannot conceive the material object that lacks primary qualities, like shape or texture. He said let's tickle a marble statue and a human being. Humans can feel the tickling sensation, while the marble statue does not feel the tickling. Thus, the primary qualities are important and awakening, while the secondary qualities can be ignored. Galileo called it natural philosophy, and we modern scientists call it physical science. According to Galileo, we cannot read the book of nature unless we understand the language in which it was written. According to Spinoza, everything behaves in accordance with strictly deterministic laws. All human choices and actions are determined logically by prior events over which humans have no control. So he felt that humans have no free will, though it is the goal of all humans. The only way to do that is to accept one's place in the infinite deterministic system. This does not free one from the web of causality but from anxiety and ignorance. Philosophical understanding brings mental calmness and composure in its wake, which itself is the supreme form of human freedom (56).

DESCARTES RENE (1596–1650)

Descartes wrote (27'19), "There is some deceiver or other, very powerful and very cunning, whoever employs his ingenuity in deceiving me. Then without doubt I exist also if he deceives me as much as he will, he can never cause me to be nothing so long as I think that I am something. So that after having reflected well and carefully examined all things, we must come to the definite conclusion that this proposition I am, I exist, is necessarily true each time that I pronounce it, or that I mentally conceive it" (Descartes 1967, I Meditation on First Philosophy II, 150). In *The Passion of the Soul*, translated by John Nottingham, Descartes speaks of the flow of animal spirits. In modern neuroscience, we talk about synapses or a synaptic knob. Descartes speaks of pores through which animal spirits can flow. We neuroscientists claim that long-term memory neurons, which consist of sets of synaptic knobs that are enlarged owing to their use, lead to an increase in synaptic efficacy. I note that we are not aware of any subject who acts more directly upon our soul than the body to which it is joined. Passion of the soul is action of the soul on the body. We need to examine to which of the two we should attribute each of the functions present in us. Anything we experience as being in us and that we see can also exist in wholly inanimate bodies must be attributed only to our body. On the other hand, anything in us that we cannot conceive in any way as capable of belonging to a body must be attributed to our soul. Philosophy was based on a hard distinction between the body and soul (29'174). Action and the movement of limbs proceed from the body and thought from the soul. Since we have no concept of thought, we have every reason to believe that thoughts present in us belong to the soul. Since our dead body is heatless and motionless, the presence of the soul creates motion and action in our bodies. Descartes amazingly described the anatomy, physiology, and mechanism of how blood is pumped and flow reaches all parts of the body, providing nourishment and oxygen to the various parts of the body and creating movement in the body. All the movement of the muscles and all sensations depend on nerves, which are like little threads or tubes coming from the brain. He differentiated the fresh, oxygenated blood, which supplies the whole body, from the unoxygenated blood, which is sent to the lungs to get oxygenated and returns back to the heart. This is due to the pulsating of the heart, which is repeated twenty-four/seven to continue the process and create movement in the body.

Animal spirit is created in the brain. Blood is constantly pumped to the brain. Blood goes to the brain directly through the arteries, and the rest spreads to the body. Blood supply to various parts of the brain makes the animal spirit. Blood never stops at one place; it moves very quickly, like the jets of the flame that came from a torch. Blood leaves the brain through pores in its substance. These pores serve as an exit for blood and an entrance for fresh blood. This nourishment leads to nerves and then to muscles. In this way, animal spirits move the body in all the various ways it can be moved. Movement of the limbs is the shortening of certain muscles and lengthening of the opposite muscles. What causes that? Fractionally small spirits come from the brain to the muscle, and contraction takes place. Fractionally, spirits leave the relaxed muscle—not that the spirits coming from the brain are sufficient by themselves to move the muscles, but the cause is other spirits already in the muscles leaving one suddenly and passing on to another. In this way, once they leave, the muscle becomes longer and more relaxed, and when they enter, the muscle, being swollen by them, becomes shorter, creating movement in the limb they are attached to. According to Descartes, there are three things to consider in nerves: 1) there is the marrow, or internal substance, which extends in the form of tiny fibers from the brain, where they originate, to the extremities of the part of the body to which they are attached; 2) there are membranes surrounding the fibers, which are continuous with those surrounding the brain and form little tubes in which fibers are enclosed; 3) finally, there are animal spirits that are being carried by these tubes from brain to muscle, causing the fiber to remain completely free and extended, so that if anything causes the slightest motion in the part of the body where one of the fibers terminates, it thereby causes a movement in the part of the brain where the fiber originates—just as we make one end of the cord move by pulling the other end.

Optics is the way light makes us see things through our eyes, which send the signal through the optic nerve to the brain from where the nerve originates. These objects are seen by the brain, which directly represents them to our soul. In the same way, we are able to hear, smell, feel, taste, and sense heat, hunger, pain, thirst, and all the rest. All objects produce some movement in our nerves, which pass the signal to the brain, causing our soul to have different sensations. Descartes argued that these movements can take place without the soul. The example he cites is that if our friend acts like he or she is about to hit us in the eye, the eye will close spontaneously, even though we think our friend is joking. The brain sends signals to our eye muscles to close to avoid injury. Differences among the spirits may also cause them to take various courses. The other cause that serves to direct the animal spirits to muscles in various different ways is the unequal agitation of the spirits and the difference in their parts. Some of their parts are more agitated than others. They penetrate into the cavities and pores of the brain, and this way, they are directed to muscles, causing agitated action. Almost all functions are performed by the body, but the soul is responsible for the creation of thoughts. There are two principles: all our actions of the soul and the passion of the soul. Various perceptions and modes of knowledge are present in our passion soul. Our perceptions have two parts. One has soul as the cause, and the other has the body. The soul is involved in imagination or other thoughts, which depend on it. We have passion in the soul. At times, we perceive whatever is noble, and we act, which is solely an "action" imagination. Thoughts are formed by the soul, like when you are thinking about your girlfriend, a beautiful place, or something pleasant. That is why we regard these perceptions as actions, rather than passions. At times, imagination arises by the agitation of spirits in various ways and upon the traces of various impressions that have preceded them in the brain, which make their way by chance through certain pores rather than others, such as illusions of our dreams and daydreams we often have when we are awake and our mind wanders idly without applying itself to anything of its own accord. Their cause is conspicuous and determinate as the perceptions the soul receives by means of the nerves, as they seem to be mere shadow and pictures of these perceptions. All the perceptions come to the soul via nerves; some of the external objects strike our senses and some the body or certain parts of the body, and some come to our soul.

Perceptions are objects outside of our body. Objects of our senses are caused by these objects when our judgments are not false. The object produces certain movement in the organs of external senses, by means of nerves, and produces other movements in the brain, which cause the soul to have sensory awareness of the object, like we see the dog or hear the sound of a car. We use vision (eyes) and hearing (ears). The brain signals the soul, and we think we saw a dog or heard a car. The perceptions of the body are internal, like hunger, thirst, or craving to eat something. To this, we can add pain, heat, and pressure felt by our body parts. The perceptions we refer only to the soul are those effects we feel as being in the soul itself, for which we do not normally recognize any proximate cause, such as feeling sadness, anger, joy, and so on. All the perceptions, external and internal, are in passion with respect to "soul." The word *passion* refers to the soul itself. After having considered in which respect the passion of the soul differs from all its other thoughts, we may define it generally as those perceptions, sensations, or emotions of the soul that refer particularly to it and that are causal, maintained and strengthened by some movement of the spirits. Perceptions are in close alliance with the soul and body. We may also call them sensations, because they are received into the soul in the same way as the object of the external senses. It is better to call them "emotions" of the soul, which are united to all the parts of the body conjointly. We cannot say that it exists in any one part of the body to the exclusion of the others. The body is a unity and is indivisible because of the arrangement of the organs, which work in conjunction with each other. Removal of one may render the body defective. The soul is of such a nature that it has no relation to the extension and dimensions or other properties of which matter, the body, is composed. It is related to the whole matter of the body of which it is composed. It is related solely to the whole assemblage of the body organ. We have no ability to conceive a half or third of the soul or the extension of the soul. The soul does not become smaller if we cut off a limb of the body.

Descartes claimed that there is a little gland in the brain that exercises its functions more than other parts of the body, though the soul is joined to the whole body. Descartes argues that the heart is not the main part where the soul exerts its primary functioning. It is the innermost part of the brain, which is a small gland situated in the middle part of the brain's substance. Through the spirits, this gland communicates with the anterior and posterior parts of the brain. The slightest movement in the gland may alter greatly the course of these spirits. Descartes explains why this organ is the seat of the soul. He adds that the parts of the body are in twos, like two eyes, two ears, two hands, and so on and so forth. The object can come together in a single impression or image before reaching the soul. He states that the single impression or image can be unified in this gland by means of spirits that fill the cavities of the brain. The soul has its principal seat in the small gland, located in the middle of the brain. From there, it radiates to the rest of the body. The mechanism of our body is so constructed that simply by this gland being moved in any way by the soul or by any other cause, it drives the surrounding spirits toward the pores of the brain, which direct it through the nerves to the muscles. In this way, the gland makes the spirits move the limb. This gland is the *pineal gland*. Based on the functioning and power of this gland, Descartes explained the various functions of the soul. He posed a question to himself: How do we recognize the strength and weakness of souls and what is wrong with the souls? It is by success in those conflicts that each person can recognize the strength or weakness of his or her soul. The stronger soul belongs to those who can, by nature, conquer the passion and stop the bodily movements that accompany it. But there are some who never test the strength of their will because they never equip it to fight with its proper weapon, giving it instead only the weapon that some passion provides for resisting other passions.

Descartes was on track until he thought the pineal gland to be seat of the soul. Neuroscientists discard it and do not accept the pineal body to be the seat of the soul, because of its anatomical and physiological functions. As described in the chakras (20'284), the pineal body represents the sixth chakra, according to Hindu philosophy. Some authors believe that this gland was located near the top of the head. In some reptiles, it is still a light-sensitive perceptual organ. The pineal gland is sometimes called the "seat of the soul" and acts as the light meter of the body, thus controlling rhythms that are influenced by exposure to light. Some believe that the pineal gland is derived from a third eye that begins to develop early in the embryo and later degenerates. The pineal gland has melatonin, which some authors have considered to have a sedative effect. As a matter of fact, I have seen many of patients taking melatonin pills for sleep. They are available as an over-the-counter supplement. Their efficacy and effects on sleep have not been established. There is some serotonin activity in the pineal gland, and melatonin is relevant to pigment cells. Both melatonin and serotonin have as a precursor L-tryptophan, an amino acid that can induce sleep, which is abundant in lukewarm milk if taken at bedtime. We do not have any scientific evidence that the pineal gland has any neurological function of significance. As per Kaplan and Shaddock's synopsis of psychiatry (page 539), melatonin secretion from the pineal gland is inhibited by bright light so that the lowest concentration of serum melatonin occurs during the day. The superachiasmatic nucleus of the hypothalamus may act as the anatomical site of a circadian pacemaker, which regulates melatonin secretion for the sleep-wake cycle. To my scientific, medical, and anatomical knowledge, there is no relationship of the soul or the sixth chakra to the pineal body. I presume that Descartes adapted this concept from chakras—chakras being the oldest. Descartes may have been fascinated with this concept. There are highly sophisticated and anatomical structures of the brain at this level of the cranium, like the brain stem, the pituitary gland, the pons, and cranial nerves, which will be discussed in a later chapter. Descartes was the first major thinker to start using the word *mind* as an alternative to the word *soul* (*anima*). He claims "I" is the mind that thinks. Thus, mental substances can think. The body moves; therefore, Descartes viewed the entire human body and brain as a machine. He suggested that animals have sensation and might have thoughts, but they lack rational thoughts like humans.

At the beginning of seventeenth century, philosophers were still thinking and believing in a self, which was the soul, an immaterial substance. By the eighteenth century, the self (soul) had become the *mind*, a dynamic natural system subject to the laws of growth and development. This was after Descartes's idea that the soul does not give life to the body. After that, European philosophers believed that the self gives life to the body, and, therefore, the self is the mind, because the thing that thinks is the mind of a person. According to Martin and Barresi, the self is a persisting thing and consists of physical and psychological parts, which develop at different stages of life (65, 463–81).

According to Locke, a person stands for a thinking, intelligent being that has reason and the capacity for reflection. The human can consider itself as "itself." It is the same thinking thing in different times and places. This is possible by its properties of having consciousness, which is inseparable from thinking. It is impossible to perceive without perceiving that we perceive when we see, hear, taste, feel, smell, and meditate. We know that we do so. It is the same identical substance that always thinks in the same person. Locke maintained the notion that personal identity consists, not in the identity of substance, but in the identity of "consciousness." Consciousness is the perception of what goes through the mind of a person. The self is the conscious thing, whether spiritual, conscious of pleasure and pain, or capable of happiness or misery. The self is not determined by identity or diversity of substance but only by the identity. Locke claimed that consciousness extends beyond the present moment. Memory is an event that creates the moment of the self being extant in the past. Memory is the glue that brings and binds together earlier and later stages of the person. Personal identity is the sameness of the rational being. Consciousness can reflect back and think that the person in the past is the same person now. Any intelligent person can repeat the idea of any past action with the same consciousness he or she had at first and with the same consciousness he or she has its present thoughts and actions—that he or she is "self" to him- or herself now. If one cuts off one's hand, there is the loss of it, and it is no longer part of the body. Thus the substance, of which the personal self consisted at one time, may be different at another time, without the change of personal identity through a part of the body that was cut off. Hence, it is the consciousness as opposed to any immaterial substance that determines personal identity.

Reid did not accept this concept of identity. According to him, "I" existed before the earliest thing I can remember, but let us suppose that my memory reaches a moment further back than my belief and conviction of my existence is a fact. If we are rational, we automatically take ownership of the past thoughts, experiences, and actions that we remember (67, 231–508). Clarke (1676–1729) defended the platonic idea that souls are immaterial and indivisible and thus immortal. According to him, consciousness is neither a capacity for thinking or actual thinking but a reflexive act. Humans know that they can think and that their thoughts and actions are their own not others'. Clarke's (68) view was that the self is unified and is a single thing. Every person feels and knows by experience that consciousness is his or her own. David Hume (1711–1776) claimed that the philosophy of human nature will be called *psychology*, a basic science to understand human behavior. As a psychologist who focused on science and abandoned epistemological and metaphysical pretentions, Hume concentrated on the self and personal identity. In his first book, *Treatise*, he argued that belief in the persistence of anything is an illusion. All ideas arise from impressions. Even when we become aware of our errors, we cannot sustain imagination. Identity in existence is a unifying substance, such as the soul. Identity to him was belief that the human is a serial bundle of perceptions that succeed each other with an inconceivable rapidity and are in a perpetual flux and movement. Our thoughts are more variable than our sight and all our senses. The mind is a kind of theater, where several perceptions successively make their appearance, pass and repass, glide away, and mingle in an infinite variety of postures and situations. Hume stated that when I turn my reflection on myself, I never can perceive this self without someone or more perceptions, nor can I ever perceive anything but the perceptions that form the self (69).

Charles Darwin, in 1838, said that the struggle for survival causes variation. The stronger ones will survive, and the weaker ones will vanish unless they adapt to the environment and exist as a new species; thus, evolution takes place in a continuum. Darwin (1872) worked on the emotional behavior of nonhumans. He added that emotional expressions like anger, despair, hatred, and love were common between human and nonhuman beings. He added that according to evolutionary theory, humans are a form of animal and there are other species that evolve on the earth as time and evolutionary processes continue in relation to environmental conditions and the need to survive. Thus, if humans have a soul, then nonhumans have a soul too. Boyle looked to the sky and compared humans to angels, but Darwin looked to the earth and compared humans to apes.

Some claimed that initially the idea of self came from human experiences of their bodily activities, which provide them with information about themselves as well as objects in the world with which they interact. Subsequently, they relate past to present thoughts. They come to identify more with ideas than with their bodies. Thereby, they developed a notion of an ego to the object of their thoughts, which they then generalize as an abstract ego or identical subject of experience that persists throughout their lives (79).

Spiritualism is the belief that the spirits of the dead have both the ability and the inclination to communicate with the living. The afterlife, or the spirit world, is seen by spiritualists not as a static place but one in which spirits continue to evolve. They believe that contact with spirits is possible and that spirits are more advanced than humans. Their belief system includes the following principles as concepts (386, 387):

- A belief that the soul continues to exist after the death of the physical body
- A belief that spirits communicate
- A belief that even after death, it is possible for the soul to learn and improve
- A belief in God, often referred to as "infinite intelligence"
- A belief that the natural world is an expression of said intelligence
- A belief in personal responsibility for life circumstances

Spirits is a branch of spiritualism emphasizing reincarnation. It is mostly practiced in Brazil

CHAPTER 2

THE ANATOMY AND PHYSIOLOGY OF THE SOUL

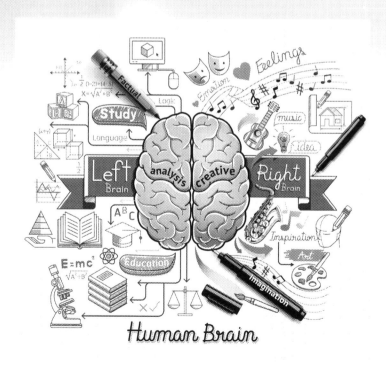

Human Brain

To help you understand the neuroanatomy and structure of the soul, I have a story to tell. One day, there was a nice gathering at Virginia Beach, and there were about fifty to sixty beautiful women partying in a posh restaurant. A bunch of friends and I decided to have some drinks. There was a full moon, the ocean was calm, and a wonderfully cool breeze was flowing from the ocean. What a pleasant day! It was as if nature knew just what to do and how to do it. Dancing was rampant after a while because of the buzz of wonderful, tasty martinis. The bartender knew what to do too. Music was blasting next door in the park. All I saw was happiness and joy flowing through the cool breeze, reminding us something good was going to happen. I was not sure what that was all about. Some of my buddies were drooling, and some had already made their moves and found partners to dance with. Some were sad, some rejected, and some still prowling to have their fair share of the bounty. It reminded me of sharks when they find a school of fish. All they want is to create commotion and have as much fish as they can gobble down. There was an enormous competition among my buddies. The good-looking and aggressive ones were enjoying the good fortune. Passion was flowing in the air everywhere. I heard songs being played. Love was in the air everywhere. What I saw made me believe that one day it would be my turn to have what I wanted. Sure enough, my eyes saw an unbelievable beauty. My eyes informed the occipital lobe of my brain about what they were seeing, and my occipital lobe responded to my eyes and asked, "What is that you want to tell me?" My eyes were wide open, excited, refusing to shut.

"You've got to listen to me, sir," said my eyes.

My occipital lobe asked, "What? What are you so excited about?"

"Sir, remember you have asked me numerous times, if you recall, almost every day, if I find a beautiful lady to call you." My eyes told my occipital lobe, "I am looking at an unbelievable beauty, like I have never seen. This one is a keeper, sir."

"Okay, can you describe her?"

"Yes, sir!" With excitement and a loud voice, my eyes described this beauty. "Roughly 105 pounds, blond hair, dark eyes, about five feet nine inches tall, smile like an angel's, beautiful breasts … What a nice round bottom! Looks like a model."

"I do not want to miss the opportunity. She gave me some looks, but I do not know what to do," replied the occipital lobe.

"You miss this chance, I will blame you for all that."

The occipital lobe called the frontal lobe, who was second in command.

"Chief, the eyes are bugging me about the beauty queen, and we need immediate action, sir. I trust my workers (both eyes). They always tell me the truth."

The frontal lobe is the second in command of the whole system and is very strict. The frontal lobe was excited and issued an executive order to the motor center to be on standby to follow orders immediately. The frontal lobe immediately ordered the hypothalamus and limbic system to do whatever needed to be done without any hesitation. Both ordered the pituitary gland, and sympathetic and parasympathetic systems to obey the orders and take action in a fraction of a second. Orders were sent through the brain stem to the spinal cord to keep the muscles ready to move in a coherent fashion. The limbic system had already informed the facial muscles to be polite and express a smiling and cordial expression. In the meantime, the motor center ordered the speech center, with full instructions received from the boss frontal lobe, to speak nicely and create a good impression. While this was going on, the pituitary gland had stormed the adrenal gland to pump cortisol and testosterone hormone secretions from testicles and provide support to prostate and seminal vesicles. The sympathetic and parasympathetic systems had ordered blood vessels to dilate in the event the boss needs an erection of the penis, who was alert and ready on command to do its best to perform its job in the event it is asked to serve. All the information was sent in a fraction of a second from the boss to these parts of the brain and the body. In return, all the information sent was returned to the boss, confirming everything is and will be perfect as ordered. The boss ordered everyone to move carefully and immediately. The eyes were informed, "Yes, go ahead, but each one of you should act as advised and as you were hired, according to the job description. I do not want anyone to meddle with anyone else's job." The final message was received. I moved closer cautiously and started the conversation with that beautiful woman. Every part of the brain and body acted like a soldier, as described by the chain of command. No dereliction of duty was the order of day. Otherwise, punishment would be severe—shame, guilt, sadness, rejection, and remorse. The whole chain of command was fully aware of anxious moments, but in my case, all the soldiers and commanders were fully trained to handle anxiety by parasympathetic hyperactivity and regulation of sympathetic activity, from regular training of the whole command and control centers. Yes, my response was getting better.

"May I buy you a drink?" I asked the woman.

"Sure" was the answer.

And the message was sent back to the boss.

"Doing well, son. Keep on. You are doing well. Offer her more than a drink. Show her who you are."

My limbic system took control of my expressions, emotions, and feelings, which were well expressed.

"What is your name?"

"Kate."

"I am Bill."

We shook hands, and conversation went on. Every move, every action, every word, and every response was monitored by my neurological system as described, and the same was true of her neurological system. Though her physiology was somewhat different than mine, the basic principles were the same. I could feel some reluctance and anxiety on my part and on her part too. We danced and romanced.

"Where do you live, Kate?"

"Nearby. In Norfolk. What about you?"

"I live in Virginia Beach."

"What you do, Bill?"

"I am a physician."

"Oh yes? I am a nurse practitioner."

My sympathetic nervous system started getting crazy while I made eye contact with her. My mouth started drying up. I am sure my blood pressure also probably went up, though I did not measure it. I could see her sweating and occasional pauses while I was conversing with her. There was instant attraction. The boss ordered me to get her telephone number before she said good-bye. I did, and the boss was happy to know that I had covered all the bases. Besides her beauty, her interaction and emotional presentation were beyond my expectations. All this happened through an electric current that moved back and forth. It was like talking on the phone, like a well-organized orchestra conducted by the conductor with precision. The boss relayed all this information to the president, the magnetic soul, instantly. All the information was preserved in the archives of the magnetic soul. It sent vibrations to the magnetic soul of Kate, which were reciprocated instantly. This was confirmed after we came to know each other further. Magnetic energy was created during the entire electric current, which carried all the information up and down the chain of command on both sides. Imagine how much electric current must have passed up and down to complete the entire process, and imagine how much magnetic field must have been created to store all this information to be used in the near future. Imagine how much transfer of information would have happened through my neurons, axons, and synapses. Imagine how many neurotransmitters would have been involved in both brains, just to get to know each other. Each and every action became thoughts, which are created by the magnetic fields of both of us. That is how thoughts originate throughout our entire life and dominate our actions. These thoughts remain buried in the archives of our magnetic field and could erupt with any external stimulus analogous to such events in future. This explains the theory of how our thoughts are originated and can erupt at any time without our awareness. You wonder why these thoughts come and go with external stimuli or without any stimulus. Merely looking at something creates thought through the visual electrical stimulus, which can trigger thoughts that have no relevance to that time. We could trigger associated thought stored in the same archives or the nearby archives stored in the magnetic field. I learned the hard way there is nothing for free. Don't think or believe that your thoughts are free. Everything needs to be paid for. In the case of our thoughts, it is the magnetic energy used to form and create thoughts. I learned in medical school that our cells and neurons use ADP and ATP as a source of energy to be able to function and survive. Trust me; to create ADP and ATP, we need source of energy for that too. If you want to know more, I would suggest you read about the metabolic chains in the body, which is just like an ocean by itself.

Both of us went to our homes, but I was burdened by thoughts about her. I learned from her that she was also burdened by thoughts about me. She said there were nervous moments, interrupted sleep, and thoughts about me while she was at work, which had nothing to do with me. At times, I felt the same way. We met quite often and started dating. Times were good, and through our mutual sharing of magnetic energy, we started sharing, caring, and blending with each other's magnetic energy. Our common interest grew every day and at every moment without us knowing what was going on. Our neurons and magnetic energy kept storing the data without our knowledge. The only thing we knew about each other was what we paid attention to. She was more attentive and analytical than I was. I learned that later. Why? There is a double connection from the right to left hemispheres of the brain in women. While I was more of a left brainer, she was both a right and left brainer. That is how we differ from each other. Women are more detail-oriented, perceptive, and sensitive. Our thoughts do not exist in a vacuum, nor are they droplets of water or fumes in the air; they have an existence of their own in the form of magnetic energy transduced from electric current generated by multiple neuronal activities.

I am sure some of you must have experienced your brain wandering from one thought to another. Sometimes you are looking at the beautiful full moon, and all of a sudden, you think of your dog or girlfriend. You wonder how and why? Our thoughts have free association and are independent of any related stimulus. They are concrete when we are attentive and operating. Then and there, your thoughts are at will. This happened to me while I was writing this chapter. I went to bed, and my thoughts started racing about this topic. I got up and started writing in the middle of the night. I did not look at the clock to avoid any interference, and I went to bed without looking at the clock. I was able to control my thoughts at will. I call these "thoughts at will." I do believe we have thoughts buried deep in the neurons of our brain, which remain inactive because they have weak magnetic energy and are overshadowed by more attention-grabbing activities. These thoughts become very active during our sleep and erupt like a volcanic magnetic energy. Our unconsciousness is in full bloom and is free to let the weak magnetic energy float to the surface in the form of dreams. The recollection of dreams depends upon the stage of sleep we are in. Richard Swinburne describes concurrent thoughts as being like sensations; they occur to a subject at some particular moment of time. But unlike sensations, they are propositional. They are normally accompanied in the subject by sensations, for example, auditory sensations caused by oneself or by others speaking or the image of such sensations, which is the vehicle of private thought. Swinburne adds that thoughts may be indicative, imperative, or interrogative in some form. Some indicative thoughts come to the subject as expressions of his or her belief; other indicative thoughts come as mere possibilities the thinker entertains or as the believed or imagined content of utterances of others. Active thoughts may be of three kinds. First, there is the case where an agent produces in him- or herself a thought as a by-product of attempting to communicate it to others with speech or writing. Second, there is the case where an agent thinks privately and repeats to him- or herself some familiar thoughts or a train of thoughts, like *I have to be at home tomorrow* or *I have to go to the bank tomorrow*. Thoughts are mediated normally by our sensations, which are not displayed publically. They bring imagined sensations. These thoughts are familiar or have been experienced through our sensations before. Third, active thoughts are those in which the agent intentionally thinks about some subject or a problem. For example, the person may think about a book or issues related to solving his or her financial or family problems. These thoughts may bring other thoughts about a boss or job and about the future of his or her children. The list goes on and on. No one can steal your thoughts unless you verbally express them to others, and the same holds true for them too. The exception is in psychotic patients and in schizophrenics. These patients may feel someone is stealing their thoughts (called "thought broadcasting") or someone is putting their thoughts into their minds (called "thought insertion").

It is important to understand the facts about the brain, which is in a dark black box with no exposure to light but has light within itself. It is a machine beyond machines, a computer beyond computers. It is a galaxy by itself. Some functions of the brain are understood, and some are beyond understanding. Though I admire neuroscientists, neurobiologists, psychiatrists, psychologists, and all others involved in understanding the unknown, I also admire philosophers and Hindu chakra writers, who imagine the unknown without any exposure to neuroanatomy or neurophysiology. Their anatomy was not accurate compared to our modern knowledge about neurobiology and neuroanatomy. The brain is made up of cells called neurons that provide the pathways by which information is received and information is given to the rest of the body. There are about one hundred billion neurons, which some estimate is thirty times the population of the entire planet. There are ten thousand miles of nerve fibers per cubic inch. A typical neuron is wired up to a thousand of its neighbors. So studying the brain is just like studying a human society and understanding the behavior of each individual in that human society and the social, economic, and political aspects of his or her entire life. As a matter of fact, it is thirty times more difficult. In unicellular organisms, like amoebas, the nucleus is the brain acting in conjunction with other organelles. In multicellular organisms, one cell communicates with other cells through chemicals. In advanced animals, things get complicated. First of all, how long does it take for the message to get from the sender cell to its recipient? It takes more time for a chemical signal to travel over increased distance; one centimeter takes 0.5 milliseconds. Blood takes about a minute to go once around the body. We have about 1,200 separate muscles. A neuron has an axon that could be a meter long and extends toward its target to make physical contact and form synapses with muscles. They make neuromuscular junctions on the muscle cell body (soma). The neuron has endless dendrites for transmission of chemical communication signals called neurotransmitters. A neuron can actually convey information at over 100 meters per second. How can they do that? They use electricity and the flow of current. This is very important to understand, because my whole explanation about the anatomy and physiology of the soul is based on this mechanism. During a visit to an American medical school, the Dalai Lama was invited to watch a brain operation. Afterward, he sat down with neurosurgeons to chat about science's understanding of the mind and the brain. He recalled the hours of conversations he had enjoyed with neuroscientists over the years and how they had explained to him that perceptions, sensations, and other subjective experiences reflect chemical and electrical changes in the brain. When electrical impulses rush through our visual cortex, we see, and when neurotransmitters rush through our limbic system, we feel something in response to an event in the outside world, sometimes as a result of a thought generated by the mind alone. Even consciousness, he recalled scientists explaining, is just a manifestation of brain activity, and when the brain ceases to function, consciousness vanishes like the morning fog. Something always bothered him about this explanation, the Dalai Lama said. Even if one accepts the idea that the mind is what the brain does and that feelings and thoughts are expressions of the brain activity, isn't a two-way causation possible? That is, maybe in addition to the brain giving rise to the thoughts, feelings, and other cognitive activities, those together add up to the thing we call a mind. Some aspects of the mind also act back on the brain to cause physical changes in the very matter that created it. In this case, the arrow of causality would point both ways, and pure thought would change the brain's chemistry and electrical activity, its circuits, or even its structure. The brain surgeon answered that the physical state gives rise to the mental state. The surgeon added that "downward" causation from the mental to the physical is not possible (367). I differ with that notion and have explained my ideas in this book extensively. I am sure someday the Dalai Lama will have a chance to read my book to understand the real science behind his question.

ANATOMY OF THE BRAIN

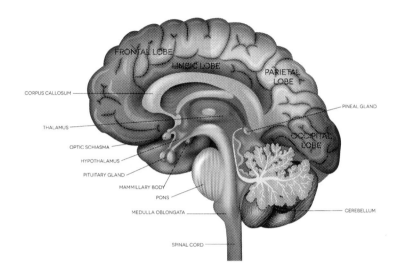

To simplify, the parts of the brain, are as follows:

- Forebrain brain
  - o Cerebrum
  - o Basal ganglion
  - o Thalamus
  - o Hypothalamus
  - o Subthalamus
  - o Cerebellum

- Brain stem
  - o Midbrain
  - o Pons
  - o Medulla oblongata
  - o Spinal cord
  - o White matter
  - o Gray matter
  - o Spinal nerves

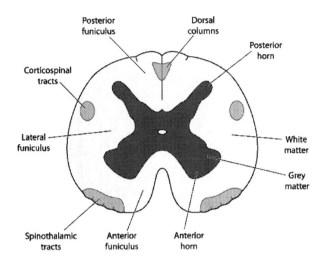

The brain is made up of neurons, axons, dendrites, myelin sheath, synapses, and brain cells with different names like neuroglia. They outnumber the neurons, which have no synapses. Macroglia may have the potential to regenerate. Astrocytes surround the blood vessels in the brain. Oligodendrocytes act as insulators for axons to form the myelin sheath. The microglia are the scavengers of our brain and act as an immune system. These are designed to detect and destroy invaders, like bacteria, and in the areas of the brain damaged by injury or stroke, they remove the debris and dead neurons. Larger axons are covered with myelin sheath, a lipid substance that improves the conduction of the action potential by acting as an electric insulator. Myelin is interrupted at regular intervals at a nodes called nodes of Ranvier.

The cerebrum has layer after layer of axons with sulci and gyri to increase the surface area and accommodate as many neurons as they can. If it were flat, then the surface area would be small. It also accommodates arteries and veins, which rush in oxygenated blood and take deoxygenated blood back to the heart. Therefore, the larger the surface area the more blood flow to the brain. It is another important fact to understand because blood has red blood cells, which have iron in the form of oxyhemoglobin. It serves multiple functions, like supplying oxygen, nutrients, and iron to increase the magnetic field in the brain, which complements the magnetic field generated by the electrochemical activity of the brain as a whole. This will be explained as we march toward the goal of achieving the physiology of the soul. As we get deeper into the layers of neurons, they become multimodal, which means they respond to more than one sensation, like the sense of vision, sound, and touch. In addition, they respond to sensations from the muscles of our body, which create desired movement. Sixty years ago, we developed a computer just like our brain, and one hundred years ago, we developed a telephone exchange, which was wired like our nervous system. We were amazed to learn about a wiring system like our brain's, but it is beyond and above to understand the complex wiring of the brain with its 10^{12} neurons and trillions of cell connections with the rest of the body. Quantum physics may explain how computer chips work, but understanding the brain can never be a molecular matter. The question of the properties of a single channel configurationally changes in the single molecules of biochemistry and biophysics.

It was known two thousand years ago that nerves acted as communication pathways between the brain and body. Galvani noted twitching in frog's legs when he touched the legs with certain metals. In the nineteenth century, it was known that nerves and muscles could be activated by electricity because of action potential. The nerves have to conduct the signal over long distances. There are channels in the membrane that open in response to small changes in voltage across the membrane called voltage-gate channels. When open, they trigger a very large voltage burst or spike of 100 millivolts in amplitude for two to three milliseconds. This dramatic and explosive event is called *action potential*. It can produce results as long as the strength of the stimulus is above a certain threshold value (below which no action potential is seen at all). Neither the amplitude nor shape nor speed of the action potential is in any way influenced by the original stimulus. This is called the all-or-none law. This is all played out by the sodium, potassium, chloride, and calcium balance inside and outside of the nerve cell, and at times, ATP-ase is used as a source of energy to complete the process. These processes are all based on the genetic makeup of the living creatures (98).

Neurologists use nerve conduction to investigate sensory and motor disorders. The clinician stimulates the nerve by placing a cathode (depolarizing) and an anode (hyperpolarizing) and then measuring the signal amplitude and signal latency. Then the researcher calculates the conduction velocity. Values are compared to normal individuals to drive conclusions about the electric conduction status of the nerve. Compound action potential in the biggest nerves' conduction is about 120meters per second or 270 miles per hour. This means a signal from the toe to the brain takes about 10 milliseconds. In small nerves, it moves 1 meter per second. Then and there, they are able to localize the lesion and the pathology of the nerve and design a treatment or look for something else to rule out other disorders of the nerve or the muscles and nerve suppliers. Our nerves are just like electric cables, which have to have a two-way source. One takes the electric current to the point it needs to go to and the other from the point of need to the main source. Our nerves are covered with myelin sheath and have nodes of Ranvier to increase the efficiency of conduction. It reminds me of the fact that when connections were established between two countries, like Canada and the United States, wires were not covered (electric and telephone wires). There was a waste of electric field with the result there was weak current to the destination. Thus scientists covered the wire with plastic material, which insulated it—just like we have in our homes to prevent wasting electricity. I was amazed to see that high-tension cables are not insulated. Why not? Again, scientists developed a system where wires were not run in a straight connection. They would jump from one cable to other and have a circuit-breaker type of system, which increased the flow of the current. It is not 100 percent protection. Did scientists learn from the nodes of Ranvier, where electric current will flow from one node to the other, or did we learn about our neurological electrical system from scientists and physicists working on electricity? Well, the bottom line is the system is most similar with the basic principles of physics and electrical conduction processes.

Well, I wish it was so simple. As we go further in learning about physiology and neuroanatomy, it gets more complicated. It is not fully understood. We have learned about neurotransmitters and synapses, the receptor sites, and the energy needed to transport various neurotransmitters and chemicals, like ATP, ADP, and so on. We know for sure that all the song and dance is about electric current. It is not only action potential or any other kind of potential but the release of neurotransmitters in response to stimuli. A neuron has an output region and an input region. The input region is carried by dendrites and the receptive region by an axon. For example, depolarization opens voltage-sensitive calcium channels, which cause exocytosis of vesicles about fifty millimeters across the neurons containing neurotransmitters that are to act on the next cell to carry information. It goes on from one neuron to other trillions, from one synapse to the other synapse, called the presynapse and postsynapse. The space between two synapses is called the synaptic cleft. Different neurotransmitters are activated by different elements. A cholinergic synapse means it transmits acetylcholine at the neuromuscular junction, which causes depolarization by sodium, potassium, and calcium channels. This facilitates the release of transmitters from synaptic terminals, causing muscular contraction. Let me list various neurotransmitters currently known to us:

- Endorphins
- Encephalin
- Oxytocin
- Glucagon
- Somatostatins
- Substance P
- Aspartate
- Glutamate
- GABA
- Glycine
- Dopamine
- Noradrenalin
- 5-Hydroxytryptamine
- Acetylcholine
- Nitric oxide
- Carbon monoxide
- ATP

Various hormones and neurotransmitters are still unknown.

These are all excitatory neurotransmitters. We need inhibitory neurotransmitters as well. We need to withdraw rather than attach, relax rather than be excited all the time. For example, if one muscle is contracting, the opposite has to relax; this is achieved by reciprocal innervations. An example is the tendon jerk at the knee when we test for reflexes. We have an inhibitory synapse with the motor neuron of the ventral horn of the spinal cord. Those of you who want to learn more, please read the neurophysiology book of your choice.

I was fascinated to learn how a sound, light, touch, smell, taste, and so on is converted into an electric current. The process by which one type of energy is converted into another form of energy is called transduction. The energy effect on a receptor cell must turn into electric energy in the form of action potential across the cell membrane, whether it is thermal, electromagnetic, mechanical, or chemical. Transduction is very important to understand as explained. In general, the effect of the stimulus energy is to alter the permeability of the cell membrane to certain ions, resulting in a flow of current and reestablishment of equilibrium. Because hearing receptors are specific to sound and noise and light receptors are for light stimuli, you cannot see with hearing receptors or hear with light receptors. This is done by an energy filter that allows certain types of energy throughout to cause an electrical effect. This principal holds its ground all the times. Neuroscientists have found specialized and peculiar receptors called *Pacinian corpuscles* in the skin and the digestive system (mesentery). In a myelinated axon, there is a sheath, like layers of an onion, called the lamellae, which shields it from every stimulus except that of mechanical formation. David Eaglman, in *The Brain*, describes his vest on page 169; "to provide sensory substitution for the deaf," he, along with his student, developed a wearable vest that captures sound from the environment and maps it to small vibrations. The motors activate patterns according to the frequencies of the sound. In this way, sound becomes a moving pattern of vibrations. Deaf people become able to translate the complicated patterns on the torso and unlock the pattern similar to the manner in which a blind person can read effortlessly. This is called synesthesia, which means a sensory experience in one modality is involuntarily experienced in another sensory modality. For example, hearing certain sounds evokes different color sensations. A sense of touch could evoke an auditory sensation through an auditory pathway. Such a mechanism was highly developed in great singers like Ray Charles and Stevie Wonder, who were blind but could play the piano like a person with normal vision. How could Ray Charles know the difference between a five-dollar bill and a twenty-dollar bill? It is all due to the highly developed synesthesia mechanism of the brain, which allows it to adopt different sensations and convert them into one that is well understood by the blind or deaf individual. My view is that there is a magnetic field generated in the brains of Ray Charles and Stevie Wonder, called the soul, which has the capability of *binding* one sensory stimulus to other sensory stimuli. Neuroscientists use the term *binding* to indicate the brain's ability to produce a unified picture of the outside world, given that vision is processed in one region, hearing in another region, and touch and motor action in different areas of the brain. All the mechanisms are able to produce results by "binding." The "soul" is a higher binding magnetic mechanism. This is solely my hypothesis.

"Who am I?" Philosophers, neuroscientists, religious sages, psychologists—all of us question, "Who am I as a physical being?" Leaving alone the brain for a moment and ignoring our soul as well, who am I as a physical mass? I can see myself; I have legs, arms, a body as a whole. I can see my face in the mirror, and when I laugh or cry, I can feel, but I can only see my tears dripping from my eyes. I can feel my tears when they touch the skin of my face. Who tells me the position and movement of my limbs, my attitude and motion relative to the earth, and what a brush from a twig of a tree feels like? I can see I am sitting in a chair with a table in front of me, talking to my friends, having a breakfast with a fork in hand; I am walking with a remote control in my hand. I can see but do not feel it. I am cooking. I see that pot and spoon in my hands, and I do not feel the spoon or the pot. I am standing and cannot maintain a posture. I do not feel I am standing on the ground, though I know I am standing on the ground. I called my girlfriend by cell phone; I did not feel it, though I know it was a cell phone. I could not feel the numbers I dialed, but I knew the number. It is only possible by the sense of touch called proprioception, which brings all these feelings in living beings. I am sorry to use neurological terms and names of the parts of brain. Neuroscientists know that all, but those who never heard of neurophysiology, what about them? I am here for them. First of all, let us discuss muscle proprioception. These are sensors like in mechanical world present in our body. In a voluntary muscle, there are two types of sensors (103): 1) muscle spindles, which send information to the brain about the length and rate of change of length; and 2) the Golgi tendon, an organ that sends signals about muscle tension or force. Both are essentially receptors. Spindles are present in all striated muscles. Roughly, in each spindle, there are about five hundred muscle fibers. The spindle is innervated by a nerve fiber. These nerves send signals about the stretch of muscle in any direction. Muscles are innervated by motor nerves, which control the actions of the muscle. It saves us from rupturing our muscles by telling us how much they can be stretched. Golgi tendon organs are similar but are concerned with any action in the tendon of a muscle (99). They register tension in the tendon rather than muscle. The nerves from both go to spinal-cord neurons and finally to the posterior spinocerebellar tract. All this process is computed by action potential and generation of electric current, whether it goes up or descends from the cerebrum or cerebellum to recognize the action. In the early nineteenth century, neurologists noted that neurosyphilis caused "tabes dorsalis," due to damage to the spinal cord neurons. It resulted in "sensory ataxia." This is due to a lack of information sent from the feet, joints, and muscles. If you ask a patient with tabes dorsalis to close his or her eyes while standing, he or she will fall down. With open eyes, the patient will be able to stand. Cerebellar disease patients were unable to maintain their balance regardless of whether their eyes were open or closed (Mortiz von Romberg). Kinesthesia is the term used for our conscious sense of the position and movement of our limbs. All these are also supported by skin receptors, which will be discussed later.

The sensory system gives outside information to the brain in its dark box. How does our body perceive and encounter various stimuli, transfer the information into electric current, and send it to the brain and then to our soul? For example, how do we know where we are sitting and what we are in touch with? This all is done by our sensory apparatus, which is assisted by auditory and visual stimuli. It puts them together for our brain and soul to process to know the facts and figures outside of our body. The largest organ in the body is the skin. It sends an enormous amount of information to our brain and protects us from any danger or damage to our body. It senses the harmful effects from outside to protect us from any damage to our limbs and body as a whole (100). It works without the senses of hearing and vision—though, in the end, they all work together to protect and give us a sense of who we are and where we are. This is the somatosensory system. Without this, our brain and soul is blind to the pleasant and unpleasant. It sends the information and tells the brain or soul what it is and what to do. On their own, they are helpless. Upon receiving the information, the brain and soul order them to take action and caution and avoid further damage. I call these system the eyes of the blind brain/soul. This system cannot see but feels more than any organ in the body. It makes us laugh, cry, scream, yell, and at times shy away from where we are. It creates a wide range of emotions and avoidance. It creates experience of a lifetime by giving information to our brain/soul to continue our future and learn how to interact with the exterior in the future. It creates a belief system—sometimes good and sometimes bad. It gives tools to our brain to avoid or enjoy pleasant feelings. It draws the attention of our visual sensory apparatus, which is guided by our brain once the information is processed. These are the cutaneous sensory receptors, which partner with our skin and send information to our spinal cord from head to toe. The spinal cord sends information to the cerebrum (cortex) to give orders through various pathways via the spinal cord in the form of electric current (action potential and through neurochemical transmitters). With all the sensory stuff being projected in front of us and providing us with "conscious sensation," it is complex and not always accurate because it is the little man in the head who decides. Is there a little man in the head of the little man, who dictates the terms and conditions of our reactions? Maybe the soul is the head man, who has the final say about all this. This system is essential for our survival and for reproduction. Evidently, it provides us the information about what, where, and how to get to the goal we need to go to, so that we can orient ourselves and set off in the right direction. Finally, we need a hint about how to achieve our goal with least effort and discomfort, avoiding the steepest landscape and crossing the river without getting wet. The order is to correct and translate from sensory stimuli to motor responses. We find that information from the sensory receptors (sensors) is immediately segregated into different pathways, reflecting different kinds of use in terms of generating movement (101). Visual sensation (eyes) localizes the objects, and then we can go toward them, reach and grasp them, or make a decision about our reaction to them. Receptors in the skin are concerned about recognizing stimuli, which need an immediate response, depending upon the stimuli, for example, withdrawing from pain, brushing off an insect or any object that is unpleasant or unwanted, cleaning food particles off the side of our face, or removing a label attached to the collar of a shirt, a pebble in the sole of your flip-flops, or an irritating bangle on your forearm. Neurons in the dorsal root ganglion of the spinal cord send axons to the sensory endings of the skin and to the cerebrum (central nervous system), thus completing wiring from the source of electricity to the point it is needed and back to the source from where it originated. The whole body's skin is mapped and supplied into specific areas, which send information back to the command center (cerebrum). The hair follicles are surrounded by pressure-sensitive Pacinian corpuscles and Merkle's disks. These provide the brain with sensitive and highly directional information about displacement of the hair brought about by contact with external objects. Now we are talking about warmth, cold, pain, deep pleasure, light, touch, and pressure, all of which are perceived by sensory receptors. For example, run your fingers across a kitchen table and close your eyes, you will feel the surface, dents, cracks, and the firmness of the table. After that, stop moving your fingers; you will feel the temperature of the surface and the firmness of the table. If I give you a hexagonal cube and ask you to close your eyes, you will turn the cube around and start counting the surfaces. When I ask you how many sides the cube has, you send a signal to the brain and are ordered to turn around all the surfaces and count each surface in the brain, one by one. The message is processed without you seeing it. The message is sent to the speech area, which sends a message to the vocal cords and to all the physical apparatuses involved in speech, and you say, "Six." What magic! You count six without knowing it or seeing it. You even describe the consistency, temperature, and smoothness of the surface and all the corners. All this information is sent to the sensory part of the cerebrum. This process involves billions of cells and creates an enormous amount of electricity and neurotransmitters involved (102). I will calculate how much electricity is produced and how much magnetic field is created by this action at a time. There is an enormous amount of electric current generated when all these processes work together, generating magnetic fields, which combine all the information together for us to complete the task as discussed. This magnetic field acts as backup energy for our neurons. When needed in the future, this energy is used by our neurons. You can call it a memory. I call it the higher functioning magnetic soul. I presume you can light an electric bulb, just for this action. All the fibers from these receptors (nerve fibers) pass through the spinal cord and reach the medulla. They terminate in the dorsal column nuclei (gracile and cuneate)—the final destination of these fibers from the medulla to the thalamus and then to the sensory neurons of the cerebrum (cerebral cortex). We humans may have a bigger cerebral cortex compared to animals, but the function of the sensory apparatus in animals is far advanced, depending upon the survival skill needed for the species. Compared to animals, our sensory system may be primitive. Let us look at ants; they communicate with their whiskers. They share information about where the food is, the safe path to travel is, whether there is any danger, how much payload to bring to the nest, and so on. The information is passed on to the entire colony, showing how to function in harmony. It is all done with a touch through the neurochemicals passed on to each other with full information. There is so much information passed on to each other that we don't have a clue. Look at a snake, which cannot hear a thing but can detect through the sense of vibration. A mouse can detect sensations with its whiskers without having a giant cerebral cortex. The list goes on and on. These sensory apparatuses are developed on the basis of the evolution of the species for survival and are passed on to their future generations by genetic transfer of information. There is constant change, depending upon the change in the environment via mutation of the genes. *Neocortex* means "new cortex" (cerebrum). It is a part of the cortex in animals and humans. About 90 percent of the cortex in humans is neocortex with 10^{10} neurons, about quarter million neurons per square millimeter. This sensory cortical mass is called Brodmann's area. The thalamus is placed right in the center of the cerebrum. Just like jam in the doughnut, it acts as a relay center for sensory information and then sends it to Brodmann's area. Motor fibers also pass through the thalamus and relay into the motor area. These work together when needed. We can sense easily when we get into the shower whether the water is hot or cold. It is sensed in any part of the skin. Thus, it prevents burning of our body parts and frostbite from the ice and also controls pleasant activities, which we enjoy, like taking a bath in the hot tub. If we touch a hot pot or stove, we immediately withdraw our hand to prevent further damage. We have two-point discrimination. If we touch our legs, one with a hot object and one with cold object, we can tell where we feel hot and cold. This is only known when the sensory part of the cerebrum is intact, depending on how and where the parts of the body are represented in our cerebrum. If a waitress is carrying glasses of wine on a tray and we pick one, she knows it was taken from the tray. So, we have somatosensory sensations, like tickle, pain, softness, itchiness, roughness, hardness, stickiness, wetness, sharpness, warmth, pressure, and so on.

THE SENSE OF PAIN AND THE SOUL

Pain is the great sensation to get your attention when you ignore your body and soul. When I say you, I mean your brain in the dark black box of your head. Though no one likes pain, every living organism has had it or felt it, either physically or emotionally. There is no way to avoid this sensation in our lifetime. Even if we do not move or if we lock ourselves in a room, we still have pain, either from sitting too long or lying too long. If nothing else, emotional pain is unavoidable. So, how can I deny it? It is my friend; I have to learn to live with it. The more I reject it, the more it bothers me; the more I accept it, the more it relieves me. Since it is my companion for life, how can I ignore it? The more I keep it close to my soul, the more encephalin, morphine-like painkillers are secreted to keep it away. The more I keep it close to my soul, the less histamine, serotonin, Bradykinin, substance P, and prostaglandins are secreted at the damaged site. Pain sensation tells me who I am, where I am, and what I am. It could be my foot, my chest, or my gallbladder. It could be any part of my body that hurts. Thus, pain reassures my soul that I am alive and I am functioning. I am not dead after all. Pain is perceived in the sensory system of the brain, and it is stored as a backup memory in our soul, which I will discuss as we go along. Pain gives us inspiration to love, to hate, and to protect ourselves and other living creatures. For example, someone in your family dies. How do you feel? You feel severe emotional pain, depending on the relationship you have. You cry and grieve. You develop empathy for those who have lost loved ones, like a wife or a husband or mother or a child. You help them feel for them. The same could hold true for you, and others help you. Therefore, your soul shares feelings with others and understands the pain of self and other souls. Once you are hurt and you are in a physical or emotional state of pain, you do realize how others feel when they are in your shoes. Therefore, pain creates a state of awareness of self and of others' existence. I had nothing to do with the First and Second World War, since I was not born; I watched the documentaries about both, and I realized how painful it would have been for millions and millions of souls. Sixty million souls died at no fault of their own. I felt pain in my soul. I felt for all of them, especially those Jews who were slaughtered, brutalized, and tortured without food and shelter. Hitler marked all Jewish businesses and shops for identification. How painful it would have been to look at the identification on the doors. It reminds me of the pain of my family in 1947, when India and Pakistan separated. My entire family was disintegrated, according to my aunt, who told us the stories of the partition of India and Pakistan in Kashmir, where my brothers, sisters, and family lived. All the relatives and friends of our family lived in the village of Sighpora. Some distant relatives were killed, and their houses were burnt. Such painful times for my family, and though I was not born yet, I still get chills when I think of these stories told to me by my aunt. My two brothers and sister were eight, six, and four years old respectively with my mom in the woods somewhere. My mom saw thugs called Kabailies, who invaded Kashmir. They killed non-Muslims, as many as they could. All came from the newly declared "Pakistan." My mom whispered to the three kids like a threatened rabbit mother. She hid them in a bush and asked them to breathe slowly and not to cry or speak with her finger on her lips. The kids sensed the danger and lay on the ground with the instinct of survival. Kabalies (thugs with guns) walked by, laughing and eating fruit. Imagine what happened to their pain then. Even if they had no physical pain, imagine the intensity of the emotional pain and fear of life and death. Fear is so powerful that the soul orders the brain to shut down all the painful stimuli and stop any neuromuscular movement. You must have seen how animals, like newly born deer, hide in bushes or tall grass when they sense the danger. The brain receives all the information, good or bad, painful or painless, and orders the body to change the course it normally takes. There are actions that need to be taken in a fraction of a second. The magnetic force of the soul, which is created by the brain, gives the order in the form of electric current, which subdues and shuts off most of the mechanisms in the body and creates a motionless status; it even ignores pain or pleasure.

Pain is defined by the international association for the study of pain as an unpleasant sensory and emotional experience associated with real or potential tissue damage. I would add to that severe emotional trauma, like PTSD (post-trauma stress disorder) due to war, rape, imprisonment, hostage situations, and other traumas. In such cases, our soul reacts to the point of reexperiencing the pain inflected by the trauma. Pain is not simply the physiological response to a physically applied stimulus but a perception, experience, expectation, and feeling of painful stimuli. The painful loss of a child or another loved one or wealth or the perceived loss of any possession can cause severe emotional pain.

I remember in the month of January 2016, Vice President Joe Biden was being interviewed by a great journalist of her time Gloria Borger on CNN. She asked him, "How do you feel about Bo?" (Bo was the son of the vice president, who was in the war in Iraq and Afghanistan. He came home and died of brain cancer. What a painful and sad event for any parent!)

Vice President Biden answered, "Look, I have lost my soul," referring to Bo. "How am I supposed to feel? Don't get me wrong; I have a daughter who is my heart." The vice president of the United States did not tell Gloria, "My arms and legs hurt," or "My brain hurts." No, he said, "My soul hurts." Why? Since the brain has no pain receptors or nerve supplies, it does not hurt, but the soul hurts until it regains the magnetic strength it has lost from any traumatic event. Even President Barack Obama, in his State of the Union address in 2016, stated, "My soul hurts when I see violence on the streets and people being killed in the United States." I am sure his soul hurts, because he did not say, "I get a headache," or "My arms and legs or body hurts." Pain is a dynamic exposure to painful stimuli, influencing the future response to the same stimulus. It is even known that pain has links to the immune system and the endocrine pathways, as well as genes underlying susceptibility to pain disorders.

It is common to feel immediate pain ("Ouch!") when someone hits you and ("Oops!") burning pain when you touch a hot stove. If I apply a blood pressure cuff to your arm and inflate the cuff to a level where I block C fibers and A fibers, which are the short and long fibers of the nerves that carry information to the spinal cord, the large fibers are blocked first and then the small fibers. Because of this, we lose the sense of pressure and the sense of touch first, and then we lose our sense of temperature, pricking pain, burning pain, and itch. In our internal organs, pain is conveyed to the spinal cord via the autonomic nervous system—like in chest pain, abdominal pain, or pain from any other organ. There is referred pain since the neurons that receive and supply the skin are from the same segment of the spinal cord, thus both skin and the organ feel pain when there is stimulus to the segment of spinal cord. For example, when we have angina pectoris (due to less blood supply to the heart), we have pain on the left side of the jaw, neck, chest, and arm because it is the same nerve supply, and if we have gallbladder inflation or pain, we also have pain on the tip of the right shoulder; this, we call referred pain. Pain neurons are located in the dorsal horn of the spinal cord. Here are some anatomical parts of the body and brain involved with an electric current that travels from the skin to the cerebrum and from the cerebrum to the skin and muscles. Visual sensation is essential in the process of avoiding any pain stimulus: skin --> spinal cord --> thalamus (also ascending reticular formation) --> primary and secondary somatosensory cortex, insular cortex, prefrontal cortex, anterior electric cingulate cortex, supplementary motor area, posterior parietal cortex, periaqueductal gray matter, amygdala, and cerebellum. The same reverses to send current to avoid pain by visual sensory involvement.

It is very interesting to know that damage to the cortex or stimulation of the sensory cortex has never been reported to cause pain, while stimulation of the hypothalamus results in acute pain, and reduced thalamic activity leads to chronic pain. In the state of excitement and intense fear, as reported by soldiers in war who are wounded and did not feel pain, there may be a general insensitivity to injuries that would certainly be painful under normal circumstances. In such situations, soldiers severely injured may not feel pain. Many studies have confirmed the lack of pain in heightened situations of fear and rage. In some instances, when we are apprehensive, there is severe and exaggerated pain, like in the dentist's office. In some cases, when pain results in hope, pleasure, and the beauty of life, it is forgiven and forgotten. While my wife had our first baby, during the process of her delivery, she blamed me for getting her pregnant and yelled and screamed, which was forgotten after my son was born. She got pregnant again and had our second son. It happened again the second time; the joy of life causes one to discard and ignore all the pain and distress. That is how all species survive to continue the life of the species. Even, at times, a simple stimulus of the skin around our sexual organs creates erotic sensations when initiated by the opposite sex. We do infer from all this that the objective identification of pain in time and space is mediated by the traditional cortical area of the parietal regions, while the emotional affective experience relates to the frontal cortex and cerebellum.

Emotional pain, though not very well understood, is a severe form of pain. While in the private practice of psychiatry, I had the learning experience of my life. During a therapeutic session with Patient A, who had lost her husband and a son in an accident, she expressed her feelings. She had slipped into major depression. In one of the sessions, I saw tears rolling down her cheeks, and she said, "I hurt, Doctor. I hurt," and she paused.

I asked, "Where do you hurt?" I wanted to rule out any other illness or cause of pain.

She said, "I cannot explain." She stated, "I wish my arm or leg was cut off. I could easily tolerate the pain, and it would be easy to explain to you, Doctor." She paused again.

I listened and felt assured she did not have an organic reason for her pain. She continued, "My soul hurts. I do not have pain anywhere else."

I thought to myself, *Her soul hurts.* I had no concept or knowledge of "the soul" and its physiology or anatomy. But it got stuck in my head. As I grew in my practice and gained experience, learning from my patients, I realized there is more to emotional pain than physiological, anatomical, or psychological causes. Sure enough, my curiosity grew up to explore more about pain and the relationship with "the soul." It is not mere electric current that flows from the source of pain to our brain and back to the site of injury. It is the disruption and depletion of the magnetic field of the soul, which is created by the electric current of the nerves and brain. This causes our soul to suffer because of the loss. We do know to a certain extent that there is a depletion of serotonin, adrenaline, dopamine, and other neurotransmitters, which we still have to learn about. Thus, there is a weak electric current in depressed patients resulting in a weak magnetic field compared to healthy, nondepressed patients. I shall discuss this in detail in the chapter on physiology and the structure of the soul. Now, I wonder how the soul of Vice President Joe Biden felt in relation to the loss of his son. It is constant and persistent memory of the loss that depletes the neurotransmitters and weakens the electric current, thus creating a weak magnetic field of the soul, which inflicts the unexplained emotional pain. I will expand on this unexplained mystery through the work of neurobiologists, psychiatrists, and physiologists under heading "Transcranial Magnetic Stimulation (TMS)" in depressed patients.

According to Gray Zukav in *The Seat of the Soul*, "When a multisensory personality looks inside itself, it finds a multitude of different currents" (30). Through experience, it learns to distinguish between these currents and to identify the emotional, psychological, and physiological effects of each. It learns, for example, which current produces anger, divisive thoughts, and destructive actions and which current produces love, healing thoughts, and constructive actions. In time, it learns to value and to identify with those currents that generate creativity, healing, and love and to challenge and release those currents that create negativity, disharmony, and violence. In this way, the personality comes to experience the energy of its soul.

Your soul is not a passive or a theoretical entity that occupies a space in the vicinity of your chest cavity. It is a positive, purposeful force at the core of your being. It is that part of you that understands the impersonal nature of the energy dynamics in which you are involved, the part that loves without restrictions and accepts without judgment. According to Gray Zukav, if you desire to know your soul, the first step is to recognize that you have a soul. If I have a soul, what is my soul? What does my soul want? What is the relationship between my soul and me? How does my soul affect my life? When the energy of the soul is recognized, acknowledged, and valued, it begins to infuse life into the personality. When the personality comes fully to serve the energy of its soul, then there is authentic empowerment. This is the goal of the evolutionary process in which we are involved and the reason for our being. Every experience that you have and will have upon the earth encourages the alignment of your personality with your soul. Every circumstance and situation gives you the opportunity to choose the path to allow your soul to shine through you, to bring into the physical world through you its unending and unfathomable reverence for and love of life.

Zukav obviously had wisdom and knowledge of the current that flows back and forth from the brain to the source of stimulus. He had the courage and intention to recognize his own soul, which encouraged him to write about the soul. My soul salutes him for this creation of knowledge and acknowledgment of the soul. Neurobiologists and neuroscientists have abolished the notion of the existence of the soul because they cannot see it, they cannot reproduce it, they cannot test it, and they have no picture of it. For those who have discarded the soul, I have a few questions: Can you see gravity? It existed way before Newton found it. He did not invent it; he *found* it. Can you see electric current? Can you see the magnetic field? I have never seen it. In the same way, you cannot see the soul. I am not inventing the soul. It has been there since living creatures came into existence. Can we measure the electromagnetic field of the human body? Yes, we can. I call it the soul. You can call it whatever you want. I will stick to my finding (not invention). Thus, it does exist. I shall discuss this in detail and prove that Zukav was 100 percent right to make his statement and write a historical book for all of our souls.

There have been several experiments conducted to assess the behavior from and response to physical and emotional pain in monkeys. By Harlow (p. 134), one monkey was put in a cage and received less attention and was punished by electrical impulse to create pain and fear. In a second cage, another monkey was well fed and rewarded with different, pleasant stimuli. Over the period of time, the monkey that received pain was socially isolated and could not mate to produce offspring; it was shy and fearful of any stimuli. It was slow to react to stimuli. The other monkey was agile, free to express itself. It socially interacted with other monkeys. It was not easily startled and was less fearful and better able to reproduce offspring. This applies to humans too. We have evidence that in the area of violence and war-ridden areas, the humans there develop fatigue or desensitization to painful stimuli. As the saying goes, "I am beaten up. How much can you beat me? Go on. I do not hurt anymore." The other spectrum is fight or flight.

According to the *Random House Dictionary*, the definition of fight or flight is the response of the sympathetic nervous system to a stressful event, preparing the body to fight or flee. It is associated with the adrenal secretion of epinephrine and characterized by increased heart rate, increased blood flow to the brain and muscles, elevated blood sugar levels, sweaty palms and soles, dilated pupils, and erect hairs. Fight or flight is a hyperarousal response to a perceived harmful event, attack, or threat from an external source. It is a genetic inbuilt response of living organisms for survival. This comes from our senses, like our sense of vision and hearing. It creates a storm of electric current, which is sent to our ascending reticular formation and to the limbic system and frontal lobe. They, in turn, create an enormous magnetic field of the soul, which sends an enormous electric response, ordering our brain to take action in milliseconds and resulting in a sudden rush of order to our adrenal glands, motor and sensory areas, and limbic system to act and take action. Thus, there is an enormous reaction, resulting in physiological and emotional responses in the body. The sympathetic system is overwhelmed; there are increased levels of norepinephrine and epinephrine, cortisol, estrogen, testosterone, dopamine, and serotonin. There is increased blood flow to muscles, including the heart; the brain; and the rest of the body to work in a uniform way, creating fight or flight. Just imagine how enormous the electric activity created in this process in a few milliseconds is. This mechanism is repeatedly created in post-traumatic syndrome, where even a small threat results in an enormous reaction. Even a symbolic threat that may not exist in reality can cause this reaction. It is an overreaction to a minimally threatening stimulus. Our soul is conditioned to respond to any threat because of its hypersensitivity. Our brain and soul are conditioned to respond to any threat, existing or even perceived, unrealistically.

In normal humans or animals, there has to be a real threat. Let me give you an example, which my professor of psychiatry explained to us while we were residents in psychiatry. He explained, "If you have a baseball bat in your hand and you are locked up in a room with a dog, if you swing the baseball bat, the dog will either run away from you or try to bite you. But if the door is open, chances are, the dog may run away. If you are chased by a black bear, chances are you will run away. If you fail to do so, you will fight to survive. This primitive reflex is passed on to us by our genes for survival. There is a reaction of the entire physical being, including increased blood clotting to prevent excessive blood loss. There is secretion of encephalin, meta-encephalin, and an opiate-like substance to prevent excessive pain. It was noted in injured soldiers who did not feel pain after massive injuries. There is anxiety and aggression. In lower, cold-blooded animals, there is a sudden change of color for camouflage to blend with the color of the background. A mother bear will protect her cubs by running away from an aggressive male bear or fight to the death. A bird will draw attention and act as if she is dead when her chicks are in danger. She will be persistent until the danger is lured away from her chicks.

SENSE OF HEARING AND THE SOUL

Hearing is also an important sense of the soul. The hearing apparatus senses vibration in the air—chirping of the birds, thunder in the sky, crying of a baby, yelling of the other people, loving and caring words of your loved ones. It gives you information vital to your survival, helping you avoid approaching danger, like a car or an aggressive dog. It also allows you to appreciate your surroundings, like a wonderful song, the beat of a drum, the soothing flow of a stream, hypnotic suggestion, and advice from our mentors or parents. Sound is propagated in the form of regular waves of pressure. Not all vibrations are sounds. They have to be audible. The frequency must be between 20 and 20,000 Hz in humans (104). But imagine the animal in which hearing is far advanced and better than a human's. A dog can hear much better than a human can. An elephant can hear at a much lower frequency. Our cerebral cortex (cerebellum) is far bigger than lower animals'; still, we lag behind them. After all, this is how we can differentiate various sounds and react to each one with anger or love, choose to avoid sitting down and having a conversation, or run away as fast as we can when we hear a dangerous sound to avoid any harm. A mother tells a child "No-no" and "Yes-yes." How can a child differentiate between the two? What a sophisticated and advanced mechanism! It all happens. Sound travels through the external ear (pinna and auditory canal), which is shaped such that we can accommodate as much sound to our auditory canal as possible. Sound is received and compressed in a small canal (the auditory canal). It gives us the actual direction and position of the production of the sound. This sound hits a thin membrane and causes it to vibrate, shaking the bony apparatus of the middle ear cavity. This membrane separates the middle part of the ear from the external part of the ear and is called the tympanic membrane. The muscles of the inner ear are supplied by the trigeminal nerve and the facial cranial nerves. The malleus is a bony structure attached to the tympanic membrane, which vibrates the incus and stapes (two bony structures). There are two muscles—the tensor tympanic and the stapedius that effectively disable the transmission system when they hear a loud sound, protecting the inner ear from damage. The inner ear is fluid filled to produce pressure waves in the inner ear, which reach the cochlea (105). In animals, a frequency below 20 Hz is called infrasound. Bats, dogs, and snakes use infrasound for hearing. Some fish have the ability to hear more sensitively because of a well-developed bony connection between the ears and their bony structure (106). It is like a hearing aid to a deaf person, which explains the vest invented by David Eagleman to provide sensory substitution for the deaf (34'169). A cochlear implant feeds signals directly to the undamaged auditory nerve, sending electrical impulses to the auditory cortex to decode the signal and make an interpretation of the nature of the electric impulse. In the same way, a hearing aid receives sounds of a certain amplitude to improve the sense of hearing in humans. Special localization of sound involves distance and direction. Distance is variable, but direction is more accurate. Both ears unify the sound by merely changing the direction of the head. The central auditory pathways are complex and not fully understood. The auditory nerve carries an electric signal to the cochlear nucleus in the brain stem, where pathways from both ears meet and information is combined into one. Here, we learn about what kind of sound it is and which direction it came from.

MECHANISM OF SOUND

Auditory nerves --> cochlear nucleus in the brain stem --> interior colliculus in the midbrain (here is the auditory startled response) -- > medial geniculate nucleus part of thalamus -- > Wernicke's area of the temporal lobe of the cortex

Here, the sound is interpreted as it is and information is processed. We hear what it is. The cortex adds to the analysis that the lower auditory system has already performed. Removing the cerebral cortex of hearing in cats and rats led to very little impairment of frequency and discrimination, but it did cause difficulties in discriminating what exactly made the sound. In addition to hearing, the eighth cranial nerve, called the vestibule-cochlear nerve, is involved in maintaining the balance of the body (108). After all this has been described, the basic principle is that in the generation of electricity in hearing, there is a magnetic field produced by the process, which is the structure of the soul. Hence, my thinking is clear that it is the final destination of the electric impulse where the magnetic field acts as a backup storage or the main controller, providing directions to the cortex's hearing area (Wernicke's area). Binding all of the sensory system is the function of the soul. Its job is to enhance the quick response, including hearing and other sensory stimuli.

SENSE OF VISION AND THE SOUL

Seeing is different than hearing. It has its own kind of *transduction* (change of one energy form to another). Scientists know light is a form of electromagnetic wave traveling very fast—with more velocity than thunder. Light travels somewhere around 300 kilometers per millisecond. In nature, most of the electromagnetic radiation is generated by hot objects like the sun, hot lava, and manmade lights. The receptors in rods and cones provide us information about the light (109). If we go from daylight to a dark room, we find it takes nearly forty minutes for our eyes to adjust. Cones are in the middle of the retina of the eye and provide detailed information about the retinal image. They are responsive to color. Rods are much more sensitive and have to group together as a functional unit of thousands, which are connected with their neuronal connections. Eyes are not only meant for light or dark but also to form an image of the outside world and send a message to the visual center of the brain. Eyes are windows for the blind in the dark black box of our brain, which forms the vision of the soul. When babies reach out to touch something they want to, it is not merely to feel the texture or shape but to learn how to see. Seeing feels so simple and easy, but it is hard to imagine what the brain has to go through to understand what exactly we are seeing. Vision has to interact with other senses to coordinate the perfect response and understanding of the external object. With enough practice from childhood to adulthood, the brain continues to learn and experience the stories told by the eyes. The eye has the most sophisticated mechanism to sense light and the intensity of light. For example, the cornea is only twenty-four millimeters away from the retina. Lenses can alter their shape and fine-tune the eye's effective focal length. This is called *accommodation*. Eyes are able to do so by having elastic and flexible lenses, which are twelve millimeters long, with cells knitted together in a series of concentric layers. It is just like jelly with a rope attached at its ends (suspensory ligament). Encircling the lens, there are ciliary muscles, which contract and relax the lenses to accommodate the light. The eye lens has no blood supply; it gets nourishment from the aqueous humor, a fluid similar to plasma.

Retina < - > optic nerve< - > tracts in midbrain, oculomotor nuclei < - >occipital lobe

Any abnormal pupil will tell us about an abnormality of the brain. The pupil has two different muscles: sphincter papillae and dilator. Both have sympathetic and parasympathetic nerve supplies. Pupil dilation tells us a lot is going on, like fear, anxiety, danger, or another change in the emotional state; sexual excitement; and much more. I am here to give an overview of the general aspects of the eye, not a detailed anatomy. Each eye has roughly 130 million receptors and one million ganglion cells. In the retina, a good deal of the neural processing of the information received has already taken place and is then sent to the optic nerve. We use our eyes for many tasks:

- recognizing objects in the outside world (brain function)
- locating where they are and how they are (superior colliculus)
- acting as a source of information about ourselves, our position in relation to the outside (all this happens in the midbrain)

Final information is relayed to the occipital lobe of the cerebrum (visual center) (110).

SENSE OF TASTE AND SMELL

This is a different mechanism in the living soul. There is a chemical stimulus that originates from outside of the body, like smell, which is sensed by the chemosensitivity of the nose (111). In the case of taste, it is the function of chemoreceptors to monitor the composition of the blood. They are used in the regulation of autonomic and hormonal functions. Our nose has one of the richest blood supplies. That is why we bleed excessively with a small ulcer or minor injury to this blood supply (an artery or a vein). We humans are *microsomatic*, which means we do not use the sense of smell to the extent that animals like dogs, lions, or elephants do. We call them *macrosomatic*. The sense of smell is a resource for survival in finding food, sensing danger, and even in reproduction. A male bull can sense hormonal changes in a female cow merely by smelling the urine or the genital organs of the female, whether she is in heat or not, which promotes survival of the species.

Animals can sense a scent from miles away because of highly developed cells contained in the Bowman's glands, which produce a lipid-rich secretion to keep the receptors' surface moist (112). The nose is lined with epithelial cells, which contain pigment, light yellow in humans and dark yellow or brown in dogs. It is presumed that this pigment may be involved in the absorption of radiation (like infrared). There are ten million receptors on the surface of the epithelium of the nose. The Jacobson's organ, which is involved in an advanced sense of smell in some animals disappears in humans after birth. The olfactory (system for smell) receptors send their own axons to and from the olfactory nerve, which forms an olfactory bulb and olfactory tracts. In animals, there is an accessory olfactory bulb, which has more prominent projections of axons to the hypothalamus, thus explaining the reception of intense sense of smells in many animal species. The olfactory tract is divided into medial (close to the center of the central nervous system) and lateral (away from the center). In humans, the lateral tract conveys the sense of smell to the cerebral cortex. In animals, the medial tract also carries the sensation of smell, because of this, their sense of smell is highly developed. The nerve fibers connect with the motor part of the brain, which controls the muscular movement of animals, allowing them to run to a source of food or away from any danger. This behavior is for survival. Many parts of the limbic system are involved in this process, which I shall discuss in the limbic system chapter. It is involved in motivation, emotion, and certain kinds of memory. In the septal nuclei and amygdale, the pleasure center is dominant.

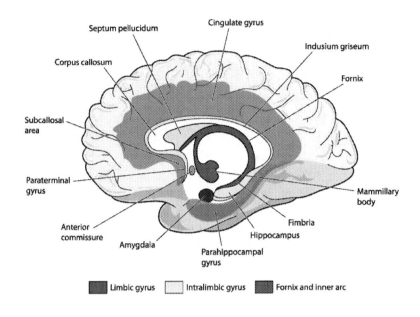

Septum pellucidum

Cingulate gyrus

Indusium griseum

Corpus callosum

Fornix

Subcallosal area

Paraterminal gyrus

Mammillary body

Anterior commissure

Fimbria

Hippocampus

Amygdala

Parahippocampal gyrus

■ Limbic gyrus □ Intralimbic gyrus ■ Fornix and inner arc

PLEASURE CENTER

When an electric impulse stimulates the pleasure center, there is a positive motivation. The hippocampus plays a part in the sense of smell. This part of the brain is associated with motivation and pleasure when stimulated by food. In the evolutionary process, secondary motivation is acquired by the stimuli through experience, learning, and the memory of olfactory motivation. In humans, there is important connection between the hypothalamus and the limbic system, which controls autonomic effects, like salivation and secretor responses to the smell of food. Also, bad smells can cause nausea and other experiences to help humans avoid such foods for the rest of their lives (113).

The sense of smell plays an important role in sexual arousal in animals and humans. Some animals have glands that secret musk and hormones to attract the opposite sex. We humans use perfumes and other products to produce pleasant smells to attract the opposite sex. Animals mark their territories so other animals can sniff to avoid hostile encounters with other aggressive animals. Even during the menstrual cycle, there are certain chemicals that attract males to mate. It is quite obvious that we humans have a huge industry of perfumes, and we always keep producing products and creating brand names. Sales are in the billions. I am stuck with one brand, because I used to get compliments from women more. My sweat glands secrete odors that make a certain combination with my cologne and produce a pleasant smell. Or it may be a chemical reaction between my body's chemicals and the chemicals in the perfume. Behavior is controlled by the nose via the olfactory bulb and various parts of the limbic system, such as the medial nucleus of the amygdale and the frontal cortex of the cerebrum. Olfactory fibers are connected to the optic tract via olfactory striae. Thus, there is a loop from the brain to the nose and sense of vision.

In a nutshell, the sense of smell controls our and animals' behavior as follows:

- Feeding—hunting, finding food, eating, avoiding dangerous foods, and stimulation of digestive secretions (this can happen even when we think of food—Pavlov's pouch).
- Sex—recognition of receptive females, triggering or suppressing ovulation, sexual attraction, arousal, repulsion, recognition of offspring, triggering maternal instinct and maternal behavior, sensing danger from predators and alarm (odors or chemicals) by other herd members
- Territory—recognizing urinal territorial marks and breeding grounds
- Social—recognizing members of the species, a group member, and social dominance.

Humans' psychological behavior is influenced by recollection of past odors, feelings, and emotions.

How different forms of smell create different responses is still unclear, but my thinking is simple. It is the olfactory center in the frontal part of the cerebrum, called the olfactory cortex, that uses its learning experiences through a genetic component or evolutionary process. As children, we are exposed to different odors, and our brain retains some of those, which creates an electric current so that there is a magnetic field of the soul. This acts as backup storage of such events and thus relates to the memories stored in the frontal lobe, which processes the thoughts and the emotions. The limbic system is an integral part of such functions. I will discuss it in another chapter. The soul may have a role to play as a supreme power to

AMAR J. SINGH, MD, DFAPA AND DANVIR SINGH

relate all these processes to our brain. My soul still has the sensation of the fragrance of roses and fruits and fresh air in the valley of Kashmir and the foul smell of my unwashed clothes. I still have the memory stored in my soul about the foul smell of putrid fruits and dirty channels full of decaying vegetation and fecal material. I still have a memory of fresh air in the vast, open forest of Kashmir. I still have the memory of the formaldehyde (used for preservation of dead bodies for dissection) we used while learning anatomy and teaching anatomy in medical school.

We can perform an electro-olfactogram (EOG) to assess the effects of various odors in humans by applying electrodes in the epithelium of the nose to record the electric potential of the olfactory cells. We still have to achieve the goal to understand. Some scientists have recorded an olfactory response through stimulation of the cerebral cortex, the limbic system, and even basal ganglia.

The adaptation of the olfactory system is not rapid, but at times, it is complete. The olfactory system can become very insensitive to particular smells. Men and women working in uncommonly smelly environments, such as sewer or gas workers, soon become insensitive to the smell around them. People are generally unaware of their own body odors. Even professional cooks have to take certain precautions to avoid insensitivity to the flavors of the food and to avoid adaptation. Wine tasters may bite on cheese to avoid adaptation.

The sense of smell is overpowered by the senses of vision and hearing in human beings.

Transduction is a process by which the sense of smell is changed into electric current or into an electrochemical mechanism, which scientists have explained as much as they could. Some claim there are hollow receptacles of molecular proportions that accept or reject odorant molecules. Each site of the receptors is the responding site in the nose receptacles (114).

TASTE

Taste has a somatosensory mechanism of texture, temperature, and pain. It is related to the large smell sensation. People with colds have a disturbed sense of taste. We humans have four main taste sensations: salty, sour, bitter, and sweet. Our taste is interconnected with the sense of smell, sense of vision, sense of proprioception, and the frontal lobe to express our emotions about a horrible taste versus a pleasant one. I am sure there is a limbic system connection, because when we kiss a beautiful girl or a handsome man, we do taste, smell, and feel the arousal of sexual excitement. In lower animals, it is far more advanced. A bull can taste and smell the urine of a cow and sense if a cow is in heat and ready to mate. Though there is verbal and nonverbal communication and posturing in some animals and birds, like changing colors, to send signals about readiness to mate, we humans flirt more prior to ovulation because there is a sexual urge at the peak to get the egg fertilized. This is a basic genetic instinct with a surge of hormones. Some amino acids and water can stimulate taste buds. Why do we crave sour, sweet, or salty flavors? In my case, I crave bitter taste too. (I grow, cook, and freeze bitter melons for the whole year.) We shall find out how, when, and why. Taste has a different mechanism, though the goal is the same—to send information to the brain, process it, and send the electric current to the taste buds and other sensory and motor system elements. Sometimes we make faces while we taste food. We sometimes say, "Wow! What delicious food!" and sometimes, "I don't like it." The threshold of preferences is under the influence of the body's state of physiological need. For example, I was playing golf on a hot, sunny day with my buddy, and I chose to walk. I drank a lot of water, but I was still sweating profusely. I barely made it to eighteenth hole. I told my buddy, "I want French fries." We went to a restaurant, and the next thing, I knew I was pouring salt onto my French fries.

He asked, "What is wrong with you? Too much salt is not good for you."

I didn't care. I ate as much as I could. I explained to my buddy that I had lost a lot of salt and I was craving salt. Sure enough, I felt good after I ate salty French fries.

"Wow," he said. "You know it better, Doc."

Sometimes I crave oranges and tangerines. Why? My body is low in vitamin C. Sometimes I crave sugar. I want an ice cream. Believe it or not, I was craving a steak once. In routine blood work, I found my whole lipid profile was low. No wonder! There is a balance between the needs of the body and the nature of the food. In obese individuals, there is a disconnect and deregulation of this system. Thus, we overindulge either in sweets or fatty foods. Where does this happen? I will explain the pathway in the body to the brain and finally to our magnetic soul. The tongue has clearly demarcated areas in the front for sweets, on both sides for salty, and in the back for bitter. That is why it takes a little longer to taste bitter fruits or food. I tasted bitter melons as a growing child, and my parents told me it is good for diabetes as it balances blood sugar. Hence, it was ingrained into my soul. As I grew older, I learned that bitter melons do have some chemicals that prevent diabetes. Hence, I learned how to cook with different Indian flavors and spices. In Asian countries, it is a novelty to cook bitter melons. In the West, anything bitter is unpleasant and noxious or poisonous. My friend took some bitter melons and his wife cooked them. The next day, while we were playing golf, he told me, "Do me a favor."

"What?"

I replied, "Never, ever give me bitter melons again."

I laughed and carried on with my play. I understood what he meant; obviously, he hated the bitter taste of the melons. I did learn about this in medical school. We tested ourselves to locate the site of taste in the region of the tongue. Tongue receptors do not send information to our brain directly since the tongue is supplied by the seventh nerve (facial nerve),the eleventh nerve (the glossopharyngeal nerve), and the fifth nerve (the trigeminal nerve), providing taste for pain (chili pepper) and hot and cold food.

Nerve fibers from these nerves go to the nucleus solitarius, which sends information to the thalamus from there, projecting fibers to the insular part of the cerebral cortex, where they are joined by the olfactory projection (smell). Fibers from thalamus are also projected to the limbic system as well.

All these chemical balances and reactions are converted into electric current and sent to the brain. It receives the information for our motor and emotional reaction and to restore the memory either in the frontal cortex or in our soul in the form of magnetic energy. This process is called *transduction*. Sometimes, ammonia is used to wake people up. It has a pungent smell. It sends a strong sensation to the brain through a strong electric current generated by such a noxious smell, which stimulates the ascending reticular formation, thus creating a strong magnetic field of the soul. This sends a strong wake-up call to a sedated person. You will find a sudden alertness in individuals stimulated with ammonia.

The tongue is not only the organ for taste or speech, but in birds and other animals, it acts as a cooling organ. You must have seen on a hot day dogs and birds opening their mouths and beaks, thus evaporating water. Evaporation causes cooling, and the animals feel relieved. The tongue also helps animals and humans to drink water and fluids along with mastication. This mechanism is accomplished both by motor function of the muscles of the tongue and the sensation of taste. Dryness of the tongue is a hallmark of anxiety, the fight or flight mechanism, and also when there is intense anger. This is controlled by the autonomic nervous system. The tongue also acts as an organ for sexual arousal, in kissing. It also feels the inner liner of the mucosa of the mouth, thus sending signals to our brain about its condition. In some cultures, it is a sign of insulting someone when we stick it out or an apologetic gesture when we gently bite it. It is an organ that is pretty active while we laugh, sneeze, or even cry. Whistling is a survival skill to help inform our group members to be alert or when we are quiet and want other members to stay quiet. It can also be a gesture of fun and joy.

How do we know whether we are sitting, standing, or lying in the bed? How do we know whether we are walking, jogging, or exercising? Though the motor system keeps us upright against gravity, in a rigid or relaxed position, we use almost all the senses available to us, regardless of what position we are in. The first source is the pressure receptors in our feet, which tell us what we need to know to determine our postural state and the position of vertical projection of the center of gravity relative to the body's support. The second source is the position of our head. The senses tell us about the position and motion of the head in relation to the outside world. Those are vestibular (inner ear) and visual systems. When we walk up the hill, we bring the center of gravity lower in order to maintain our balance. We may lean forward when the center of gravity is shifted; then we use our feet. This is called a stepping reaction. When I perform yoga in a mountain position, I stand on one leg with the other leg flexed against the knee of the first leg. I am standing on one leg with the extension of the hip joints. I keep my toes spread and anchored to the yoga mat. In the beginning, it was tough. I would fall and use the step of the flexed leg. Then I learned to extend my arms like the wings of a bird and focus my vision on one spot with full concentration and the breathing technique. Then I was able to stand for a sustained period of time to get the full extension of the hip and leg on which I stood. In jogging, the center of gravity is ahead of the body, thus continuous motion prevents falling on the ground. It sounds very simple, but it is more complex, since there are many sensory systems involved in the process, like the vestibular system (internal ear). Semicircular canals inform us about the angular position of the head. *Otolith organs* give us information about our position relative to the effective direction of gravity. Here, the vestibulo-ocular reflex is maintained in conjunction with the position of the eyes, subject to the outside world. The vestibular canals are very sensitive and give advanced warning that one is about to fall over. If we sit in a rotating chair or spin ourselves and go around and around, our eyes move to the opposite direction in relation to our head. This cannot go on forever; the eyes are going to reach their limit of rotation. This smooth counter-rotation of the eyes in one direction is interrupted as intervals by a quick flick in the other direction, giving rise to what we call vestibular nystagmus. If the chair is suddenly stopped, there is a reverse nystagmus. It may produce an inappropriate postural response, which is vigorous enough to throw us on the floor. All the other controls of posture that try to keep us upright fail. If we attempt to stand up after having been rotated in a revolving chair, our head on one side, there is an adaptation of the canals that falsely signals that we are falling in the opposite direction. This reflex actually makes us fall over again (115).

The sense of vision and sense of hearing (vestibular system of the inner ear) work together, and they travel together in the midbrain and communicate with each other. They share common pathway before they reach the cerebrum. The vestibulo-cochlear system (ears) send all the information to the temporal lobe while the sense of vision (eyes) relays information to the occipital lobe. In the retina of the eye, we have neurons that are specialized to the movement of the retinal images across the retina. This is called the visual proprioceptive system. Due to the motion of outside objects, there is enough stimulation of these neurons. This sense is a very powerful one. We have experienced ourselves sitting in a train at the station while another train moves off. Our eyes follow that train and move in the direction of the moving train. Our head moves along with the eyes, thus stimulating the semicircular canals in the internal ear. That is why, at times, we have nystagmus and dizziness. If we sit in front of a moving drum with black and white stripes, after a while, we feel nystagmus. We call it optokinetic nystagmus.

Many of you will raise the question, "How does the brain know when there are two systems—the eyes' and ears' neurons firing at different rate? Well, both create an electric current and send it to their respective centers (visual and auditory centers in the cerebrum). The answer goes back to basics. These two systems work together, and the brain operates by learning from previous experiences. My view is that both centers of the cerebrum

Median Section of the Brain

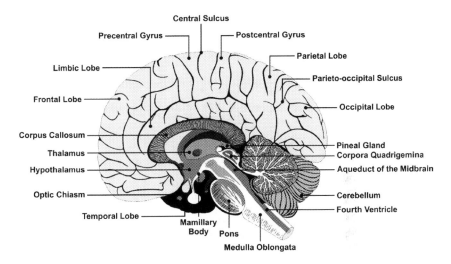

Central Sulcus
Precentral Gyrus
Postcentral Gyrus
Parietal Lobe
Limbic Lobe
Parieto-occipital Sulcus
Frontal Lobe
Occipital Lobe
Corpus Callosum
Pineal Gland
Thalamus
Corpora Quadrigemina
Hypothalamus
Aqueduct of the Midbrain
Optic Chiasm
Cerebellum
Fourth Ventricle
Temporal Lobe
Mamillary Body
Pons
Medulla Oblongata

Once these fibers reach the cerebral cortex, they are sent back to the part of the brain mentioned earlier, which is called the descending reticular formation. These axons reach to the spinal cord after passing through the various parts of the brain mentioned earlier via the reticulospinal tract, which regulates the spinal reflex and also modulates the sensory input by gaining synapses in the spinal cord. These axons form synapses with the autonomic nervous system. I may add all the axons from the visual sensory system, auditory sensory system, pain sensory system, proprioception, and taste and olfactory sensory systems are connected to the reticular formation. They all pass through thalamus, hypothalamus, and other parts of the brain mentioned in the pathways of each system in previous chapters. I am of the belief that the motor system (muscles and all the joints) are also connected with both the ascending and descending reticular formation, thus forming a unit complex of functioning when stimulation causes alertness. This system operates twenty-four/seven. The descending reticular formation is more active than the ascending reticular formation during sleep. This helps us to rest and relax without the disturbance of arousing stimuli from our surroundings. Various organs in our body communicate with the reticular formation via the autonomic nervous system. For example, when you have a gallbladder stone, kidney stone, or appendicitis, you wake from sleep with an alarm and feel severe pain, to the point some scream, cry, and beg for help. This is quite easy and obvious while you are wake. If the reticular formation is depressed by anesthesia, the sensory stimulus still produces activity in specific thalamic and cortical areas but does not produce general cortical arousal.

Many parts of the brain are aroused when stimulated by the external factors around us (color, noise, shape, location, and other sensory stimuli). It is suggested by some neurobiologists—and I agree—that binding of all these processes and functions of neurons and the stimulation of various parts of the brain leads to conscious actions and conscious recognition, which is abolished by lesions or destruction of the midbrain cerebral cortex and reticular formation. They work together to maintain our consciousness. In stroke patients, after recovery, consciousness and alertness are intact but are slow. When there is destruction of the midbrain, there is a coma state, where the individual does not respond with various reflexes, like the corneal reflex. There is no withdrawal to pain stimulus. Since the 1960s, it has been the death of the brain that has been called the death of a person. It was described as a permanent loss of cognition, consciousness, memory, and thoughts. In brief, the death of the brain was the death of a life. There were discussions about "bodily life" and "personal life." Body life was and could be sustained by life-support measures in the medical world, but what about "personal life," which has come to an end (35-17). Well, there could be both cerebral hemisphere destruction and also brain stem destruction. In that case, the whole brain is dead. But let us look at different aspects of death. Let us presume a brain stem lesion or damage (both reticular formations are intact); in that case, we may not have cognition, thoughts, or consciousness, but the person responds to pain stimuli and the reflexes in the eyes are intact. The digestive system and other organs are functioning but consciousness does not exist. This person is just a nonfunctional person unable to remember judge, reason, act, enjoy, worry, think, create, distinguish between right and wrong and outside and inside, and remember who is who—spouse, children, friends. Thus the person has lost his or her "personal life" but has bodily life. The same takes place in a persistent vegetative state (PVA). My view is simple. When the cerebral hemispheres are damaged, the electric current stops producing a magnetic field, which is energy I call the soul. Though the brain stem, where reticular formations are, and the rest of the body have an electric current still passing up and down, it is very weak and not enough to produce enough magnetic field; thus, the soul is weak to the point that it cannot create enough strength for the body to function to the level of normalcy. The cerebrum and its neurons generate and receive enormous amount of electric current twenty-four hours a day, seven days a week; therefore, it transduces an enormous amount of magnetic energy, which makes it possible for the body to function normally. I shall discuss it, at length, in the anatomy of the soul. Stupor and obtundation are lesser grades of depressed consciousness. Sleeping and waking cycles are regulated by the reticular formation and structures in the hypothalamus and brain stem. Nerve cells in the reticular formation of the pons begin to discharge before the onset of sleep. Lesions of pons close to the trigeminal nerve nuclei produce a state of hyper alertness and much less sleep through secretion of serotonin and norepinephrine, which control the stages of non-REM and REM sleep (118). Reticular formation axons and dendrites are located near the third, fourth, and sixth cranial nerves and the motor ascending tracts through the pons, which help us to be aware of waking, chewing, grooming, suckling, coughing, swallowing, sneezing, and expression. The reticular formation is connected to the cerebellum and basal ganglia. The reticular formation regulates the heart rate and generates the rhythm of breathing. This is learned from Ondine's curse. It is a rare congenital disorder with a brain stem injury. In this case, breathing is no longer automatic. Patients have prolonged apnea when they fall asleep.

The limbic system is a master brain by itself within the vast central nervous system of living creatures. It defines its rules but is still ruled by the cerebrum. It tries to rule its domain, but its domain is ruled by the cerebrum. It thinks it is independent and a creator, but it is dependent and monitored. It tries to run its own government but is governed. It thinks on its own, but its thoughts are thought through. It tries to memorize, but its memories are memorized by the cerebrum. It serves for basic survival functions, but they are watched closely. Its guide and master are in the extension of the gray matter of the cortex buried between the two lobes of the cerebrum. It serves as an agent of basic survival, like feeling behaviors, fight-or-flight responses, aggression, expression of emotions, and autonomic system, endocrine, and sexual functions. It is the ancient part of the brain, which we share with other animals. It connects with the brain stem and sends axons from neurons to the cortex. It also receives axons from the cerebral cortex, which then descends to other parts of the spinal cord and cerebellum. The axons from the cerebral cortex form a common association among various sensory apparatuses. The hippocampus is within the limbic system and plays a crucial role in spatial reasoning, problem solving, and memory. In the 1930s, the hypothalamus was recognized as a part of the brain connected with the autonomic nervous system. It was included in the limbic system because of its contribution to our emotions and feelings (119). In the *Journal of Biomedical Science and Engineering*, dated October 28, 2015 (Princples, Anatomocal origin and Application of Brain waves; A Review, Our Experiences and Hypothesis Related to Microgravity and questions on Soul)an article explained the basis of performing ECOG (electrocorticography). It was noted that the limbic system and reticular formation created enormous brain waves that were recorded in the laboratory. As mentioned, the reticular formations are mainly for consciousness and are connected to the limbic system. I would like to mention some of the parts of the brain that are very essential for our emotions, behavior, and day-to-day functioning:

- Hippocampus
- Dentate gyrus
- Amygdala
- Parahippocampal gyrus
- Cingulate gyrus
- Subcallosal gyrus

The dentate gyrus is one of the few regions in the brain that produce new neurons throughout adulthood in a process called neurogenesis. The septal area is the pleasure center of the brain. This is a thought-provoking anatomy and physiology of the brain. I wonder if people with psychiatric disorders, like antisocial personality disorder, borderline personality disorder, narcissistic personality disorder, and paranoid personality disorders, and even terrorists who kill and blow themselves up have abnormal connections within their brains or if there is an alteration in the connections due to stress and grave external environments.

For the amygdala and hypothalamus, I would really prefer to discuss the anatomy of this part in a somewhat detailed fashion because it will explain a whole lot. This area has much to do with how and why behaviors change under stress.

The amygdala and hypothalamus nuclei are very complex. A disturbance in the primary functions of these two areas can lead to the following:

- Bizarre eating and drinking behaviors
- Changes in sexual behavior—some monkeys become hypersexual and even mount same-sex monkeys
- Altered grooming and self-care
- Defensive and even offensive postures—in animals, when hunger stimulates this part of the brain, such postures are predominant; if you watch wild animals, like lions, cats, and foxes, all lean and hide with full concentration on the prey, which is weak and appears vulnerable (As the saying goes, hungry lions make kills more often than the well-fed ones.)
- Sudden changes of passive behavior to aggressive behavior
- Loss of memory and in some cases profound effects on memory

They are responsible for autonomic responses and mechanisms, like increased heart rate and increased circulation to the parts of the body ready to react, for example butterflies in the stomach or an increased frequency of the urge to defecate or urinate (going to the bathroom). I remember my days while having final exams in medical school. I used be jovial and smiling with my fellow students, who did not like my behavior and told me to shut up and walk away from them while they were cramming with their books just before the exam. What was happening to me? I used to go to bathroom with increased frequency, every ten minutes. It reminded me of a great pathologist William Boyd, whose book we used during our pathology classes. He wrote, "[The] stomach is a loud speaker for your organs in the body. When they are distressed and cannot speak, [the] stomach speaks for them by increasing the peristalsis causing vomiting and increased urge to defecate." I did have loose motions. Yes, that was how I responded. On the surface, I appeared very confident. My soul expressed my fearful feelings during my exams. How they would end was unknown to me. The same thing would happen in an oral exam, at the mere thought of how I would be able to perform. William Boyd also stated, "When your eyes do not cry, your stomach cries," by which he meant, when you cannot express your feeling and fear of the unknown, it causes upset stomach and vomiting. This is explained anatomically by the limbic system and autonomic nervous system.

The septal area is fairly large in animals. The olfactory and limbic system are connected with this area. It is responsible for pleasurable activities along with the hypothalamus, epithalamus, and midbrain. Dopamine is the key neurotransmitter involved in pleasurable activities. Antipsychotics reduce the dopaminergic activity in these areas. Some neurobiologists have established limbic system causes for the feeling of euphoria that may lead to narcotic addiction.

A lesion in the amygdala can modify, inhibit, or unleash the behaviors. A lesion in the lateral amygdala causes expressive and irresistible eating, which can cause bulimia. The stimulation of the medial amygdala (toward the center) can cause anorexia nervosa. Patients feel that they are fat and do not eat. It is a wrongful perception of the body. We neurobiologists are learning about the parts of the brain that cause various disorders. As we learn more about the neuroanatomy and neurophysiology of humans with the experiments conducted in animals, neurological lesions or diseases will continue to teach us more and help us to understand our brain and soul. Anxiety is also caused by hyperstimulation of this part of the brain. In some patients, an amygdalectomy reduced antisocial traits but caused hypersexuality.

There are three types of memory: immediate recall, short-term memory, and long-term memory.

The hippocampus is the part of the limbic system that is responsible for converting short-term memory into long-term memory (up to several days). Some neurobiologists claim that the temporal lobe of the cerebrum is responsible for long-term memory, which I will expand on, explaining the functions of the cerebrum. A lesion of the hippocampus has produced retrograde amnesia (an inability to register new long-term memory), which means new information cannot be retained to be recalled. The dorsomedial nuclei of the thalamus and mammillary bodies are integral parts of the registration and recall of memories. The navigation of routes and recall of places are achieved by stimulation of the hippocampus (122). Thus, we are aware of the fact that the hippocampus is involved in future forecasting.

As mentioned, the dentate gyrus is the only part of the brain involved in the regeneration of neurons. Some claim that the lack of neurogenesis (formation and regeneration of neurons of the brain) causes depression. This is something new I learned. Some argue that antidepressants increase neurogenesis in the dentate gyrus (123).

The autonomic nervous system is connected to the entire body and has two subsystems, which take information to the brain. They provide very important information about various parts of the body. This system supplies nerves to vital organs and tissues, like heart muscles, smooth muscles, and blood vessels; all the organs in our chest, abdomen, and pelvis; and the secretary glands. Fibers bring information to our organs and take information to the brain through the spinal cord. Higher centers modulate the functions situated in superior spinal centers like the brain stem nuclei and the hypothalamus. The heart has its own nervous system. Still, both the sympathetic and parasympathetic systems have control of our respiration and heart functions. The nerve supply to our motor muscles is directly through the nerves coming out of the spinal cord. In the case of the autonomic nervous system, there are preganglionic neurons located in the intermediolateral gray column of the spinal cord and axon relay to the ganglion, from where postganglionic axons distribute neurons to the destination and target organs (32, 1).

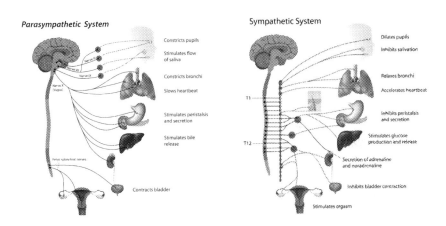

Let me simplify the sympathetic nervous system.

Preganglionic fibers, from the thoracic and lumber regions, form sympathetic chains called a trunk, which sends axon to a chain of sympathetic ganglia. These are ganglia are a) the superior sympathetic ganglion, which supplies fiber to the papillary dilator (eye); (b) the lachrymal glands and basal glands; (c) the submaxillary and sublingual glands; and (d) the parotid glands. The thoracic level (T1 to T5) sends fibers to the heart and lungs.

The celiac ganglion supplies sympathetic fibers to (a) the stomach, (b) the liver, (c) the pancreas, and (d) the spleen. T9 and T10 supply to the adrenal gland.

The superior mesenteric ganglion supplies to the small intestine and colon. The inferior mesenteric ganglion, from L1 and L2 fibers, goes to (a) the colon, (b) the kidney, (c) the urinary bladder, and (d) the sex glands. The superior mesenteric ganglion also supplies to the pancreas, (b) spleen, and (c) adrenal medulla.

The cardiac and pulmonary plexus supplies the heart and lungs.

The inferior mesenteric ganglion sends fibers to a) the pelvic blood vessels, (b) colon, (c) the kidneys, and (d) the urinary bladder.

The hypogastric plexus supplies to the sex organs.

The cervical C1, C2, and C3 supply to the head region and to skin glands, smooth muscles, and blood vessels of the head.

Sympathetic nerve supplies follow the course of blood vessels and reach their final destination.

I will discuss the functions and how this regulates various bodily functions. The parasympathetic system has a different pathway. We call it the craniosacral parasympathetic system, which means parasympathetic supply comes from the brain stem (medulla), sacral region, cranial nerves, and the sacrum (S2, S3, S4). Since the spinal cord ends at the second lumber region, it sends nerves all the way from the lumber region, which comes out of the vertebral openings. Parasympathetic and sympathetic fibers follow along the motor nerves. The spinal sheath ends up at the end of the sacrum bone and is attached to the bone. This long tail of sheath is called cauda equine. It does not carry any nerves but anchors to the sacral bone for support to the spinal cord. The brain does not have any pain receptors or nerve supply, but the dura matter, which covers the brain, is supplied by the autonomic nervous system.

The second system to understand is the *parasympathetic nervous* system. There are *gray matter nuclei* in the brain stem (midbrain II and III, medulla oblongata). Parasympathetic axons travel from these nuclei through (124) a) the third nerve, or the oculomotor nerve; (b) the facial nerve (VII); (c) the glossopharyngeal nerve (IX), and (d) the large wandering nerve that needs clear attention because a lot of research has been done—the vagus or tenth nerve. The second system is mainly in the pelvic region.

Axons from the brain stem nuclei are the main centers for the nerves. The Edinger Westphal nucleus is the center for the oculomotor nerve. It sends fibers to the ciliary ganglion, which supplies the papillary constrictor and ciliary muscles.

The facial nerve originates from the superior salivary nucleus, which synapses with the sphenopalatine ganglion and supply fibers to the lachrymal and nasal glands (eyes and nose). Through the submaxillary ganglion, it supplies the sublingual glands and submaxillary gland.

The inferior salivary nucleus sends axons to the optic ganglion supplies the parotid gland.

The dorsal motor nucleus of the vagus has a vast supply for organs in the thorax abdomen. A few of the organs are as follows: heart, lungs, stomach, liver, pancreas, spleen, small intestine, and colon.

Pelvic parasympathetic innervations go to the colon, kidneys, adrenal medulla, bladder, and sex organs.

All the fibers go through the hypogastric plexus. There is no direct supply to the organs mentioned. All the fibers from these nerves go through ganglia for the oculomotor nerve. Axons travel through the ciliary ganglion.

The facial nerve synapses in the sphenopalatine ganglion. The glossopharyngeal nerve goes through the otic ganglion. The vagus nerve goes through the hypogastric plexus in addition to ganglia.

Sympathetic and parasympathetic nerves form a plexus to create a common sharing of information, thus working together whenever there is a stimulus—pleasant, painful, or noxious. Some of the plexuses briefly discussed include the cardiac plexus, which is innervated by both the vagus and sympathetic nerves, supplying to blood the vessels of the heart, SA node, and the covering of the heart, the pericardium. The smooth muscles of the heart are supplied by both systems (125). The pulmonary plexus supplies all cells of the lungs, like blood vessel cells and smooth muscles of the bronchi. The celiac plexus (solar plexus) supplies almost all organs of the abdomen. The hypogastric plexus and pelvic plexus supply the rest of the pelvic organs' vessels, seminal vesicles, and prostate—all female and male sexual organs.

The pain sensation is carried by the sympathetic and parasympathetic nervous system in all the internal organs in the chest, abdomen, and pelvic organs. Pressure and proprioceptor sensation is carried by both of these systems.

Visceral afferent pathways are associated with sensations such as hunger, nausea, and visceral (organ) pain. Referred pain to the skin is carried from visceral organs to the nerve roots of the same spinal segment that supplies the organs, for example, heart pain angina and myocardial infarction pain may be referred to the left arm because the nerve supply to the heart is shared by the skin of the left arm through T1 through T5. The same process is involved in a gallbladder stone; pain is referred to the right shoulder or clavicle area. In pancreatic and kidney pain, the sensation is referred to back in the lumbar region.

The pathway to the brain stem from the spinal cord gets sensation from baroreceptors stimulated by pressure from the visceral organs, like bloating of the stomach or intestines or any swelling. In the same way, we have a chemoreceptor that sends information about oxygen and carbon dioxide levels, which are located in the medulla and get stimulated by these changes. The regulation centers for reflexes, heart rate, respiratory rate, and the rhythm of blood pressure are all located in the medulla oblongata and pons. Pupillary reactions, like in the accommodation to the sense of light, are integrated in the midbrain by the third nerve nuclei. The hypothalamus is the master mind regulating the autonomic nervous system (both the sympathetic and parasympathetic nervous systems). It responds to external and internal changes in the environment since all the fibers from the midbrain are terminated in the hypothalamus. The posterior part of the hypothalamus is involved with sympathetic function, while the anterior portion is involved with parasympathetic function (126).

The limbic system is known to be the visceral brain, since it is closely linked with the hypothalamus. The limbic system controls the visceral sensation (the sensation from different organs) and is expressed in the form of emotional reactions, like sexual behavior, fear, aggression, eating, the response of the cardiovascular system and gastrointestinal system, urination, defecation, erection of hair, and papillary changes (pupil and eye). As we discussed earlier, most of the sensations, sensory organs, and information is interconnected here in hypothalamus and limbic system. From the limbic system, different fibers are extended to the cerebral cortex, which initiates emotional expressions like smiling and blushing in the face when we are exposed to good or exciting news. A lot more shall be discussed about the higher functions of the brain. But we have gathered all the information together to be shared in the hypothalamus and limbic system. We will find even our motor system is also communicating with the autonomic and sensory system, as discussed in the previous chapter. Overstimulation of the vagus nerve can cause a low heart rate or hypotension (low blood pressure).

The current concept of the gastrointestinal tract is that it has a collection of neurons associated with its functioning. Some neurophysiologists and anatomists call it an "intrinsic nervous system of the gastrointestinal tract." It can function relatively independently but is modulated by the central nervous system. This part of the enteric nervous system is a collection of loose meshworks of neurons that regulate the gastrointestinal motility and the secretion of acid and mucous in the stomach to balance the pH. In the case of the small intestine, it increases the motility of the smooth muscles, which helps to increase vascular (blood) supply to the gut and respond to the inflammation of the gut. There are about one hundred million neurons grouped together in the ganglia around the gut. The ganglia are interconnected with each other and form the mesenteric plexus (Auerbach's plexus), which is located under the mucosal layer of the gut and is arranged from the lower end of the esophagus to the rectum. The second set of ganglia, which supply the pancreas and gallbladder, is called Meissuer's plexus. It supplies to blood vessels and to the pancreas for secretion of insulin and helps with the regulation of the gallbladder, common bile duct, and cystic duct to expel bile juice upon stimulation from the duodenum when the food arrives there. The vagus nerve and sacral parasympathetic nerves supply the whole gut and act through acetylcholine. Why is there such an arrangement? Whenever there is a lesion in the central nervous system, the gut has independent functions; though, in normal events, it is controlled by the nervous system. The parasympathetic nervous system functions through acetylcholine as a neurotransmitter secreted by pre- and postganglia. The sympathetic nervous system works through a neurotransmitter called norepinephrine. Though epinephrine is secreted by the adrenal gland, it does not act as a neurotransmitter in the case of the gut. Norepinephrine is secreted by postganglial neurons only. Other neurotransmitters involved in the functioning of the gut are substance P, somatostatin vasoactive intestinal peptides, adenosine, and adenosine phosphate (127).

The pituitary gland is an important part of the brain. It secretes life-saving hormones and regulates many hormones in our body. There is a rich connection between the hypothalamus and the pituitary gland. The pituitary gland has two lobes. The posterior lobe is called the neurohypothesis, and the anterior part is called the adenohypophysis. Neurons in the supraoptic and paraventricular nuclei send axons to the posterior lobe of the pituitary. The axons transport herring bodies and regulate oxytocin and vasopressin. Once these hormones are secreted, they circulate through the rich vascular plexus around the pituitary gland. The anterior pituitary lobe receives axons from the nuclei of the hypothalamus, which produce hormones, including releasing factors and inhibitory hormones. The hypothalamus weighs about four grams and is about 0.3 percent of the total brain weight.

The hypothalamic nuclei induce hunger and the sensation of satisfaction of hunger through the satiety center in the ventromedial nuclei when the blood sugar level reaches the optimum level after we eat food. Damage to these nuclei cause anorexia and sever weight loss, while lesions on the satiety center leads to overeating and obesity.

The posterolateral and dorsomedial areas function as sympathetic activating centers, while the anterior area activates the parasympathetic activating center.

BODY TEMPERATURE

The autonomic nervous regions cause the constriction or dilation of the blood vessels, thus conserving or losing the heat. A fall in temperature can cause shivering, thus increasing body temperature by muscular movement and by contracting the blood vessels. I am sure we all have experienced this when we are suddenly exposed to cold weather in a snowy or icy-cold area. The body has to maintain a temperature of around 98 degrees F to have normal functioning. Overheating or overcooling can cause damage to cells and changes in metabolic functions. When there is heat, we get a message from the hypothalamus via the autonomic nervous system, which causes sweating and thus loss of heat. This is called a thermoregulatory system. It's like a thermostat, which is sensitive to the changes and fluctuations in the temperature. Fever or hypothermia is the result of irregularity in this region of the brain. This balance soothes our soul and maintains the balance in our day-to-day life. Extremes of temperature are a noxious stimulus to our soul. This is explained on the basis of abnormal electric current in the nervous system. We can further explain this on the basis of the action potential generated at the cellular level.

WATER BALANCE

The hypothalamus stimulates vasopressin secretion from the pituitary gland by activating the osmoreceptor in the third center near the supraoptic nucleus. Osmoreceptors respond to change in osmolarity. Their activation creates a burst of action potential that travels through the neurons of the supraoptic nucleus. This stimulates secretion of vasopressin. A lesion in the hypothalamus or pituitary makes it unable to regulate secretion of vasopressin, therefore causing increased secretion of water. This increases the thirst, causing diabetes insipidus due to the imbalance of sodium concentration. The anterior part of the pituitary gland secret hormones through the hypothalamus. It secretes a stimulating hormone, depending upon the need of the body under normal conditions. The pituitary gland has a direct effect on sexual hormones, the thyroid gland, and the adrenal gland (128).

CIRCADIAN RHYTHM

Body functions, like the regulation of temperature, secretion of corticosteroids, and oxygen consumption, are influenced by light intensity. The suprachiasmatic nucleus works as an internal clock. There are two gene cells in this nucleus called "clock and per," which control the wake-sleep mechanism. When we have light, there is a wake signal. Light causes the stimulation of the suprachiasmatic neurons, regulating metabolic and electric activity, which stimulate the secretion of neurotransmitters. This mechanism keeps our brain and body on a day and night schedule, like clockwork. The pineal body is attached to the hypothalamus by the pineal stalk, which also secretes melatonin and regulates the sleep-wake mechanism of our body.

MOTOR NEURONS

In order to understand the action potential and electric current generated by the neurons that supply the muscles, we must recognize that both skeletal and smooth muscles work in groups. Neurons supply fibers to more than one muscle cell, hence action potential is generated as a group of muscles. This electric current has to be at an optimum level to generate the movement of the muscles. Some neurobiologists focus on one neuron and one cell to explain the action potential, which in this case is not true, because we need billions of neurons and millions of muscle cells to get the desired movement. We need the collective action of both to produce enough electric current for the desired action of the muscles. Motor neurons are large, with a long axon. Each control-scattered group of individual muscle fibers is called a motor unit. The spinal reflex is caused by the fibers that enter the spinal cord from the region of the body.

The descending pathway from the cerebrum goes to the brain stem, medulla, and these structures in the brain stem:

- Reticular formation
- Vestibular nuclei
- Red nucleus
- Tectum
- Direct fibers to the cerebellar cortex

Each of them has specific function to describe the normal activities of life. Understanding these functions will explain how, why, and when we exhibit various actions and behaviors. Therefore, it is important to understand the entire journey of the fibers (axons) from the neurons of these parts. Let us understand the reticular formation, which will explain the anatomy of consciousness, alertness, and the sleep-wake status of our life.

The reticular formation (RF) is formed by diffused aggregation of cells interspersed with fibers going in all directions. It is full of axons and dendrites woven and intertwined with one another, with long axons ascending to the midbrain and cerebral cortex and down to the spinal cord. There are nuclei made out of a clump of neurons in order to increase the activity and electrical current together and so they can work cohesively as a unit. It is the oldest part of the brain, receiving ascending and descending information to and from spinal cord to the cerebral cortex through the thalamic nuclei.

In the middle of the pons, nerves are large. They are called megnocellular nuclei on the lateral side (away from center). These nuclei are in close association with the third, fourth, sixth, and seventh cranial nerves in order to create coordinated movements, like walking, chewing, grooming, suckling, coughing, swallowing, sneezing, and facial expressions. Even conscious eye movement is coordinated here. The reticular formation has ascending and descending fibers from the superior colliculus. The reticular formation projects fibers to the cerebellum, basal ganglion, somatosensory system, substantia naigra, and vestibular nuclear and motor cortex. Through these connections, multiple tasks and functions are performed simultaneously by our body.

The vestibular sensory system's neurons have connections with the reticular formation and form other tracts, sensing the movement of the head and direction of gravity, thus maintaining the posture of the body. The lateral vestibular nuclei form the descending tract. They are motor in nature, sending motor excitation to the spinal tract. Some of the fibers of this tract are inhibitory. These control the extension of muscles rather than the flexion of muscles. The vestibular nuclei, along with the reticular formation, are closely associated with the cerebellum and higher motor fibers. The cerebellum has control over spinal cord motor nuclei. The reticular formation condenses with visual sensory and vestibular axons and coordinating conscious awareness of both functions. Red nuclei are situated in the upper part of the pons and the midbrain and are connected to the cerebellum which is not associated with sensory input or output. It is more prominent in animals than humans. It also is connected with the spinal cord and controls the flexor group of muscles in the spinal cord. When stimulated by electric current, it causes flexion of the muscles of the upper cervical group.

The Cranial Nerves

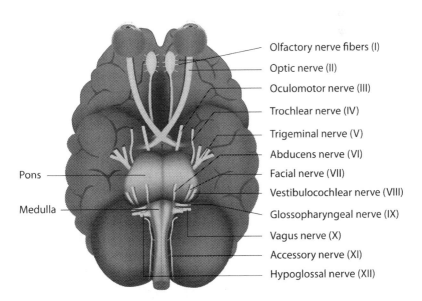

Olfactory nerve fibers (I)
Optic nerve (II)
Oculomotor nerve (III)
Trochlear nerve (IV)
Trigeminal nerve (V)
Abducens nerve (VI)
Facial nerve (VII)
Vestibulocochlear nerve (VIII)
Glossopharyngeal nerve (IX)
Vagus nerve (X)
Accessory nerve (XI)
Hypoglossal nerve (XII)

Pons

Medulla

The superior colliculus forms a motor tract called the tectospinal tract. It lies in the roof of the fourth ventricle. Superior and inferior colliculi are two parts that integrate vestibular and visual sensory input and ascend to the cerebral cortex.

Corticospinal tracts are important for executing movements of the muscle when needed, since they get information from all sensory tracts. The corticospinal tract has the longest axons, since they start from the cerebrum and extend to the end of the spinal cord neurons. Half of the axons come from the frontal cortex, including motor neuron fibers; these fibers end in motor neurons of the spinal cord and excite neurons by using glutamate as a neurotransmitter. These cause movement in all the muscles of the body, including in the arms, legs, and trunk. The upper-end fibers fan out to form an internal capsule. They pass through the thalamus and basal ganglia. Henceforth, there is a close connections to the reticular sensory system. That may contribute to conscious awareness of any movement and explain the status of the body and any response to verbal, auditory, visual, pain, tactile, and other sensations. These all contribute to the anatomy and physiology of consciousness. I shall repeat the concept in the chapter on consciousness and the conscious. Any damage or disconnection of the spinal cord causes flaccid paralysis, loss of both voluntary movement and muscle tone below the site of the lesion. This is called spinal shock and can last for days or months. All the muscles below the lesion are flaccid.

Decerebate rigidity appears when there is a lesion or section at the level of the colliculi. There is a generalized stiffness of muscles and hyperactive reflexes. Consciousness is lost, the response is absent, and there is no sensory input from the vestibular nuclei. This explains the bodily death versus personal death. We provide life support to the body or biological life and sustain it. In this case, the "personal life" appears to have come to an end, since the human as a person can be deemed dead. Normally, brain death, where due to brain stem and cerebral hemisphere death, is the whole-brain definition of human death. The definition of death is destruction of the cerebral hemispheres (cerebral cortex) and consequent absence of higher brain functions, such as consciousness and the ability to think, feel, and be aware of others. Once the brain stem is dead, there is an irreversible loss of essential integrative functions and of self-consciousness or personhood (17–35).

We need to understand the way our muscles work and give us a structure of the self being. Muscle spindles send signals to our cortex about the length and rate of change of the length. While working out, we use our muscles to lift weights and pull or push the weights to develop the muscle tone. Our own body weight works to maintain the tone of muscles due to working against gravity, which maintains muscle tone. If there was no gravity, we would be crawling flat on the surface of the earth. When our body attains an erect posture to walk or jog, we are gaining muscle strength. Muscle spindles tell us how much we can stretch them and how much weight we can lift. Gravity not only helps our muscles; it also helps our bones and joints to maintain their strength and the appropriate structure of our skeleton. This way, our muscle spindles avoid any tears or extra stretching to avoid spraining.

Our motor system faces a fundamental and frustrating dilemma, like learning exactly how much weight we can lift and how much energy we need to pick up a specific weight. This involves a specific position of our limbs, the position and angle of our joints, the speed and velocity of our movements. It is difficult for our muscles and limbs to understand. *Load*, in simple language, means a force against which our muscles have to operate. When the command is sent to motor neurons depends essentially on the difference between the resultant force of contraction and the load on the muscles, so we cannot tell how much movement will occur in response to a given command, unless we know the load as well. Ultimately, the motor system creates the best possible estimate of the force it needs to generate at every movement in order to achieve what it needs to achieve, like lifting, moving, or manipulating. For this, it needs as much information as it needs and as quickly as possible. The muscles, joints, and receptors in the skin give us information about the consistency, shape, and slippage—smooth, spiky, or irregular—in order for us to have a grip on the load. To do this, we need the cerebral cortex and its intelligence to comprehend and understand. If we are to manipulate the outside objects, like lifting, moving, and throwing them, we not only have to understand the object; we also have to know our own strength and the capability of our body and the control we have. To lift a case of beer, we have to understand the weight of the case of beer, our movements, and the strength of our joints and muscles. When I have to pick a log of wood, I use all the senses needed. For example, if I see log of wood is long and heavy, I will move it, touch it, and feel it. Can I pick it up or not? I use my experience and intelligence to either pick it up or not. Well, if it is more than I can pick up, I have two choices—not to pick it up or ask for help and use other hands. This is the reasonable thing to do. Or I may go ahead and pick up the log of wood and end up hurting or spraining my back or other muscles. I used free will to do that and did not use my intelligence. That is how the macho image of oneself ends up hurting one. It is not the muscles' fault. It is merely ignorance on my part.

Let us look at golfers. If they are pros and have had the experience of hitting the ball with perfection, they use their intelligence to hit the ball. If one is not an experienced golfer, then one does not hit the ball where it is supposed to go, resulting in frustration. In the case of pro golfers, there is muscle memory, which comes with repeated practice. They have to use perceptions and register the length of the shot to reach the target. This is done by keeping one's eyes on the ball and hitting it in such a way that the ball takes flight. The movements of the joints and muscles and confidence have to be perfect to make a perfect shot. It requires total focus and concentration. How to swing? How far to swing? How tight to hold the club? How close to hit the ball? How much divot to take after hitting the ball? Our muscles and our cerebral motor and sensory centers learn this art. The coiled motion of muscles is a form of our spindles. It is not only muscle power that defines the perfection of the shot but the frontal lobe, which thinks about what exactly needs to be done. The occipital lobe envisions the depth and distance of the target. The limbic system controls the emotional aspect of game—how confident one feels and how passionate or how angry one feels at the time of making a shot. How do you feel about the previous shot? Though the mechanics of the shot are controlled and performed by muscles and motions of the joints, it is all accomplished by the coordination of all the centers at the cortical level and limbic system. It is the feeling of the ball and the swing of the club.

This reminds me of a book written by Tiger Woods entitled *How I Play Golf*. At the Masters, Tiger set the record of four consecutive majors. He watched his father hitting the ball in his garage into a net. He developed his swing, starting with how much pressure to put on the golf club or how tight or loose to hold a putter. He developed the memory of how hard to hit the ball. This started with the receptors in his skin and the Golgi spindles of his tendons. Tiger was a keen student of the game, keeping his focus, tenacity, and courage when he was eight years old. Tiger Wood writes, "From the beginning, I was taught many aspects of golf, that it was much more than just hitting the ball, finding it and hitting it again. It was a constant learning process with experience." He learned fundamentals like never getting the club past parallel on the backswing, which are essential for playing the game properly. Tiger discovered that early success helped to boost his confidence and created sense of competition. He admires all the great golfers like Sam Snead, Ben Hogan, Arnold Palmer, and Jack Nicklaus.

What made him a great golfer was pure learning of muscle movements and repeating the same swing. All of his senses were involved—the pressure receptors, the Golgi spindles of his muscles, his autonomic nervous system, and his neurological system—in summary, his entire body and soul. Though his brain and muscle memory did the mechanical tricks to make him a great golfer, his soul executed the total result of his action. Over the years, his conscious efforts and the practice of the electrical activity of his entire nervous system, which was stored in his soul in the form of a magnetic field, kept him going on, even during his failures. Tiger Woods had been infatuated with the game since his father first put a golf club in his hands when he was a toddler. Ball and club became his playmates. The feeling of his solitude and self-reliance enhanced his attraction to the game. Tiger Wood relates to great golfers of that time Arnold Palmer and Jack Nicklaus. The game had the same appeal to them. It creates a sense of independence. As the saying goes, you play golf against the golf course; once you beat the course, it is easier to beat your competitor. Ultimately, it comes down to you—how well you know yourself, along with your limitations and confidence. It is always good to know what you don't know. Conscious awareness of not knowing what you don't know creates awareness to know what you want to know. It is important in all aspects of life to understand and acknowledge what you don't know. Accept it. That will create enthusiasm and the courage to learn the unknown. Consequences come after the action, sometimes good and sometimes bad. Learning how to accept them and improve upon them is the key to success. Sometimes, the game comes so easily that you hardly believe every swing is natural and perfect. It causes a seduction to the game of golf. Sometimes you envision a perfect shot, but it turns out to be a disaster. Figuring out what went wrong is the key to correcting the next shot. Getting angry and frustrated is not helpful. Slow down your thoughts about the shot, and let your soul guide you to the next shot. Tiger talks about the great Ben Hogan, who stated he had only four good shots in one week of golf. Tiger, having won twelve rounds, stated that he "had only one perfect shot.(37,p5)

All the great athletes have to start somewhere. The truth starts from a system, which neurophysiologists call the servo-assisted system. This system is highly advanced at its optimum functioning level. At times, muscle spindles provide an error signal (which is a discrepancy between actual and desired length) that is used directly in the stretch reflex to correct the response and indirectly to modify the ballistic programs for future action. Our cerebral cortex (motor, sensory, visual, and vestibular systems) sends a signal to our spinal cord not only about the desired length but also its estimate of the force needed to achieve that length, which is derived from our stored programs (muscle memory) and previous experience. For example, when I play golf, I am aware of the fact that a full swing of a nine iron will hit the ball between 125 and 130 yards. This experience and knowledge makes me swing the nine iron when I am 125 to 130 yards away from the hole on the green. The same holds with other clubs, like an eight iron for 140 yards and a seven iron for 150 yards. The actual distance varies with the age, skill level, and physique of an individual. The sensory receptors are an integral part of achieving the goal by assigning the weight of the club. Enhancement of this ballistic system gives rapid feedback to guide all athletes in attaining perfection in their respective fields like basketball and tennis players.

Let us think about a small and simple task. Imagine you are holding a glass of wine and your friend is pouring wine in that glass. There are many muscles involved in this simple action. There is a constant stretching of muscle, and the weight of the glass goes up as the wine is poured. The brain continuously monitors the situation and decides at every instant exactly how much direct excitation to send up to the spinal cord to keep the hand steady. It would be simple to send the information once and for all—not only for the force needed but the desired position of the hand coming from the spinal cord to get on with the job of adjusting the force to the load automatically, by sensing the extent to which the actual position of the wineglass matches the brain's command. This compensation is called follow-up servo (130). The main muscle acts as a slave that follows any length changes signaled to the intrafusal fibers of the muscles. The simple servo model saves the brain from having to worry about such a small matter. The brain simply thinks in terms of desired effect and leaves the lower level to get on with its work, figuring out how to achieve it. Servo-assistance is explained on the basis of the fact that there are two separate signals sent to the spinal cord by the brain. One is a position command that tells muscles via Y-fibers and muscle spindles what length is needed to hold the glass of wine. The other command is for the force needed to estimate the load and to hold the glass of wine. This information is obtained from receptors in the skin and the Golgi tendon organs of the muscles. In this case, past experience and special senses, like vision, are integral parts of obtaining such information. It is essential to be aware of such force.

I used to slam the door without paying any attention. Then my wife made me aware of the fact that I would eventually break the door with the way I slammed it. I immediately become aware of the fact that I needed to take a little time to close the door slowly and cautiously. I now close the door gently. Sometimes, out of anger, we slam the door without paying attention to it. Sometimes, we want to send a message to others about how angry we are. I learned when I pick tomatoes from my garden to cut the stem with a scissor or knife and place the tomatoes in the basket gently without damaging the fruit. This involves some cognitive functioning, including memory of past experiences and muscle memory.

CEREBRAL CORTEX

The human cerebral cortex is an evolutionary miracle. It is the supreme functional organ. It has a very complex structure formed by the neurons, axons, and dendrites. It initiates movement of the body. All the sensations are received and analyzed, creating functions that include comprehension, conjunction, concentration, reasoning, problem solving, abstract imagining and planning, consciousness, and conscious thinking and speaking. It is involved in higher functions, like reasoning, monitoring, shaping adaptive and maladaptive behavior, prioritizing and sequencing actions, and coordinating elementary motor and sensory functions into a coherent and goal-directed stream of behavior. It is very difficult to understand our vast complex mechanisms—how the motor system and other systems work. It gets complicated. How do we know what the appropriate strength of the stimulus we need to get an appropriate response and behavior? There is a sensory response as soon as we stimulate the motor nerves. When we pick a cell phone up in our hands, there are millions of neurons put to work, coordinating actions—bringing your phone to your ear and allowing you to talk to your friend. The brain is stormed with a barrage of stimuli from the skin to the tendons, joints, muscles, ears, mouth in looking at the phone, positioning the phone at the right place, pushing the buttons, and talking to your friend. Moreover, the brain is determining how to hold a conversation about a planned subject. At the same time, you are looking for a pen to write down the number for another friend.

Then your doorbell rings. Now your entire body has to move and keep your dog away from the man who rang the bell. You get up and go to the door with your phone on your right side. You tell your friend to hold on, and you open the door. "What can I do for you, sir?" You have to restart the entire train of the thought and be calm, not to be disrespectful to your friend.

The man sees you are on the phone and says, "Oh, I am sorry. I will call you or come back later."

Again, you have to start a new story. The entire functioning of your body and brain has to be changed so you can restart your conversation with your friend. By this time, billions of body cells and neurons have started firing the electric current to all parts of the brain and body involved in this action. How much action potential is generated? How much magnetic energy is generated by the rush of electric currents? I will discuss this in the chapter about the soul. One lesson we have learned is that there is infinite knowledge to gain about our brain and its functions. Our actions, thoughts, and performance are very well organized under normal circumstances.

This is all achieved by what neuroscientists call "hierarchical organization," like in any other organized system, including our military, a corporation, or any governmental entity that is intended to carry out effective action. Higher up, it starts with the cerebral cortex, the cerebellum, and the basal ganglion, depending upon what kind of movement needs to be performed. Coordination among these higher centers is essential to carry on the wide range of movements and their characteristics, like rate, rhythm, strength, and force. We still have to understand this complex functioning of the body, and as our neurophysiology and neuroscience techniques are improved, we will learn more and more.

Let's look at when we want to pick up a small baby. First, we look at the baby and understand that we have to be tender, gentle, and soft to hold the baby at safe parts of his or her body. We don't grab and use excessive force compared to picking up a sofa or a log of wood. We have to be very discreet and use appropriate force. We have to grip and touch to make sure the baby is safe and comfortable—unlike we would with a log of wood. If the wood falls, it does not matter, but if a baby falls, it matters a lot. Any harm to the baby is unacceptable. So we think and plan. Our cerebral cortex makes the decision in both frontal lobes to pick up (thought and process) the baby. We involve motor areas and basal ganglia. Basal ganglia initiate the movement to pick up the baby and approach the baby. Then, we must reach for the baby to pick her up. We use our motor area and cerebellum. The third part is we grasp the baby. Here, our motor area orders the muscles involved to grasp. Our sensory system, like our baroreceptors, sensors in the skin, and Golgi bodies of the tendons and muscles, along with sensory receptors tell us how much pressure is needed to get hold of the baby, to hold her safely and make sure she won't fall. If too much force is applied, the baby could be hurt. We use the visual sensory system, working together, to make sure the baby's position and posture are correct, that the baby is not upside down or horizontal. Thus, we pick the baby and hold her in our lap, making sure the baby is comfortable and not squeezed or held loosely to avoid a fall. My view is that there is extensive action potential and electric current generated in the neurons of the frontal lobe motor cortex, basal ganglion, cerebellum nerves, joints, muscles, skin receptors, and visual sensory apparatus. The electric current emits a magnetic field, which is a soul. This guides the entire process of this act of perfection. Slight changes in our electric current—whether too much or too little—will not allow us to complete the full act.

Once the baby is in our lap, we want to make sure the baby is comfortable and happy. We try to play, look at the baby, and maybe smile or make peek-a-boo gestures. We have to make perfect movements and gestures. The baby has to be comfortable. If not, the baby will cry and be unhappy or fearful. It is now the baby's motor system, sensory system, cerebrum, cerebellum, and basal ganglia that have to function together to attain her body posture in your lap. You interact with the baby; she looks at your face and feels your emotions. It is all done by the magnetic soul of the baby and your magnetic soul energy. It depends on these energies interacting and blending with each other. If there is a lack of blending and compatibility of the magnetic soul, the results could be that the baby will become annoyed or start crying. Or you yourself will not feel comfortable (magnetic soul). Thus, you pass the baby to her mother or caretaker or place her in the crib. After this process, you think, *What happened? Why did the baby cry?* Is it that she did not like the way I picked her or my expression? Now a different thought process or muscle movement takes place. Your neurons are still firing. You feel bad, or you justify your gesture there. Billions of neurons and body cells are firing. Your own autonomic nervous system and limbic system kick in to stimulate your emotions and feelings. This is how we understand what, where, when, why, and how. Consciousness is an integral part of the process; thus, the reticular formation is essential for the completion of the process.

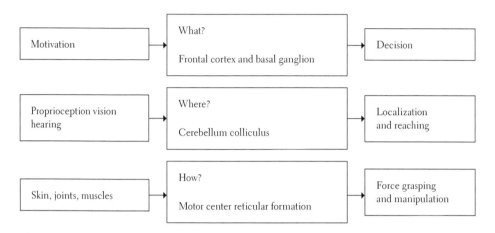

Let me expand on this aspect and make it simple to understand. The primary motor cortex receives precisely the kind of information needed to manipulate objects and has accurate electric current to descending connections to be able to control force and velocity with precision and speed. It is the desired position of the limbs translated into detailed instructions about the force needed from time to time, in order to achieve the result. If there is damage to this region or damage to the sensory system of the skeleton, one can plan and reach perfectly to pick up the baby but will be clumsy. When it comes to reaching the last stage of lifting the baby, individuals with damage to the cerebellum may have problems with motion and desired action. The distance to reach and pick up the baby is misjudged. The person may overshoot or oscillate. Motion is broken into incomplete components, in spite of the fact he or she is conscious. In the case of basal ganglion damage, for example in Parkinson's, movements may be executed, but the patient is conscious of the difficulties of getting them started or stopping them. A patient with frontal lobe damage may have difficulty planning and making decision about whether the baby needs to be picked up by holding the arms or grabbing the baby. Precision will not be adequate and perfect.

PRIMARY MOTOR CORTEX

Many neuroscientists were interested in finding out about the effect of electric stimulation to different parts of the brain, and sure enough, they were able to find the motor area that caused movement and sensation in the limbs. In 1975, Wilder Penfield produced movements in the limbs of patients by stimulating the cortical motor area with an electrode. Penfield observed the neural impulses that resulted from stimulation by the electrode. He could not conclude whether it was an electrode or something behind the scenes, such as an empirically undetectable human soul or God, that caused the capabilities of the neuron to conduct electric impulses and extend this current to the other neurons further down, which caused movement of the limbs. Neuroscientists finally found that there was a conveniently accessible region in the middle of the cerebral cortex, and an electrode produced movement in the opposite side of the body. Hughlings Jackson studied stroke patients and paralysis of the various parts of the body postmortem and found a correlation between the parts of the cortex damaged and the paralyzed parts of the body.

This is very important to understand the pathways—what, where, how, and when. The connection with the reticular formation will explain the conscious effect of the movements, though it comes from the motor and sensory area. The reticular formation is involved in consciousness and unconsciousness. We are aware of what we are doing. For example, if we are carrying a log of wood on our shoulder, we are aware of the log of wood and our conscious awareness about the log of wood. Thus, the question is does free will come from the motor and sensory area, or does it originate in the thalamic nuclei. My view is it comes from both. The thalamus works with the cerebellum, basal ganglion, reticular formation, and colliculus. They all work in harmony to create free will and consciousness of the free will, which gives feedback to our soul. The soul is the magnetic energy generated by the electric current in these parts of the brain as mentioned. It is important for philosophers or those who have religious beliefs about the soul to understand, as it will give some answers to questions about mystic beliefs about the soul and free will. The corticospinal tracts end in the motor neurons of the spinal cord, which finally reach their destination through the spinal nerves. Those who want to learn may read *Gray's Anatomy*. This is a brief explanation to justify the mechanisms I discussed. For example, in monkeys, the motor cortex is dominant in the area presenting arms and mouth because these parts of the body are mostly used in day-to-day activity. In pigs, the area representing the snout for performing various functions is dominant. A cerebellar lesion produces a subtle type of movement disorder rather than paralysis. The current concept about the cerebellum is that it has grown out of the brain stem as an adjunct to the vestibular system. There may be some functions involved in the area of intelligence. The cerebellum is dominated by the spinocerebellar and corticocerebellar tracts. The cerebellum has massive Purkinje cells and numerous dendrites. It stores and executes specific sequences of action by means of gradual processes in which the sequences are first generated consciously while the subject is attempting to master the task as a result of repetition, which is gradually taken over by the cerebellum by itself. Here, movement takes place in a sensory context, some of which will be due to feedback from the last movement. Every time we carry out a motor act, it results in a kind of echo that comes back to us through our senses. For example, when we play a note on the piano, we get feedback from proprioceptors, spindle tendon organs, joint receptors, nerve endings from the skin, and visual and hearing sensory apparatus. Each note that is played consequently generates a particular action.

The same mechanism takes place when we first learn to ride a bicycle. Once we are able to maintain balance on a bicycle, there is enhancement of learning every time we ride it, which leads to the memory of riding a bicycle. If we do not ride bicycle for a while, this memory will come back, and we will be able to ride the bicycle much easier without too many falls, like we had the first time. It is essential to have vestibular learning (internal ear). Vestibular learning is an essential aspect of the neuroscience to learn in order to understand the enhanced functions of the cerebellum. As mentioned, the vestibulo-cerebellum is joined by the visual information system through mossy fibers. Marr's model explains that visual information is involved in postural responses, with the eyes' movement through a direct reflex route via the vestibular nuclei and oculomotor nuclei in the brain stem and Purkinje cells of the cerebellum. Thus, it enhances the motor movements in the cerebellum, both in the form of input and output mechanisms. Both the brain stem and the cerebellum are integral parts of the brain for explaining the coordination of such information shared by the cerebellum and brain stem. We are learning now that the cerebellum is involved not only in learning about movements but also teaching. It learns to predict errors before they actually occur; these errors, whether real or virtual, are then used to modify the behavior of the circuit in the brain stem (131).

As mentioned earlier, the cerebellum seems to support the vestibular system by endowing it with intelligence. It signals new opportunities and avoids threats, which need the brain's full computational resources. It also stores models that are out of use and may need modification. The basal ganglia include a) the globus pallidus, b) the putamen, c) the caudate nucleus, d) the striatum, e) the substantia Niagara, and f) according to some neuroscientists, the subthalamus. These are interconnected. They project fibers to the thalamus and then to the motor cortex and superior colliculus, which control eye and head movements. These basal ganglia have neurotransmitters, mainly dopamine, gamaminobutyric acid, serotonin, substance P, and acetylcholine. Basal ganglia are connected to the limbic system, which is mainly concerned with the motivational and emotional part of functioning, possibly through the nucleus accumbens. The functions of the basal ganglia are poorly understood, but they have disinhibitory actions on the motor system.

Parkinsonism is caused by the destruction of the dopaminergic pathway between the substantia Niagara and the putamen. In Parkinson's disease, there is a poverty of movement (akinesia), particularly expressive movements, which are apathetic in appearance. There is a loss of associated movements, like swinging of the arms when walking. The patient may blink less often than one would normally. There is a shuffling gait, and they are slow to walk. They have no defect in their peripheral motor apparatus. There is an impairment in initiation of the movement but not in execution of the movement. Once movement is started, it may be difficult to stop; this is called preservation of the movement. There is an increased rigidity of the muscles. Tremors of the hands are present at rest but disappear as soon as voluntary action is started. Though we have not understood how exactly basal ganglia work, through experiments in lower animals and the diseases caused in humans, we have come to understand some of the functions. Basal ganglia clearly execute movements that are strategically planned and initiated.

The cerebral cortex is the network of neurons related to the initiation of movement by receiving sensation from the body, from our all sensory systems and sensory organs. The cortex has a special function in comprehension, cognition, communication, reasoning, problem solving, obstruction, imagining, and planning. It is the neuron group that basically defines us in its entirety. All the information sent is finally processed here. I call these executive functions. When we have a problem we need to reason through, understanding what is good, what is bad, what is right, and what is wrong, the prefrontal lobe is the master. This part of the brain receives all its information through the reciprocal connections with the rest of the brain parts (15 of 30). The definition of *reasoning*, according to dictionary. com, is a "set or process of a person who reasons; the process of forming conclusions, judgments, or inference from facts or premises; the reasons, arguments, proofs, etc., resulting from this process."

Reason is defined as "a basis or cause, as for some belief, action, fact, events; a statement presented in justification or explanation of the belief or action; the mental power concerned with forming conclusions, judgments, or inferences; sound judgment, good sense; normal or sound power of mind, sanity; logic, a premise of an argument; philosophy; the faculty or power of acquiring intellectual knowledge, either by direct understanding of first principal or by argument; power of intelligent and dispassionate thought, or of conduct influenced by such thought; to think or argue in a logical manner; to form conclusions, judgments; to urge reasons which should determine belief or action; to convince, persuade by reasoning; to bring a change in someone's opinion through presentation of argument and to convince; to be clear, obvious or logical."

Reasoning and abstract thinking start from our childhood with a healthy genetic makeup in our frontal lobe, which is able to reason it through with developmental processes. At birth, a human children are helpless, and as they go through the milestones of life, like crawling, walking, and talking and with the sensory development, they are able to develop reasoning and decision making. In animals, there is an innate instinct in their offspring. A chick that is recently hatched starts pecking for food and seeds. A baby deer or caribou gets its strength in a matter of hours and starts running to avoid predators. In humans, there is a rapid growth of neurons and connections of dendrons and axons. The human brain shapes itself to the world into which we are born. It adapts to every ecosystem around us. For the first two years in humans, the wiring of the neurons occurs at a rapid pace. There are trillions of synapses in the brain of children, which is double the number of synapses in adults. So there is an enormous electrical current created, which absorbs as much information as possible through the sensory system. Children learn the meaning of no and yes when we stop them from doing things that are harmful, but at times, they do things regardless of our telling them not to. I remember my older child's stubborn behavior. We had a hot wooden stove in our house to heat the house. My wife and I always tried to keep him away, but one day, he touched the hot stove and burned his fingers. Yes, after that, he never went close to the stove. I am sure he had a reason not to touch the hot stove again. His pain and touch sensations and vision retained the memory of the hot black stove for his entire life. It all happens with the connection of trillions of neurons and conscious awareness of reticular formation. By the age of two years, two million new synapses are formed every second in an infant's brain (8, 34). Which synapses stay, and which will go? This is the unsolved mystery, but synapses that get strengthened and have fully developed circuits will stay and generate enough electric current and action potential. They continue growing and developing enough action potential strength. They remain active, thus enhancing and learning to carry on reasoning capabilities. My view is that those neurons or the connections of dendrites that remain dormant are the anatomical site of the unconscious part of our life, which I will discuss in detail later. What we hear and also what we see remain a part of our memory. It continues the process as our axons are myelinated and continue developing with dendrites and connections.

Some neuroscientists claim that 50 percent of our neuronal connections are pruned as we mature. The brain is a relentless shape-shifter, constantly reshaping and reconnecting with dendrites of the neurons. Because your experiences are unique, so are the vast detailed patterns in your neural network. They continue to change our whole life. Comprehension and cognition are developed by the experience and stimulus from the environment in which children grow. Language and communication are integral parts of the cognitive functions. This comes from parenting, schooling, teaching, reasoning, and processing. The frontal lobes are the main parts of the brain. They determine the extent of use of knowledge and how it is used in real life. Bilateral lesions of the frontal lobes are characterized by changes in the personality (frontal lobe syndrome) and how a person interacts with the world. It has been studied in brain trauma, infarcts, tumors, lobotomies, multiple sclerosis, Pick's disease and other related diseases. These patients exhibit slowed thinking, poor judgment, decreased curiosity, social withdrawal, irritability, and an apathetic indifference to experiences that can suddenly explode into impulsive behavior. If one lobe is impaired, the other side of the lobe can compensate for the functioning with high efficiency, so that it sometimes goes unnoticed. Frontal lobe dysfunction may be difficult to detect by means of highly structured neuropsychological tests. The intelligence quotient (IQ) may be normal since neuroimaging studies have shown that the IQ seems to require mostly parietal lobe activation (15–30). For example, during administration of adult intelligence scale revised tests (WAIS-R), the highest level of increased metabolic activity during verbal tasks takes place in the left parietal lobe, whereas the highest level of increased activity during performance skills occurred in the right parietal lobe. In contrast, frontal lobe pathology may become apparent only under unstructured, stressful real-life situations.

There is a famous case reported in neuroscientific literature of Phineas Gage, a twenty-five-year-old railroad worker who was working with explosives and accidentally drove an iron rod through his head. He survived, but both frontal lobes were damaged. The patient was followed by J. M. Harlow, MD, in 1868. He found dramatic change in his personality; he suddenly started using the grossest profanity and was impatient with advice, restraint, and conflict with his desires. He worked with the iron bar in his head. His friends described him as happier than before, more carefree, less inhibited. How do we explain this? My view is that his soul was intact, though he had frontal lobe damage. His neurons still continued generating electric current, which in turn created enough of a magnetic field, a form of energy that I call the "soul." This gave feedback to his neurons, and therefore, he was able to function at a reasonable level. He had enough sensory stimuli that enhanced his magnetic soul. There were experiments conducted in monkeys in which a lesion was inflicted in the frontal lobes. It demonstrated that anxiety was reduced, and monkeys worried less when they made mistakes during the learning tasks (244–38).

The prefrontal lobe is highly developed in humans, as compared to other primates. The prefrontal lobe has diverse output, which extends to the hypothalamus as well as to the basal ganglia, subthalamus, and midbrain. It receives connections from the thalamus limbic system, which are the site for emotions and motivation. The prefrontal lobe has the highest functions of intelligence, morality, and possibly religious belief and contributes these functions to our soul, which gives feedback to the prefrontal lobe and acts as a form of reserved magnetic energy, for whenever it is needed to perform desired functions. Though pain is perceived at the thalamic level, the prefrontal lobe acts as if pain is not emotionally expressed. A patient may complain about pain but may laugh about it. One may feel the pain but may not sense it. Emotional pain may be in the form of lack of anxiety about it.

As mentioned earlier, all the high-order functions are executed by the frontal lobe, like reasoning, abstraction, planning, and initiating activity; monitoring and shaping of behavior, ensuring adaptive actions; inhibiting maladaptive behavior; prioritizing and sequencing actions; problem solving; and coordinating elementary motor and sensory functions into coherent and goal-directed behaviors (132). Damage to this area of the brain causes a variety of dysfunctions. Lesions in the dorsolateral part of the frontal lobe cause patients to become indifferent; they have abulia, apathetic, mute, and motionless behavior. Patients with orbitofrontal area damage are not inhibited and appear labile (they experience changes in their moods from high to low). They are irritable, inattentive, and easily distractible with impaired judgment, loss of social skills, and loss of inhibitions. Damage to the medial part of the frontal lobe can cause akinesia (a lack of spontaneous movement) and make victims apathetic. Injury to the basal part of the frontal lobe can cause loss of memory. These frontal lobe syndromes are due to damage to both sides of the frontal lobe. They have difficulty with language comprehension, communication, abstract thinking, and thinking of the right words and a lack of coordination in the sequence of muscle contractions necessary to produce intelligible sounds and to assemble words into meaningful sentences. The right hemisphere leads in interpreting three-dimensional images and spaces in addition to arithmetic and designs. In most right-handed people, the left hemisphere is dominant. Right-handedness occurs in about 70 percent of people; the rest, about 30 percent, are left-handed and right-hemisphere-dominant (39, 257).

How do we coordinate our complex and very precise actions and thinking of day-to-day life? This burning question is a quest for humans to understand. Our knowledge remains inadequate, and the mechanisms are not fully understood, in spite of the fact we have made enormous progress in the field of neuroscience. We are proud of ourselves for functioning far more superiorly than animals. We can think and produce our ideas in a functional way. We humans have been able to put pieces of metal and plastic together and make them fly (airplanes, rockets, satellites, airspace systems, the Hubble telescope), to go to moon, and to learn about Mars. We have made metal to float on water and travel in ships. We have made cars and created science to use to our benefit and create efficiency and comfort for our lives. The list goes on and on. In a nutshell, we humans created our imagination into practicality, while animals have not been able to do so, though some animals are more agile, stronger, and have far advanced sensations. Some can smell, see, hear, and feel things humans cannot; for example, many can sense the magnetic field of the environment. Some can see ultraviolet light. With their tongues, snakes can understand the environment far more than we can. This is all due to the rudimentary part of their brains being far advanced compared to ours. But we have a very advanced cerebral cortex, which has created all I described. This is the only difference in what we call the "new brain." In humans, there is not only an extensive expansion of the cerebral cortex neural tissue but a dramatic change in the relative proportions of the cortex devoted to different functions. Unless and until we have an adequate and appropriate level of stimulus, our brain does not respond. In other words, if we do not have an adequate electric current created by action potential, the appropriate actions and functions cannot be created. Weak action potential and weak electric current will not produce the desired function. This, according to my view, will not produce enough of a magnetic field to give the adequate required strength to our soul. Certain areas in our cortex are associated with specific functions. Thus, the area designated for vision, if damaged will cause only a defect in the sensation of vision, like the posterior part of the cerebrum. A defect in the motor area will cause an impairment of motion, like paralysis in stroke, though patients with stroke can see and hear. There are areas called "association areas." Cortical neurons can change their function to help us cope with a change in functional demand. The cortex would be a group of specialists in a hospital setting with the astonishing way they communicate and their network, by which they can share their ideas and function cohesively to carry on the work and produce a healthy required result.

The cortex is divided into a) the frontal cortex, b) the temporal cortex; c) the parietal cortex; and d) the occipital area.

The following diagram demonstrates their relationship.

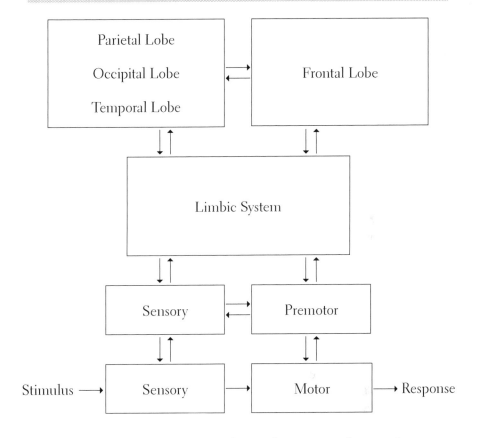

Many neuroscientists want to lump these areas of cortex into one, like the parieto-temporo-occipital cortex (PTO). This part of the cortex responds to an outside stimulus for the behavior simultaneously, like the movement of the hands, mouth, or eyes or hearing influenced by attention. There is an intimate association of motor and sensory areas. Especially when we grip an object, there is an instant movement of the muscles to hold the object. Also, when we see someone doing something that we want to do, our reaction is also dominated by visuoparietal association. Recent studies attribute this to mirror neurons. They enable one to learn tasks by watching them but also to understand what someone else is doing. When you see someone doing something that helps us to predict an outcome, we tend to apply that to ourselves. Some have attributed empathy to mirror neurons.

Dr. Andrew Weil, in a *New York Times* book review stated, "I once heard a Hindu yogi tell a group of western scientists that 'all of the brain is concerned with the mind, but not the entire mind is in the brain.'" To hear a western neurosurgeon say something similar is most remarkable. A scientist examines the evidence before she or he presumes to draw conclusions.

Wilder Penfield, a neurosurgeon who performed numerous experiments while operating on his patients, was convinced that there is energy, which he called the mind. It is a function of the neuronal brain. As he learned more about the brain, he found that there are semiseparable mechanisms within the human brain—there are sensory and motor and other mechanisms that may be called psychical like speech, memory of past streams of consciousness, and capabilities of automatic interpretation of present experiences. The brain has an amazing automatic sensory and motor computer that utilizes the conditioned reflexes. There is a high-level brain mechanism that is most closely related to activity, which humans have referred to as consciousness or the mind or the spirit. In my view, the mind or the spirit is the magnetic energy called the soul, which has functions of the higher brain. Though Penfield describes the mind and the spirit, he remained shy of mentioning the soul. He could not see the soul, but he felt there was an energy that controls and contributes to the functions of the neuronal brain. He raised the question, "Does the brain mechanism account for the mind? Can the mind be explained by what is now known about the brain? If not, which is the more reasonable of the two possibilities that human are based on one or two elements? Penfield remained very hopeful that this mystery would be solved based on scientific understanding. He wrote, "I predict that true prophets will rejoice, and they will discover science a long-waited ally in the search for 'Truth' mind is a very distinctive reality."

In Thayer lectures in 1950 at Johns Hopkins, Wilder Penfield described operating on patients in order to cure them and finding out things about the cerebral cortex and the mechanisms of the higher brain stem that turned a suspicion or a mere notion into a vital hypothesis. Dr. Penfield became more and more convinced that the mind was something in its own right, that it did things with the mechanisms at hand in its own way, that it had energy of its own. His scientific experiments aligned him with prophets, poets, and philosophers who emphasized the spiritual element in humans. In 1934, Dr. Penfield and his associates at McGill University established the Montreal Neurosurgical Institute. While working with his colleagues for more than thirty years, he directed scientific and surgical teams toward solutions of many unanswered questions about brain—such as causes of epilepsy, how one learns language, and how the brain remembers. While in the operating room, observing the responses of the patients to gentle electrical current applied to the temporal lobe, he became aware of the fact that it was possible to produce, artificially, a curious state of automatism. During this procedure, the patient became unaware and verbalized inappropriate comments. One patient was heard to say that "time and space seemed occupied," made semipurposeful movements, and later had no memory of the events at all. The same was found by Hughlings Jackson in epileptic seizure patients. His team concluded that it could have been initiated in the deep temporal lobe from neurons of the amygdala. It was evident that electrical stimulation produced a train of complex events in the brain that seemed to isolate the patient's awareness and memory recording from motor and sensory activities. This operation was performed to remove scar tissue in a seizure patient. About seven hundred operations were performed during Dr. Penfield's extensive work. He concluded that there is something that characterizes the mind as distinct from the physical brain.

Hippocrates, the father of scientific medicine (42, 185), studied humans in health and disease and added the moral code: "I will use treatment to help the sick according to my ability and judgment, but never with view to injure or wrongdoing. I will keep pure and holy both my life and my art." Hippocrates. in his lecture, left us with the recognition of moral, spiritual, physical, and material notions. According to him, some people say that the heart is the organ with which we think and that it feels pain and anxiety. But this is not so. People ought to know that from the brain we have pleasures, joys, laughter, and tears. Through it, we think, see, hear, and distinguish ugly from beautiful, the bad from the good, and the pleasant from the unpleasant. To consciousness, the brain is a messenger. The brain is the interpreter of the consciousness, and epilepsy comes from the brain when it is not normal.

These were great souls who recognized and gave us the wisdom and knowledge to keep looking for the answers in our quest to understand the soul. They recognized the energy beyond the neuronal stimulus that created an electric current, which answers all our functions of day-to-day life. We know now that the brain does not act mysteriously as a simple and uncomplicated whole. It has within it many partly separable mechanisms, each of them activated by the passage of electric currents through the insulated nerve fibers. The definition of *mind (spirit)* from *Webster's*

Dictionary is "the element in an individual that feels, perceives, thinks, and additionally has free will and power of reasoning." Neurons are connected and integrated together in gray matter and all vibrate with an energy that is under control. They are disciplined like a vast symphony orchestra, while millions of messages flash back and forth to numerous functional targets. However, when there is any abnormality, neurons fire like thunder and an electric current of clouds, sending this force to rest of the body and causing to have an epileptic seizure. Many neuroscientists and neurophysiologists focus on one neuron or a body cell and get discouraged. They are unable to say or write that it is due to billions of neurons firing together to create a massive action potential, thus completing the complicated action or function of our body. Dr. Penfield and his associates, while operating on their patients for epilepsy, with electrical stimulus created a dream state (21, 40). These were not dreams; these were electrical activations of the sequential consciousness, a memory that was activated and laid down during the patient's earlier experiences. The patient "relived" such experiences, which he or she had been aware of in the past, like a moving picture flashback. This flashback was reported by a conscious patient. As an electrode touched the cortex of a female patient, she reported that she was in her kitchen listening to the voice of her little boy (21, 40), who was playing outside in the yard. She was aware of neighborhood noises, such as motor cars.

Another patient reported that he was sitting in a baseball game in a small town and watching a little boy crawl under the fence to join the audience. Another was in a concert hall, listening to music. He could hear different instruments. Dr. Penfield stimulated the same spot of the cortex, and the patient could hear the melody of the song. In another patient, when the electrode was touched to a point, she felt a tingling in the left thumb. At another spot of the brain, she felt tingling in the left side of the tongue, and at another area, there was movement of the tongue. When he stimulated another area, the patient reported, "I heard something; I don't know what it was." The same area was touched with an electrode again without warning, and the patient reported, "Yes, sir, I think I heard a mother calling her little boy somewhere." The patient was asked to explain, and she reported it was somebody in the neighborhood where she lived. She added that she herself was somewhere close enough to hear. When he touched at another spot, the patient responded, "I heard voices down along the river somewhere. I think I saw the river." The stories go on and on. That is how they stimulated the motor, sensory, auditory, and speech areas of the cortex. Dr. Penfield was astonished; he called these responses "experiential."

This has led us to the understanding of physiology, electric stimulation, and of the patterns of neuronal discharge in an epileptic stimulus (31, 40). It has also led us to understand the recorded memory, which was stimulated with an electric current. Dr. Penfield called it the "memory cortex" or "interpretive cortex." The brains of 1,132 patients were explored during the surgical process for the treatment of epilepsy and seizures. Dr. Penfield goes on to explain two mechanisms after learning from the electric stimulus of the regions of the cerebral cortex; there is a brain mechanism, the function of which is to send neuronal signals that interpret the relationship of the individual to his or her immediate environment. The action is automatic and unconscious, but signals appear in the conscious (34, 35, 40). The program comes to a computer from without; the same is true of each biological computer. Purpose comes to it from outside its own mechanism. This suggests that the mind must have a supply of energy available to it from independent action. This analogy, I assume, explains the magnetic soul, which I suggest is called the mind. There is an enormous magnetic field generated by the electric currents created by the neurons, which travels to the entire brain. I am of the opinion that our magnetic soul has an integral role to play in the functioning of our brain. I shall discuss this in detail in the chapter on the structure of the soul. Our soul gives direction to our brain in advance. This higher mind mechanism is the (soul) magnetic energy essential for consciousness. Our soul gives us this energy when we wake up from sleep to our consciousness. Our consciousness is absent while we are asleep, but neurons keep firing the electric current to keep our body functioning. The magnetic field remains activated while we are asleep. The highest mechanism is closely related to the mind; it is truly a functional unit proven by the fact that epileptic discharge in gray matter forms a part of its circuits and interferes with its actions selectively. During epileptic interference, consciousness vanishes. That is to say the mind goes out of action with the highest brain mechanism. The mind has energy. This form of energy is different from that of neuronal action potentials. Does the mind have a memory of its own? Dr. Penfield would say no. Our soul, which Dr. Penfield calls the mind, has the capability of opening our memory files from the brain anytime it needs through the control of magnetic energy. My view is clear about the magnetic energy that is interacting with our neurons and the brain and body; I call it the soul. Hughlings Jackson, in 1872, used the phrase "physiology of the mind." We would someday explain the mind (315–339).

Charles Sherrington stimulated the cerebral cortex with an electric current, which activated the motor mechanism, and there was a facilitation effect (50–74). I. P. Pavlov explained the conditional reflex. A dog was trained by frequent association of sound and food to salivate when a bell was rung. The dog did not know this before then. How did it happen? Two mechanisms took place—the unconditional effect, which is the sight of the food, and the conditional stimulus, which is the sound of the bell. The third effect was salivation. There has to be chain of neuronal action. Either pathways existed before or new connections were developed to achieve the desired effect. There have to be neurons that activate the salivary glands. When the dog hears the bell, electric current is passed to the auditory area and the visual area for the image of food; then both fire the current to the autonomic center in the brain stem to cause salivation. This became an automatic phenomenon. All electric currents do produce magnetic fields. My view is the magnetic soul could coordinate the whole process through a magnetic stimulus sent to all the three centers, thus becoming a conditional phenomenon (46, 38, 258). Let us presume there is a neuron C, which controls the reaction from an unconditional stimulus (UCS). Neuron B and neuron A respond to a conditional stimulus (CS). Both send electric current to C; thus, neuron C produces the response (R) of salivation.

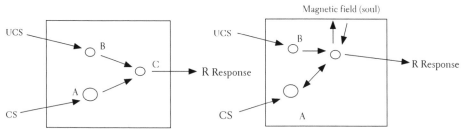

Ivan Pavlov studied this in a conscious dog. He described a conditioned reflex that the animals acquire because of anticipation. It can also be applied to human beings. Sometimes, the thought of delicious food creates salivation and the secretion of hydrochloric acid and mucous in our stomachs. One can conclude that conscious attention adds to the brain action that would otherwise have no record. One may assume that it is soul, the (magnetic field), the highest brain mechanism, that initiates the brain's action associated with that decision.The mind reasons and makes new decisions. It understands. It acts as though endowed with energy of its own. It can make decisions and put them to effect by calling upon various brain mechanisms. This could only be brought about by expenditure of energy, which in my view is the magnetic field (soul). It creates all these mechanisms. I concur with Dr. Penfield; it is the magnetic soul, which he called the mind. The constant electric current causes constant magnetic energy, which I refer to as the soul. You may call it whatever you feel.

If there are two elements, then energy must be available in two different forms. There is a force that is made available through neuronal conduction in the brain. Is there a force that is available to the mind, which has no such circuits? Can chemical actions in nerve cells result in brain action, on the one hand, and in mind action, on the other? Electricity was first revealed to science while it was being conducted along the nerves of living organisms. Physicists might well consider our questions seriously today and thank neurophysiologists for discovering the nerve conduction of electricity.

The highest brain mechanism switches on this semi-independent element, which instantly takes charge during wakefulness, and switches it off in sleep. Does this seem to be an improbable explanation? It is not so improbable, to my mind, as is the alternative expectation—that the highest brain mechanism should itself understand, reason, direct voluntary action, and decide where attention should be turned and what the computer must learn, record, and reveal on demand. In the case of either alternative, the mind has no memory of its own as far as our evidence goes. The brain, like any computer, stores what it has learned during active intervals. All of its records are instantly available to the conscious mind throughout the person's waking life and in a distorted fashion during the dreams of the half-asleep state. A century of scientific progress has passed since Hughlings Jackson suggested that there were high levels of functional organization in the brain. He seemed to consider the highest as most closely related to the mind. Since his time, various partially independent mechanisms have been identified and mapped in the cerebral cortex and the higher brain stem. None of them can explain the mind. The mind remains a mystery.

My definition of God is the sum total energy of the universe and energy created by living beings. We humans have contributed the maximum to this universe by means of understanding science and applying it to the maximum use, through construction of planes, ships, the Internet, items of luxury and items of destruction, like nuclear and other destructive weapons. We do justify that in the name of self-defense of the territory. We humans come and go, but advancements continue and inventions carry on. Artificial intelligence will take over major functions of our brain and body, but it is the decision of our brain and the soul to achieve that. There will be change in our human species, since artificial intelligence is endless. Only in the case of modern humans does this not destroy it. Science and the processes of science and culture existed way before we found them. I did not invent the soul. It existed since the day living creatures came into existence. Newton did not invent gravity. It existed forever. He found it. We did not invent electricity. We found it. In the same way, godly forces existed way before humans described God in their own cultural and religious beliefs. Humanity has no cause to fear the truth. It can, in the end, only fortify the valid creeds by which we live. Deep in our nature is the urge to explore, to learn, and to adopt a creed that will give us reassurance. The common person has a personal credo too. It is apt to differ, if only a little, from that of his or her fellows. And therein lies the strength and hope of the race. The facts and hypotheses discussed here may well be of use in many fields of specialized thinking, such as religion, philosophy, and psychiatry, as well as physics, chemistry, and medicine. Whether the mind is truly a separate element or whether, in some way not yet apparent, it is an expression of neuronal action, the decision must wait for further scientific evidence. We have discussed here only one piece of that evidence. But since it is incomplete, one must consider two hypotheses of explanation.

After understanding what Dr. Penfield was trying to say, it is obvious to me to assume that the mind is magnetic soul energy, which is a form of energy generated by electrochemical mechanisms, as we know them at the present time. Though you are not with us, my soul congratulates your soul for creating a concept that I find myself privileged to explain to humankind, regardless of their profession. Yes, your soul and the souls of those whom I admire still follow your wisdom and knowledge. They will be happy to read my work. You were concerned your fellow biophysicists may laugh at your work. It is fine. Some will laugh at my work too. As long as it creates a framework to conduct further research and find the answers, laughter is a pleasure for me and so be it for your soul. When one physician proclaimed that a peptic ulcer is caused by bacteria, the whole world's physicians laughed. In medical school, a professor of surgery, while teaching us about the treatment of peptic ulcer, laughed at this notion. We, the students, laughed too. Now we know how to treat peptic ulcer with antibiotics and antacids. Millions of surgeries were performed by cutting the stomachs, duodenums, and branches of the vagus nerve supplying the stomach, merely for money or out of ignorance. Millions of humans suffered from the side effects of such surgeries. What a tragic time of misinformation.

An excellent book written by Stewart Coats and Charles Taliaferro is *A Brief History of the Soul*. They wrote that so far we have questioned the assumption made by those who raise the conservation of energy objection to dualism, that causation must involve a transfer of energy from cause to effect. However, does granting this assumption spell a defect for dualism? It is hard to see why it should. After all, the conservation of energy principle applies to closed physical systems; a soul could introduce energy into it. If introduction of this energy requires an energy loss in the brain, a system that is equal to the amount of energy introduced by the soul, then that loss would entail a redistribution of the lost energy into some physical system.

Well, it is a valid statement raised by both philosophers. As I have already explained, the soul is a magnetic energy generated by the electrochemical energy enabling us to function in our brain and in rest of the body. Thus, there is interaction between the magnetic energy of the soul and the neuronal mechanism and functions that create the result. Though there is waste of energy, there is constant regeneration of action potential, as long as we are functional units. For example, we are awake and move around or work. There is electrical current constantly present to complete the movement of the functional unit (humans or animals). We constantly have to be conscious and alert. There are trillions of neurons and body cells firing electric current and generating a magnetic field (soul), which interacts with the neurons to create a thought, desire, motivation, and much more. Dennett claims that the mind is composed of some nonphysical and utterly mysterious "stuff." I think he is referring to some mysterious energy (57, 24). Our organs are problem solvers. In fact, all organisms are highly active problem solvers and explorers of their world (153–158).

CHAPTER 3

THE DEFINITION OF THE SOUL

T he soul is the sum total magnetic energy generated by the electrochemical mechanisms in the brains and bodies of living creatures.

For example, when we hear a sound or a voice, our hearing cells cause an electric current by the mere vibration of the eardrum of the hearing apparatus. This change from sound to electric current is called transduction. This transduction takes place in all of our sensory apparatuses. Once the vestibular nerve is stimulated, the electric current reaches to the cortical hearing center in the temporal lobe, as discussed in detail in chapter Anatomy and physiology of the soul, through stimulation of various neuronal paths in the brain. This current generates a vast magnetic field. Again, let us look at the visual-sensory apparatus. Light photons stimulate the rods and cones and the optic nerve, which creates an enormous firing of billions of neurons and the rest of the cells in the body when we respond to this stimulus. This current reaches the final destination on the occipital lobe of the cortex through the pathways discussed, creating a response by billions of cells, thus generating an enormous magnetic field. The same holds true of the sense of taste, smell, pain, pressure, touch, and temperature. These currents are simultaneously creating electric current in billions and trillions of cells, thus sending electric current to their respective centers in the brain. There is an action potential created in the cells, and, as I said earlier, they not only send information to their receptive centers; they also receive information back from the respective unit of the body for action to achieve the desired result. We are conscious, except while we are sleep. Even in our sleep, our brain remains active, and neurons keep firing since rest of the body has to continue functioning (heart and other organs). While we are conscious, our reticular formations and all sensory apparatuses keep firing and producing electric current in order to maintain a constant conscious status. In our sleep, our brain uses less energy compared to while we are conscious. There is a constant magnetic supply to our soul, whose primary energy is magnetic energy. Some neuroscientists think that action potential is not enough. Let us see why it is sufficient to keep us in a state of constant consciousness and in a moving functioning unit, like thinking, desiring, wishing, making decisions, remembering, interacting with our environment, learning comprehending, reasoning, judging others, understanding ourselves and others, and acting as an individual, father, mother, son, daughter, neighbor, teacher, student, and whatever your functional responsibilities are.

Action potential occurs in several types of animal cells, including neurons, muscle cells, and endocrine cells as well as in some plant cells. In muscle cells, the first mechanism is action potential for contraction. In the pancreas, insulin secretion is made possible by the cells (58, 49). Action potentials are generated by special types of voltage-gated ion channels embedded in a cell's plasma membrane. These channels are shut when the membrane potential is near the resting potential of the cell, but they begin to open when the membrane potential increases to a precisely defined threshold value (62, 192). In some types of electrically active cells, like neurons and muscle cells, the voltage fluctuates frequently. It takes the form of an upward spike followed by a rapid fall. These up-and-down cycles are called action potentials. In some neurons and cells, this up-and-down cycle takes place in a few thousandths of a second.

In muscle cells, this lasts for a fifth of a second. In plant cells, it may last for three seconds or more. Typically, the excitatory potential from several synapses must work together (in billions and in some cases trillions) at nearly the same time to provoke the action potential. Some neurons do not need such stimulus to fire. They spontaneously depolarize their axons and fire action potential at a regular rate "like an internal clock" (for example, the heart's sinoatrial node and atrial-ventricular node). This is known as pacemaker potential. It also occurs in the brain, where conscious alertness is needed while one is awake (63, 115–132). The resting potential in the neuronal cell is -75mv (64). After depolarization, the action potential in a neuron is almost +55mv (64).

Now, the question we have to ask ourselves is how to compute how much electric current is produced when a stimulus is applied. There are a trillion other cells in our body. The action potential could be measured by applying simple multiplication. Let us assume the action potential lasts for 2 to 4 millisecons (ms) with a refractory period of 1 to 3 ms. This is just one neuron, for the sake of example. While we perform an action, let's say jogging, playing football or tennis, and working out, not only are the muscle cells active; the whole brain is active. There is action potential generated. I will calculate the electric current produced as follows:

1mv = 0.045 volts
4ms = 0.004 seconds

In one second, we produce
0.045 volts X 60 = 2.7 volts
0.004 seconds X 60 = 0.24 seconds

Thus, in 0.24 seconds, we produce 2.7 volts for the sake of argument. Then how many volts we will produce in one minute, one hour, twenty-four hours, one month, one year, a lifetime?

This is the story of one neuron in your lifetime. There are billions of neuron activated with each action so keep multiplying. How many billions of volts are produced in our lifetime? It sounds very simple, but there must be other variations. I leave that to be solved by the physicists and mathematicians. I hope someone will answer the question, how much magnetic field is created for

- each action
- each hour
- each day
- each month
- each year
- a lifetime

Therefore, my argument is simple; we produce an enormous amount of electricity and an enormous amount of magnetic soul. Thus, this energy, which is called the mind, is the magnetic soul. This will explain us how the brain and magnetic soul work together to produce a unit called a human—the self and all others. I beg someone to help me with accurate math to resolve the mystery of the soul or whatever you want to call it. I will stick with the name "the magnetic soul."

In an article "Beyond Good-Bye," Sean Carroll, who is a physicist, raised a question; our knowledge of life after death is dramatically incomplete with everything we know about modern science. The author of the article says that people who claim that a soul persists after death would have to answer what particles makes up the soul, what holds them together, and how it interacts with ordinary matter? (385). My answer to him would be as described in this book extensively.

Given its conservation throughout evolution, the action potential seems to confer evolutionary advantages. One function of action potentials is rapid, long-range signaling within the organism; the conduction velocity can exceed 110 meters per second, which is one-third of the speed of sound. For comparison, a hormone molecule carried in the bloodstream moves at roughly eight meters per second in large arteries. Part of this function is the tight coordination of mechanical events, such as the contraction of the heart. A second function is the computation associated with the generation of actions and reactions. Being an all-or-none signal that does not decay with transmission across the distance, action potential has similar advantages and functions as digital electronics.

My magnetic soul is satisfied and relieved to write about it, and my heart is pounding faster since my autonomic system is overloaded and causing my heart to beat more rapidly. Well, it will settle once my magnetic soul settles down to its normal level and my neurons come to a refractory period of action potential. T. H. Bullock and G. A. Horridge in, 1965, described and explained the scientific physiology of action potential (66). William Powluk, MD, MSc., an assistant professor at John Hopkins Medical School, has written a lot about the magnetic field of the body and magnetic treatments for his patients suffering from various illnesses.

According to him, humans are souls with bodies, not bodies with souls. True health only comes when the soul is balanced. Health does not equal happiness. Happiness does produce health. Magnetic fields can be as strong as surgery or as gentle as quantum fields. Ultimately, the soul and the body are electromagnetic. All magnetic fields interact when the body (or the soul) is out of balance in the electromagnetic field. Electromagnetic therapies can help to restore some or all of these imbalances. Before the body gets into a state of serious imbalance, unless there is sudden trauma, it must go through progressive stages of imbalance, from energetic imbalance through physical imbalance to a physiological stage to a pathologic stage. The latter is organ or tissue death. Magnetic fields work in earlier stages of imbalance. With severe imbalances, more drastic measures are usually required, such as surgery and chemotherapy. The magnetic field may only be very helpful as a complementary modality of treatment. Therefore, magnetic fields can be used across the spectrum of health states. Because of this, they can be dramatically helpful in preventing energetic imbalances from day-to-day stresses caused by modern life. These stresses gradually accumulate and, like a grain of sand over time, can create a desert. The body and soul have their own wisdom and can rebalance themselves if left alone and not overwhelmed inappropriately. The unthoughtful use of magnetic fields can create an imbalance by not allowing the body to modulate itself homeostatically. Individuals can become proactive in managing stress, doing long-term health maintenance, and slowing the aging process with simple daily use of magnetic fields. Static magnetic fields are already widely used. Now European pulsed electromagnetic home systems are becoming available to the consumer (73, 1–5).

I may compliment you, Dr. Powluk, for your highly intellectual thinking and approach to the body and soul. I think you are the first doctor who thinks like me and has enough evidence to research more in the field of medicine and health in general for everyone. My goal is to create enough thinking among neuroscientists and other medical professionals to learn more and pay attention to this concept of life as a whole. Moreover I would desire for every human being to learn and pay attention to the body and soul. In an article available online (http:/www.drpawluk.com/education/about_dr_pawluk), he wrote, "Stepping outside the traditional 'House of Medicine' was not a simple or easy decision. I was risking the ridicule, censure and quizzical looks of my peers. Well, may I refer you to Dr. Penfield, who also felt the way you feel. I understand." But to create clearer thinking and begin moving forward with the concept of a magnetic soul, we should create further research. That is how we have grown in medicine, and moreover, that is how we will grow in the future, with this new concept of human thinking and future treatments for humankind. I will be writing more about transcranial magnetic stimulation for depression and other indications approved by the Food and Drug Administration (FDA). There are various therapies that attest to this view and the future of magnetic field theory, as well as applications of the same in various modalities. I am sure, after people read my book, some will laugh; some will say, "Oh well, I don't know"; and some will say, "Yes, we should do more research," if they like it. I am of the view that we should not be discouraged to inform our colleagues and the rest of humankind of what we believe in. Let's let them make judgments for themselves (74, 1–4). A journey of many miles starts with the first step. If you never start, you will never find the end. If you continue, you may find something. Once you find something, good or bad, at least you know what you do not know. That is the only way you may want to know.

John Jo McFadden (75, 262–270) expressed his views in an article on conscious electromagnetic field theory. He proposes that consciousness is a manifestation of the brain's electromagnetic field (CEMI). The key feature of the brain's electromagnetic field is that it is capable of integrating vast quantities of information into a single physical system and thereby accounts for the *binding of consciousness*. Let me explain what the binding problem is. It is a nightmare for neuroscientists to explain. How is the brain able to produce a single unified picture of the world outside of us, given the fact that the electric current comes from the senses of vision (eyes), hearing (ears), touch (skin), pain, smell, and taste (tongue) from different sensory apparatuses, which send electric currents to different parts of the brain? How this is all brought together? Though the interconnectivity of all these neuronal axons and dendrites of the neurons can explain the binding, my view is that in addition to the interconnectivity, there is the heart of the explanation—the soul, or the magnetic field, brings all the sensations together and makes it easier. It is the fastest way of bringing it all together, occurring in fractions of seconds, and makes us perceive what we perceive from outside and produce a single unified picture by synchronized firing of the neurons, which causes a unified electromagnetic field. Thus, it is the soul, which is a magnetic field, that facilitates the binding of information. McFadden also proposed that the digital information from neurons is integrated to form a conscious electromagnetic information (CEMI) field in the brain. Consciousness is suggested to be the component of this field that is transmitted back to the neurons. It communicates its state externally. Thoughts are viewed as electromagnetic representations of neuronal information, and the experience of free will in our choice of actions is argued to be our subjective experience of the CEMI field acting on our neurons.

The brain's neurons are densely packed, with 100,000 neurons per square millimeter, so the field adjacent to the neurons will not be independent but form a complex overlapping field made up of fields of millions of neurons in the vicinity. Thus, the neurons in the cerebral cortex and hippocampus will amplify the magnetic field generated by the electric current, spreading to the designated area of the brain and beyond. In a busy brain, it is very likely that many neurons will be in a state that the electromagnetic field of the neurons generates. It will influence neural dynamics. A piece of indirect evidence for the suggestion of an electromagnetic field of the brain may be gained from the electromagnetic field applied to the brain from external fields. In humans, the evidence comes from the sensitivity of the brain to relatively weak electromagnetic fields applied to it by the use of transcranial magnetic stimulation (TMS). In TMS, a current passes through the coils placed on the scalp (head) of the patients to generate a time-varying magnetic field that penetrates the skull and induces an electric field in the neurons of the brain. Though the exact mechanism is still unclear, it is assumed that electrical induction of the local current in the brain tissue modulates neuronal firing patterns.

A magnetic field is generated when an electric current is passed through metal. The experiment explains it to us in a simple way. First, a metal rod was connected to a wire and electric current was passed through the metal rod from a battery. There was a magnetic field generated around the metal rod, which was weak. Then, it was thought that if we surround the rod with coils, there would be an increased magnetic field. Still, the magnetic field was not strong. Inventors replaced the metal rod with an iron rod, and suddenly, the magnetic field was much higher than before, because iron is a better conductor of electric current. This is the basic principle in the human brain and body. When an electric current passes through the nervous tissues, a magnetic field is generated. Anatomically, it is obvious that our brain has sulci and gyri in order to pack the neurons together and increase the number of cells compared to what a flat surface could accommodate. Thus, sulci make room for the vascular supply of blood. Our blood has oxyhemoglobin, which has iron. Iron enhances the electric current, which increases the magnetic field in the body. Arteries are surrounded by the autonomic nervous system, which also enhances the generation of the magnetic field of the soul.

Freud created the structural theory of the mind. The id is unorganized and instinctual. Infants are born with this instinct. The ego has three components—the conscious, preconscious, and unconscious. The word *ego* is used in regular English conversation to mean "a person's sense of self-esteem or self-importance." We sometimes say, "He or she is egoistic." Freud used this term to analyze the part of the mind that mediates between the conscious and the unconscious, the part responsible for reality testing and the sense of personal identity. When we say someone has "a big ego," we are saying that he or she is too full of him- or herself (www.vocabulary. com). Freud gave it a different meaning. According to him, the ego is the executive organ of the psyche (*psyche* is a Greek term used for the mind, soul, and spirit). It controls motility, perception, contact with reality, and defense mechanisms. The ego modulates and delays the expression of drive. Freud believed that the id is modified as a result of the impact of the external environment on the drives, needs, and desires. The ego appropriates the energies due to the pressure from external realities for id to do its work. As the ego brings influences from the external world to bear on the id, it simultaneously substitutes the reality principle for the pleasure principle. Freud explained that conflicts occur between the id and the outside world, only to be transformed later to conflict between the id and the ego. The superego establishes and maintains an individual's moral conscience on the basis of a complex system of ideals and values internalized from parents. The superego then serves as an agency that provides ongoing scrutiny of person's behavior, thoughts, and feelings. It makes comparison with expected standards of behavior and offers approval or disapproval of these activities. This process occurs unconsciously.

The *ego ideal* is often regarded as a component of the superego. It is an agency that prescribes what a person should do, according to internalized standards and values. The superego, by contrast, is an agency of the moral conscience that proscribes and dictates what a person should do or not do. From an early age, one continues to build an early identification through one's contact with admired figures, who contribute to the formation of moral standards (aspirations and ideals) (317, 31, 159–166). Freud attributed the pleasure principle to an inborn tendency of the organism to avoid pain and to seek pleasure through the discharge of tension. The reality principle is a learned function, closely related to maturation of the ego. This principle modifies the pleasure principle, like postponement of gratification or delaying instant gratification. I admire Freud for such a wonderful concept given at his time. Though he was a neurologist by training, he lacked all the scientific tools to assess the functions of the brain, like FMRI and other relevant advancements in neurobiology and neuroscience. At present, we neuroscientists agree that the basis of all the sensory motor and emotional expressions is the electric current transfer from the source of origin to the source of destination (described in detail in the chapter on the anatomy and physiology of the primary soul). In addition, all the cells of the body and neurons of the brain need energy and create electrical energy to promote any action, reaction, or emotion. Freud described the ego as an agency or an organ of the psyche. It does not explain the neurophysiology or neurobiology of emotions, actions, or reactions. It is just an imaginary theory that has no scientific or biological support. I do admit to the existence of the ego, conscience, consciousness, and unconsciousness, as explained in detail in the chapter on the soul and consciousness. These mechanisms are based purely on scientific basis. My view on his theory is based on magnetic energy (soul) created by the electrical impulses in our brain and body. Ego, consciousness, and unconsciousness do not exist in a vacuum. They all need the energy of the neurons at the synaptic level. Expanding upon his theory of the ego, the energy of the magnetic field produced by the different parts of the brain is designated for the different functions, like motor, sensory, emotional, and other behaviors. Let's give him credit and borrow the ego concept. To me, this involves the frontal lobe, the parietal lobe, the occipital lobe, the limbic system, and the other parts of the brain as a whole combining all the required functions and the behaviors through the binding mechanism of the brain to produce the required reactions to internal and external stimuli. So I would suggest the ego part of our magnetic energy creates the functions of the organism (as suggested by modern ego psychologists) including the following:

- Control and regulation of instinctual drives
- Judgment
- Relation to reality
- Object relations

According to Herman Nunberg (1931), the synthetic function of the ego is to integrate drives and elements into an overall unity, which involves organization, coordination, and generalizing or simplifying large amounts of data received by the organism. Modern neuroscientists call it combining theory. Heinz Hartmann described primary autonomous ego functions. According to him, it is a rudimentary apparatus present at birth, which develops independently of intrapsychic conflict between the drives and defenses. These functions include perceptions, learning, intelligence, instructions, language, thinking comprehension, and motility (31, 159–160). I argue all of the above need energy in order to develop to their full form. What is that energy? It is the electric currents that carry all the information from either side of the stimulus and to the receiver for the required actions. All the mechanisms generate magnetic energy, which interacts with the neurons of the brain to achieve results.

The term *defense mechanisms* was coined by Freud and his daughter Anna Freud. In this mechanism, any information that is potentially threatening to the integrity of one's ego is deflected unconsciously by various psychological mechanisms. Let us look at common defense mechanisms.

Denial, for example, is the refusal to accept reality or fact. The person acts as if a painful event, thought, or feeling does not exist. Modern psychologists and psychiatrists still believe that denial is an unconscious part of the ego. I argue that denial has conscious and unconscious parts.

For example, when I asked a patient, "Do you drink and how often?" he replied, "Almost every day." There was no denial. He knew he is drinking every day. My second question was, "Do you think you are an alcoholic?" His answer was "no," which is from the unconscious part of the ego. Another example is I had a patient who had a heart attack (myocardial infarction). I asked him what happened. His answer was "I had a heart attack." My second question was, "How did it affect your health?" He replied, "Oh, I'm fine. Look at me now. I'm healthy. Now, let's get beyond that.

In a court of law, a judge asked a defendant, "Do you plead guilty?"

The defendant answered, "No, Your Honor, I do not plead guilty."

Is it unconscious? He may be innocent or guilty, but he knows. Let's look at the Fifth Amendment (319) I 1791, which states,

> No person shall be held to answer for a capital or otherwise infamous crime, unless on a presentment or indictment of a grand jury, except in cases arising in the land or naval forces, or in the militia, when in actual service in the time of war or public danger, nor shall any person be subject for the same offence to be twice put in jeopardy of life or limb, Nor shall be compelled in any criminal case to be a witness against himself nor be deprived of life, liberty or property, without due process of law; nor shall private property be taken for public use, without just compensation.

Well, a friend of mine was going through divorce. He pleaded the Fifth. He knew everything he had done. Is it an unconscious outcome of his ego? No. My view is quite the contrary. His denial was a purely conscious mechanism of his frontal lobe, parietal lobe (motor area), sensory system, and limbic system. He heard and saw an attorney asking him questions. His hearing and vision sent an electric current to the parts of his brain. He processed it and sent back the electric current to say, "I plead not guilty." He used his voice, lips, and expression. He used the electrical energy created by his magnetic energy (the ego is part of that) after processing the information with his higher neuronal functions (magnetic energy of soul). Is it unconscious? There are numerous examples. Let us think about it (31, 161–12). Some of the unhealthy mechanisms are the following:

- Projection
- Distortion
- Acting out
- Blocking
- Hypochondria
- Introjections
- Passive-aggressive behavior
- Projection
- Regression
- Schizoid fantasy
- Summarization
- Controlling
- Displacement
- Dissociation
- Externalization
- Inhibition
- Intellectualization
- Isolation
- Rationalization
- Reaction formation
- Repression

Healthy defense mechanisms include the following:

- Altruism
- Anticipation
- Asceticism
- Humor
- Sublimation
- Suppression

I would like to explain some of defense mechanisms and try to write them in simple language.

Projection is when an unacceptable inner impulse or action is shifted to outside of the self. In psychotic disorders, it is a delusion about external reality. It may take the form of hallucinations, like voices are telling me to do what I did and what I am doing.

Distortion is replacing the experience of external reality to suit inner needs, usually wishful fulfillment, like having feelings of graciosity, superiority, or entitlement.

Blocking occurs when tensions arise from unpleasant thoughts and stimulating impulses and we inhibit the impulses or thoughts.

Introjections occur when we internalize the characteristics of the loved objects to ensure closeness and constant presence of the object to avoid anxiety. In the case of the loss of a loved object, introjections nullify or negate the loss by taking on characteristics of the lost object.

Projection is common in normal individuals and mentally ill individuals. In normal individuals, it is the attribution of one's own acknowledged feelings, thoughts, and actions to others—for example, "I did not do it. He did it." It may take the form of misinterpreting motives, attitudes, feelings, or intentions of others.

Regression is returning to an earlier stage of development or childish behavior in adults. This reflects a basic tendency to achieve instinctual gratification. This is often the result of a disruption of equilibrium at a later phase of development.

Somatization is the conversion of emotional conflict into physical symptoms.

Displacement is the purposeful unconscious shifting of impulses from one object to another object, with the purpose of solving a conflict. For example, I might say, "It was not my idea. It was his or her idea or thoughts."

Externalization is a general term referring to the tendency to perceive in the external world and in external objects components of one's own personality, including instinctual impulses, conflicts, moods, attitudes, and styles of thinking.

Intellectualization refers to the control of affects and impulses by way of thinking about them instead of experiencing them. There is excessive thinking to defend against anxiety caused by unacceptable impulses.

Rationalization is the justification of attitudes, beliefs, or behaviors that might otherwise be rationally unacceptable through an incorrect application of justifying reasons or the invention of a convincing fallacy.

Reaction formation is the expression of unacceptable impulses in antithetical form (opposite). This is an expression of the impulse in the negative. It is an aspect of obsessional characters (318).

My experience in psychiatry makes me feel that defense mechanisms have neurobiological origins and have both conscious and unconscious parts. Some are used by mentally ill patients and some by normal humans.

They may be the result of the function of the "ego," which is seated in our magnetic energy of the soul.

A thoughtful article by Sandeep Vaishnavi, MD, PhD (320), explains that it is important to understand that thinking of psychiatric symptoms in terms of neural circuits, in the same way neurologists consider neurological symptoms to be correlated with damage to the neural circuits, might be a better approach if someone has had a stroke, Parkinsonism, or a brain tumor. Whatever symptom a patient has, a neurologist can pinpoint the site of a lesion in the brain and design the treatment accordingly. I am of the opinion that once we have enough modern tools, like (FMRI, TMS) and all advanced diagnostic tools, psychiatry will merge with neurology and be call neuropsychiatry.

THE NERVOUS SYSTEM AND THE ELECTRIC POWER STATION

Some of you may be wondering what a power station has to do with our brain. It makes it easier for me to explain to those who do not have enough knowledge of human anatomy and physiology. Our nervous system works just like a power station. For example, if there is a power station in Buffalo, New York, supplying power to the whole state of New York, it produces an enormous amount of electric power, which creates an enormous magnetic field. This power station supplies electric power through high-tension wires to a grid system. These high-tension wires also create massive electromagnetic fields. Once the grid system is operational, it supplies power to the city of New York, through its own grid system. This grid system is connected to transformers in various neighborhoods. Finally, power reaches your house, which has a breaker system of its own. The reason for that is your house needs different voltages in different areas. Some appliances need 220 volts and some need 120 volts. Some areas, like the kitchen, must be set up to operate a microwave oven, dishwasher, and freezer, and some areas need only light, so it must be configured in such a way that electricity is evenly distributed, depending upon the need of the house through the circuit breakers. The wires get smaller and thinner as they move away from the power station, to avoid any surge or overload of power. This is a well-organized and well-planned system. If one circuit breaker goes off, you will lose power in that designated area without disrupting the rest of the house. So life is comfortable. You can enjoy watching TV, cooking, having a hot bath, and numerous pleasures provided by electric power. Someday, this electromagnetic field may be used as a source of energy, by converting it into electric power. While building such infrastructure—the power station, the long and complicated connection system of wires, and the grid system—there are codes developed by countries, states, and cities in order to prevent any damage and to increase efficacy. If a power station is damaged for any reason, the entire area loses power. There is a total blackout. There is chaos and confusion. Life becomes miserable. In that case, we either repair or look for other sources of power. Let us presume high-tension wires get damaged by an ice storm. We lose power in the designated area of supply. Let us say a city. Then that city does not have power. The entire city is paralyzed until repairs are done. The same holds true for your neighborhood and your house.

Our nervous system is structured the same way. The only difference is that we have two-way systems, which I will explain as we understand how our brain works. Our brain is a power station, which produces electric current that flows to the rest of the entire body. The current travels from the brain to the spinal cord and then to large nerves (high-tension wires). These nerves get smaller and smaller as they reach the destination of supply, like the electric system's wires. The nerves get smaller to a precise size to tolerate the electric current and supply an adequate amount of electric current to produce desired functions. These wires have their grid system and a wide range of connections through ganglia. This current flows from head to toe and to each organ of the body. The principle is the same, like power from an electric power station to your house. If the brain gets damaged, then power is shut off to the rest of the body. We are devoid of all the functions of the body, until the brain is repaired and attains normal function. Our brain, nerves, and organs produce current in two ways: current generated by our brain to be sent to the destination where it is received to produce the desired function, like muscle movement; and current sent back to our brain full of information, like pain, touch, pressure, temperature, and more. This system does not exist in a man-made electrical system. We have two-way systems. If our high-tension wires are damaged, then we have paralysis of the area the nerve supplies. For example, if our spinal cord is damaged, we develop paraplegia of both legs (loss of power to a city). There is no to and fro information between the legs and brain. Our nervous system generates an enormous electric current, which produces an enormous amount of magnetic energy, which I call the magnetic soul. You can call it whatever you want. In order to honor human souls who have looked for scientific explanations of the soul for centuries and since the inception of human intelligence, I will stick to this concept of the soul. Man-made electric systems have codes to follow; if they do not, the project is cancelled. In the same way, we humans and living beings have a genetic code to follow. If it is not followed, we develop genetic disorders of the nervous system. This is all in our DNA and RNA.

CHAPTER 4

STRUCTURE OF THE SOUL

The primary soul involves the entire nervous system, including the autonomic nervous system, as well as the vascular system and lymphatic system.

The secondary soul involves all the organs of the body, including the ears, eyes, heart, lungs, liver, kidneys, and all other organs of the body, like those of the gastrointestinal tract, the sexual organs, smooth muscles, bones, and the rest of the structures.

The tertiary soul involves the musculoskeletal system and the rest of the parts of the body, like the skin.

Thus, the soul plus a body equals a complete human being, which has a self and a soul.

I discussed the action potential and the nervous system in the previous chapter. In the secondary soul, the heart is the strongest generator of action potential. The heart's magnetic field is estimated to be five thousand times stronger than that of the brain. It can also be measured several feet away from the body with a SQUID-based magnetometer (80). A presentation by McCarty and coworkers has demonstrated that this magnetic field can influence the cerebral and cardiovascular functions of other individuals while in they are in direct physical contact or even a few feet away, as assessed by ECG (electrocardiogram) and EEG (electroencephalogram) recordings. This has been explained by many scientists. Some have proposed that the heart actually plays a major role in generating and integrating the flow of energy in the body (81).

A superconducting quantum interference device (SQUID) is a very sensitive magnetometer used to measure extremely subtle magnetic fields, based on superconducting loops of Josephson junctions. It is used in various studies in biology. Magnetoencephalography (MEG) is used to measure neuronal activity in the brain. It is also used in magnetogastrography, to measure the weak magnetic field of the stomach. It can be used in tracing the path of orally given drugs. In the clinical field, it is very helpful in diagnosing and for risk management of heart diseases. New SQUIDs are used as detectors to perform magnetic resonance imaging (MRI) and are used in other fields, like underwater exploration (82).

The principal function of the heart is to serve as a pump to supply oxygenated blood received from the lungs. This goes on twenty-four/seven while we are alive. Any failure of blood supply leads to death of the tissue. The heart has to supply oxygenated blood to itself to keep functioning. Any disruption leads to the death of its own muscles. Blood supply is not enough for this pump to work; it needs a constant electrical supply. It is a unique pump. It repairs its own arterial system through a mechanism called angiogenesis. Its inner layer is called the endothelium and secrets numerous enzymes and chemicals, which keep blood vessels dilated and keep the blood from clotting to avoid coagulation. The enzyme-endothelium-derived relaxing factor (EDRF) is also secreted by the endothelium. In addition, endothelial cells also secrete a group of growth factors that induce generation of new blood vessels and keep the pump healthy (84, 946–47). This is the only pump I have ever heard of that produces its own electric power, makes its own repairs, and feeds itself. It has its own brain, called the sinoatrial (SA) node and atrioventricular (AV) node. They are connected to each other. The AV node sends the nerves to the ventricles. They are called right and left bundle branches. These give rise to Purkinje fibers in the muscle cells of the heart and endothelium. The connection between the SA node and AV node is called the internodal pathway. The whole system is called the electrical conducting system of the heart. It plays an important role in broken-heart syndrome. There is no such diagnosis because no insurance company will pay for this diagnosis when doctors bill for it. So why even bother to diagnose such an illness, which is not recognized by the AMA? The fact is many people have died because of broken-heart syndrome. The mechanism of death is due to overactivity of or overstimulation of the vagus nerve, which causes a slow heartbeat. In the elderly, it can cause a sudden blockage of the conducting system of the heart, causing the heart to stop pumping blood to the brain and the rest of the body, which leads to sudden death.

I was watching CNN on December 29, 2016, and learned that Debbie Reynolds had died twenty-four hours after the death of her daughter without any cause. They were both among the great actresses of their time. It drew my attention because I have known many elderly couples who died within a short period of time of each other. How does it happen? My presumption is that the sudden demise of a loved one causes a sudden surge of magnetic energy, which triggers overstimulation of Vagus nerve due to that excessive discharge of acetylcholine. This inhibits the conducting system of the heart from pumping blood, causing sudden death. This is the shock to the soul that explains the whole process.

During my time of teaching anatomy in medical school for three years, my research was on comparative anatomy of the conducting system of the heart. I still remember the SA node cells under microscope looked like a bunch of grapes, jumbled together and working in harmony to produce electric current. I never completed the research since I left the country. I feel honored to have dissected the brain, heart, and human body, fiber by fiber. Learning and teaching students about the human body was a passion and satisfaction in my life. It gave me great insight and understanding about the organs of the body and how they look and function together to create a complex and advanced human being.

As far as the action potential of the heart is concerned, it is the song and dance of sodium ($Na+$), potassium ($K+$), chloride ($Cl-$), calcium ($Ca+$) ions and various chemicals and energy sources. I do not want to get into too much detail, since we would need several volumes of books. For those readers who are interested in knowing more, I recommend reading about the physiology and anatomy of the heart. I will briefly discuss the electric mechanism, since it contributes to the magnetic soul. Though the heart has its own brain (SA and NA nodes), it is connected to our primary soul in "the brain" by the sympathetic and parasympathetic (vagus nerve) systems. The sympathetic nervous system increases the heart rate by increasing the firing rate of the action potential, while the parasympathetic nervous system decreases the firing of the action potential, thus decreasing the heart rate (85, 327). Though the heart center is located in the lower brain stem, both the sympathetic and parasympathetic systems are ascending and descending connections from the heart center to the brain stem and to the hypothalamus, which are connected to the limbic system. Does the heart send constant information of its beating twenty-four/seven to the higher centers and when there is any emotional change? Yes, it does. Our heart is informed about those emotional states. It beats harder when we meet our girlfriend or boyfriend, whom we love. It is all done by electric current, which sends or brings the information to the higher centers and the heart. In a fight-or-flight response, the same mechanism takes place. The heart is ordered via the sympathetic nervous system to pump faster and faster to provide enough blood and oxygen. My view is there is a constant electromagnetic energy supply to our brain, which maintains consciousness. Does it explain why when we are in distress or experiencing emotional trauma we sometimes say, "My heart is broken"? Or when a woman broke up with her boyfriend, she says she is heartbroken? If a husband or wife dies, we use the phrase, "My heart hurts." Yes, it is through our sympathetic and parasympathetic system, from which our soul receives constant magnetic energy, either in sorrow or happiness. The heart is thus part of our secondary soul. It is constantly in touch with our primary soul (the brain). I think all the emotional reactions and responses are combined by the binding theory of the soul.

Bjorn Nordenstrom, in his book *Vascular Interstitial Closed Circuit* (1983) (VICC), wrote that there are numerous circuits, ranging in size from meters to microns, that utilize both ionic and electronic electricity and produce an electromagnetic field with varying frequencies of amplitude and wavelength. He believed that chi, the energy of life in ancient Chinese medicine, is analogous to or perhaps the same as the electromagnetic energy found in the biological closed electric circuit. It is the ying and yang components, the positive and negative electric charges of the closed-circuit ionic flow. During the healthy state, chi flows through prescribed pathways (meridians) in the body in an orderly fashion; this includes the VICC and other interstitial channels, which may be thought of as corresponding to these meridians (86, 87).

Dr. Nordenstrom describes a circulatory system that is based on spontaneously occurring electric potentials. Potential gradients have long been known to develop in normal organs as a result of metabolism and in injured or diseased tissues because of hemorrhage or necrosis. The electric current is conducted by a biologically closed electric circuit (BCEC), blood plasma, and interstitial fluid. The vessels act as insulators for electric current, like electric cables (86, 97). However, many physiologists have questioned this explanation. My view is that our blood vessels have sympathetic and parasympathetic nerve supplies, which usually surround and supply the nerves to the blood vessels (arteries and veins). This could explain a viable mechanism of conduction of electric current to and from the central nervous system. Electrical signals arising in the SA node stimulate the atria to contract and then travel to the AV node, which is located in the intratrial septum (87). The heart cells share the electric current freely in a synchronized fashion and thus contract the ventricles to pump the blood to the heart and rest of our body. Heart muscles have similarities to neurons and muscles of the body, because they generate action potential in order to maximize the efficiency of the conducting system of the heart.

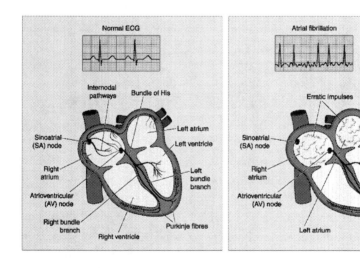

Now you may ask why I am writing about the heart. It is because my view is that the heart and all the other organs act as secondary souls. There is no argument that the heart generates enormous amounts of electric current constantly until death. Thus, it generates enormous amounts of magnetic field, which contributes to our soul and is a source of enormous energy. Moreover, a pacemaker is used to regulate and stimulate the electrical conducting system (ECS). Defibrillators are used to give a shock to the heart to regulate its beating, based on electric current. This magnetic energy contributes to our soul, which could have stimulated the thoughts of some philosophers to claim that the heart is the seat of the soul. The electrocardiogram is based on an electric current generated by the heart, which not only tells us about the health of the heart but also various diseases of the heart. Based on the fact that the electric current generates a magnetic field, the heart is a strong generator of the magnetic field, which I call the soul. There is a strong bonding of our magnetic field when we hug somebody out of love or passion, provide comfort, and make love. The truth from us and others is displayed by such actions, and compatible souls get stronger and bond with each other. I have never hugged someone I do not like or someone I hate. I have never hugged my enemies or perceived enemies, because my soul is not compatible with their souls. Our magnetic fields are at different wavelengths. This makes me believe that the seat of our love lies in our soul.

Lungs are the partners of the heart. Together, these organs give life to our soul. Without their continuous work, the soul would not exist. Breath is the parana (energy in Hindu philosophy) of the soul. Each breath gives us oxygen and takes carbon dioxide out. Oxyhemoglobin is the fuel for our life, along with other nutritive products in the blood. We have 18,000 to 20,000 breaths per day and average 5,000 gallons of air. That is thirty-five times (88) more than we drink or eat by weight. We can live without food and water for days, but without breathing, we would last no more than a few minutes. Each breath nourishes our heart, each cell in the body, and our brain (primary soul). Without air, we cannot speak or digest our food. The average person can hold two pints of air per breath. In yoga, the emphasis is on regulating the breath to relax the muscles, and in meditation, the focus is on patterns of breathing to reach the spiritual level of the soul by ignoring the sensations. Though we breathe continuously, to the point we become unconscious of it, being aware of breathing makes us conscious of our existence. As long as we are alive, it is with us. We can't leave our office or home without it. It is always with us, no matter how we feel and where we are. Some people have difficulty breathing while they are anxious, enraged, or frightened. They breathe faster and faster and more and more shallowly and wind up hyperventilating, which causes a lack of oxygen and too much carbon dioxide. This brings on feelings of light-headedness, often accompanied by feelings of pressure in the chest due to a lack of oxygen resulting in an overwhelming wave of fear or panic. When you have panic, of course, it just makes it much harder to get control of your breathing. People who experience hyperventilation can think they are going to have a heart attack and are going to die. Sometimes, they black out, which is dangerous enough. Some people pass out. Passing out is a frightening experience. The basic groundwork for meditation is to focus on breathing and become aware of it. Doing this, we feel the air as it flows in and out through our nostrils; we feel the belly as it moves in and out. Paying attention to your breathing means paying attention to yourself and nothing else, like your job, financial problems, needs, greed, and other stressors existing in your life. Becoming aware of your breathing means feeling the sensations associated with it and attending to the changing qualities of those breathing sensations.

Breathing is regulated by the respiratory center in the brain stem and by the concentration of oxygen and carbon dioxide. One-fourth of the oxygen is used by our brain in spite of the fact that it is one-fifth of our body weight, roughly weighing three pounds. Hindus believe that the breath is the gateway between the mind and body. The whole system of yoga is built on breathing techniques, called pranayam. It is designed to expand consciousness and the purity of the body. Yogis make a distinction between the breathing (satula parana) and the subtle movement of energy that results from the breath (sukshma parana). We can then direct that energy toward specific areas or chakras through visualization or the use of posture. My view is that this is redistribution of the magnetic field energy of the soul to enhance the yoga postures. Breathing exercises are essential to practice for meditation and to reach to the spirituality of soul. They are briefly described as follows:

1. Deep breathing—sit quietly and inhale and exhale deeply.
2. Breath of fire—this is rapid diaphragmatic breathing, using fast, short breaths created by the contraction and relaxation of your abdominal muscles. It helps to build abdominal muscles and with the motion of internal organs to increase energy for their respective functions. It increases the blood circulation to organs and pushes gas and waste products from the gastrointestinal system, which is discussed in the chapter on meditation and the soul.

The secondary soul provides existence to our soul through the connection of our primary soul (brain). The stomach, liver, pancreas, kidneys, sexual organs, vascular system, lymphatic system, and the rest of our internal organs provide our secondary and primary souls the resources for real existence and growth. This is true of all animals and other living creatures.

Let's look at our gastrointestinal system. I shall focus on the stomach, and you will understand the rest. The stomach is a highly abused organ of our body; we put everything into it by mouth. We load it up with hot dogs, hamburgers, vegetables, fruits, and sweets to the point it cannot tolerate them. Even though it is full, we still push it to the limits. At times, we fill it to the point it will blow up. But the stomach is a resilient bag. It will protect you and save you by throwing up excess food. This is how we get fat, unhealthy, or malnourished. This organ works hard to the point that it goes beyond its limits. It secrets mucous, which is alkaline, and hydrochloric acid, which is acidic. Both are extremely irritants and can burn the finger if it is dipped in these juices—as I learned in first two years of medical school in the department of physiology. We never listen to our stomach or what it wants, but we want it to work for what we want, in spite of the fact it gives us life and provides nutrition by turning noxious foods into healthy, absorbable food. It churns and churns, pulverizing the food we ingest to the smallest particles so our intestines can absorb them to give us life. We used to cut it to treat duodenal ulcers and staple it for obesity, though it has nothing to do with hunger. We were so ignorant that we cut millions and millions of stomachs for peptic ulcers. Now we give an antibiotic and antacid. We do not cut it anymore. The same happened to the uterus. Millions and millions were cut open for fibroid tumors and irregular bleeding for money and monetary gain. Shame on those who did it for the sake of money.

This story crossed through my soul after I wrote the preceding paragraph. One day, the stomach argued with the soul and told it, "Stop filling me with your desires for food."

The soul told the stomach, "I am the master. I want you to do what I demand you to do."

The stomach asked, "Is that the way you think about and treat me?"

The soul said, "Yes, you are a sack of potatoes and nothing else."

The stomach said, "Okay. I will show you."

The soul ordered the mouth to send the stomach anything the soul wanted. As a rebellious act, the stomach vomited it all up. This went on until the soul started feeling weaker and weaker. They had arguments, and the soul went on its own away, looking for various foods, like beef, chicken, and fruit, but it was unable to have anything. The stomach went on its way, looking for food but was unable to touch anything. The soul went to its gurus, masters, asking for advice.

The guru answered the soul, "Oh! You ignorant one, where is your wisdom? You cannot survive without the friendship of your stomach. Go back home and apologize to stomach."

The soul came back and asked the stomach to forgive it.

The stomach said, "Not so fast, Master. You have to meet certain conditions like you must treat me with respect. You must not call me a sack of potatoes. Don't force me to digest whatever garbage you desire. Keep your desires limited and tolerable to me. Give me healthy food to digest so as I can serve you properly. Let me consult my friends, like the liver, pancreas, spleen, and kidneys to see if they agree with these conditions. Then I will be your friend and not annoy you."

The stomach consulted its friends through various nerves and the celiac plexus (sympathetic nervous system). They all agreed, and the soul was informed about this decision. The soul honored the decision and gave up. It supplied only healthy food and limited its desires for the pleasures of life. They remained friends and produced a healthy body and healthy soul. The moral of the story is if we engulf ourselves with too much food or unhealthy food, we become obese. Two little makes us weak and frail. There has to be a balanced approach to fulfilling our desires and greed; thus we can produce a healthy human being.

Nausea and vomiting may occur independently. They love each other. They are closely allied and presumed to be mediated by the same neural pathway. The act of vomiting is under the control of two functionally distinct medullary centers. The vomiting center is located in the dorsal portion of the lateral ventricular formation. The chemoreceptor trigger zone is located in the area postrema of the floor of the fourth ventricle (147). The vomiting central controls and integrates the actual act of vomiting. It receives afferent stimuli from the gastrointestinal tract and from other parts of the body, like the higher brain stem and cortical centers, especially in the internal ears' vestibular apparatuses and from chemoreceptor trigger zones. Each individual person has a respective response. Different people respond differently. Some are very sensitive, and others are less sensitive. The vomiting center is located near other centers, like the respiratory and vasomotor centers, and all these centers are involved in the act of vomiting and trigger autonomic centers (146). Once the electric current of noxious stimuli is received, there is an electrical current spread to respective areas, which generates the magnetic energy (soul). This combines all the stimuli in the act. Even the electromagnetic energy spreads to the visual and motor areas. That is how abdominal muscles are contracted at the same time. We see someone vomiting, and we feel nauseated and throw up too. This is the soul's magnetic energy controlling other magnetic energies (soul), thus creating a cascading effect. Under normal conditions, there is constant interaction between our soul and stomach through the pathway of the vagus nerve and celiac plexus. The stomach communicates with the liver, pancreas, and spleen through these nervous system pathways and through chemical levels in the blood like blood sugar. The stomach not only digests the food and any other bacteria, it also regulates the entire process of digestion through the gastro-hepatic reflex and gastro-colic reflex. The chemoreceptor trigger zone responds to noxious chemicals in the blood, like drugs, alcohol, toxins, and numerous other understood chemicals. Nausea and vomiting are hallmarks of pregnancy. Psychogenic vomiting is associated with numerous psychological and mental disorders, like anorexia nervosa and bulimia. The stomach and the whole system are commanders in chief of the secondary soul. They not only feed the physical body but also our soul. In Spanish, wise people often explain it as in the following: "Panza llena corazon contento," which means "A full belly makes a happy heart." I will add to that. "Panza llena corazon content y alma tambien," meaning it also makes a happy soul, as mentioned earlier.

The liver shares its connection with the rest of the organs. It is a very friendly organ. It shares information through the vagus nerve and celiac ganglia and through the blood supply. It is supplied by the portal vein, which takes all the nutrients, good and bad, from the gastrointestinal apparatus. Whatever is absorbed from the food and any other substances, the liver is the authority for deal with it. Its cells, called hepatocytes, are the metabolic and burning furnace of the liver. They do not say no to anything that is supplied to them. They are sacrificial and do not care if they die. We ingest alcohol or other drugs, which are sent to liver. There, the cells burn alcohol to aldehydes, which may kill these hepatocytes and turn into fibrous tissue, causing cirrhosis of the liver. These warriors burn and excrete anything that is fat soluble and change it to water-soluble products. The liver generates proteins and helps our immune system and red blood cells. When the cells are dead, new ones regenerate and even grow in size. It is well known that when one part of a liver lobe is removed surgically for any disease, the rest of the organ grows in size and continues its daily routine work. Many drugs we take are rendered very effective by metabolizing them or rendered ineffective by this process. The liver's biliary system provides us bile juice for digestion of food. This juice is stored in the gallbladder. There is a constant communication with the duodenum. When small portions of food pass from the stomach, a message is sent to the liver to contact the gallbladder to send bile juice immediately. These are all soul mechanisms. The liver is very realistic when it comes to sexuality. It burns excessive estrogen and keeps our figure and identity as a male or female. In the case where the liver is damaged, men grow breasts and lose their libido. The same holds true in women; it burns testosterone and protects them from developing masculine features.

Kupffer cells produce valuable water-soluble proteins for synthesis of various enzymes essential for our body and soul. Hepatocytes give us low-density lipoprotein, which is healthy cholesterol. The liver is a common site for metastatic cancers from several abdominal organs because of the portal vein, which drains blood from these organs and sends it to the liver for purification. The liver plays a major role in the metabolic process of amino acid synthesis and degradation of proteins, carbohydrates, and cholesterol. With the advancement of medicine, liver transplants have been done with reasonable success. To understand the functions of the rest of the organs of the body, please refer to a book of anatomy or physiology.

TERTIARY SOUL

This part of the soul involves the musculoskeletal system and skin. Muscles give us strength; bones and joints give us a structure and form. Though our soul can live without legs or arms, it will be devoid of its complete form. Our muscles and joints create an enormous amount of electric current and magnetic field. Without this field, our soul is devoid of extra energy to feel complete in its entirety. Most of this apparatus is covered in the chapter on the anatomy of the primary soul.

This part of the soul gives shape, form, height, and who we are in reality. Oscar Pistorius, a South African athlete, ran in 2005 Paralympics and won a gold medal. With new artificial-limb development, we can move our joint merely by thinking about any movement we want to make. It is the magnetic soul energy process that commands our neurons in the brain, thus causing such movement. We can develop phantom limb syndrome. Usually when a leg is amputated, we still feel the pain in the amputated limb. It could be due to retained memory of the leg in motor and sensory areas, which triggers the magnetic field. This could indicate that it is our soul that perceives the pain. Though there are no studies available to support this at this time, meditation could be one of the modalities of treatment. It operates through our soul and its magnetic energy. It is very well described by Dr. V. S. Ramachandran, who treats patients with mirrors in front of them to adapt to the reality and existence of the other arm. I do not know if his outcome is 100 percent or if it is a result of the placebo effect, which is 33 percent. I do not confirm or deny his claim. I leave this for him to explain.

CHAPTER 5

SOUL THE SEAT OF LOVE

ove has been the center of living animals. Do the heart and lungs contribute to our love? This question has been raised by philosophers and wise religious leaders. My view is that in addition to our brain centers (the limbic system, frontal lobe, and cerebellum), the heart, lungs, and rest of the organs that constitute and are part of our secondary soul play a major role and are major contributors of magnetic energy to our soul, thus sharing commonality and enforcing further strengthening of the basis of love. This is why we say, "I love him or her from the bottom of my heart" and "My heart beats faster and faster and my breathing gets deeper and faster when I think of my love (boy- or girlfriend). Mere thought can induce such a reaction. Sexual intimacy is part of love but not love by itself. Even other organs are part of love and react to it. We get butterflies in our stomachs when we meet each other at the initial stage of our love. Every sensation contributes to our soul, which is an energy generated by those sensations. I call it magnetic energy. We fall in love (love at first sight). How is that? It is the strength of the magnetic souls of two individuals blending and accepting the feelings of love. We call it the chemistry of love.

I had a burning desire to understand the origin of love. During my research, this is what I found in a book written by Richard F. Thompson (289, 6). A prokaryote is a single-celled organism that lacks a nucleus. The majority of the DNA in these cells is found in the region of the cell called plasmid which makes it is easier to transfer DNA to other cells or other bacteria. Many biologists think that the ancestors of mitochondria were free-living bacteria that at some point entered into other cells and became symbiotic, engaging in mutual helpful relations with the cell. The cell depends on the mitochondria to supply it with energy. The host cell provides the mitochondria DNA to survive. The most intriguing part of this story is about the mitochondria, which in the cells of your body come from your mother. The egg cell from the female has mitochondria, but the sperm cell from the male does not. The mitochondria are in the tale part of the sperm, which upon fertilization is shed. The sperm's mitochondria do not transfer to the fertilized egg. Hence, when you were first formed as a fertilized egg, all your mitochondria came from your mother's egg cell. As your cells divide and multiply, so do your maternal mitochondria, and they become part of the cells. It has been going on since before *Homo sapiens* evolved or even when life came into existence. This fact led molecular geneticists to study the mutation rate of the genes in human mitochondria.

My view is that mitochondria are the soul of the cell. Without mitochondria, the cell cannot survive in our body. The most prominent roles of mitochondria are to produce energy for the cell (ATP) (phosphorylation of ADP) through the use of oxygen, which regulates cellular metabolism. This happens through the citric acid cycle or the Krebs cycle. Mitochondria were first described by Richard Altman in 1890. He called them bioblasts. Warburg gave them the name of mitochondria. Why is this important? The soul of the cell is the mitochondria. Without this, the soul of the cell cannot survive. So I am of the view that this is the first connection of the fetus and mother. It is the time that the life of fetal cells is the soul from the mother. The attachment of the fetus to the uterus is not only the cause of love and the ultimate bond to the mother; there is another factor, which is ultimate; in each cell of the fetus, there are mitochondria of the mother. Therefore, I say the soul of the mother lies in each cell of the fetus, which is the strongest seat of love for the mother for her offspring. It is the ultimate integral part of our soul. I was under the impression that the love of a mother existed only because of the fetus being in the womb of the mother for nine months, and the womb nurtures the body and soul of the fetus. Our mother's soul is deep-seated in the mitochondria of our body, which remains with us until we die. No one can deny or take it away from our body or soul until we die.

I asked my boys while we were swimming in the pool, "If your mom and I were drowning, who would you save first?"

Both verbalized loudly, "Mom! Mom!"

Of course, I asked, "Why? You don't love me, or you think I am strong and can defend myself and your mom cannot?"

Both answered, "No, Dad. She is our flesh and blood."

I did know then and they did not know about mitochondria. The soul of the cells dictated the instinct in them. Now I understand. The same holds true for any female who is a mom. She will die for them and care for them, no matter how good or bad they are. This is the science of a mother's love. A mother's love knows no boundaries or territories. I call it the love of compassion. In neurotransmitter language, I call it "estrogenic love" or "oxytocinogenic love." There exists nothing in between love and reasoning or justifications. Instincts and cellular mitochondria take over all pitfalls and failures of the children. I call it "glorified love," love without gains or losses. The motive is pure love, without any tainted flurries of emotions, anger, or pain. Pain is absorbed by every mitochondrion of the cells in the body of the mother. All the cells in the body of a mother's soul shut the mitochondria of the cells off in the brain. All the mechanism that creates anger, aggression, and hate are shut down by the soul of each cell of the body of the mother. It is not what she is doing; it is the nature of genetic instinct through the mitochondria passed on to the offspring in the form of the mitochondrial soul of the cell. She cannot help it or avoid it and forget it forever. This also happens in some animals. A mama bear is left alone to take care of her cubs because of this physiological and anatomical relationship between the mother and her offspring. Papa bear, in contrast, does not love his child or children. The father can abandon the child or children and move on. Sometimes, the father will discipline the child or children by "tough love." I call this "testosteronic love."

In my experience, if a mother's love is unconditional, it can become pathological if the mother is an enabler for certain behaviors that are unacceptable. The father tries to set limits, and the mother may confront the father's intervention and be overprotective of the child or children. This creates severe marital conflict and even divorce. I have learned from two cases. I am sure there are many more such cases. Case A came from an affluent family and started playing video games from sixth grade on. The son would sleep all day and be up all night. His grades started deteriorating. The father intervened, but the mother said, "He will grow out of it." His

SAT scores were at the bottom. The father had desired his son to go to a decent college and grow up to be what he wanted to be. There were many confrontations between the father, mother, and son. It became a dysfunctional life for the parents. The son justified his behavior by saying that he would go to community college and then transfer to a better college; it took him three years to finish two years of community college. The behavior of the son remained the same. He would sleep during the day and be up all the night, screaming and talking to other players, playing video games. This went on until the son was twenty-three years of age.

One day, the son came to his father and asked if he would help him to get through college in Northern Virginia. The father's joy knew no bounds, and he said, "I will do anything for you."

The son went to college and shared an apartment with a friend. His father paid his regular college tuition and expenses were. The father was happy for the rest of the few years. It was after three years when the father questioned it. "The college was for two years, and you are going on for three years. What is that?"

After three years, the father learned that his son never attended classes. He decided to cut him off, and the son moved to his aunt's house. Every time the question of a job was raised, the son played games. "I have to take a drug test. My friend is a recruiter." That went on and on. The son was twenty-nine years old with no job and no education, and still, he exhibited the same behavior. He would sleep during the day and play video games at night. The mother protected and continued to enable him. He had a few jobs lasting a few days. The father resolved his anger and grief and gave up. The mother made up excuses for him. All the time, the only way the father could resolve his grief and anger was by withdrawing and not acknowledging the existence of his son. All the efforts of his father were in vain. The mother still supported her son financially and emotionally. The father questioned such behavior, but the mother continued confronting the father and justified her son's behavior. The family fell apart, and the son continued playing video games, knowing his mother would continue providing support. He had the perception that his parents would get divorced and he could live with his mother. This was pathological love, which not only destroys families but the life of the children too.

Case B was the same. It resulted in the son living with the father and mother until the age of thirty. He was still playing videogames. His mother was an enabler, and his father was distant and unhappy, keeping the peace.

There are many parents who have such stories of the modern age and Internet video games. There is a devastating addiction to video games, in which the lives of beautiful and intelligent young men and women are destroyed. These children develop no social skills. They are lonely, immature, and lack relatability. In low-socioeconomic families, these kids end up in jails, and the suicide rate is very high. This is the curse of a mother's love in some unfortunate children. Success is only possible when both parents confront the problem together and set limits. As these children grow, they learn how to divide their parents, destroying the lives of their families and their own too.

There are times when we do not have feelings of love, because there is a lack of intermingling of the magnetic energy of the soul. We sometimes say, "Oh, we did not have chemistry with each other." A healthy heart and healthy lungs make a healthy soul. They send positive waves to each other beyond the involvement of the senses. It is the sixth sense, "the soul which perceives it and feels it" (89).

Love is an English word, and we have to stick with it. We could call it *amor* in Spanish, *payar* in Hindi, and so on and so forth in different cultures and different languages. The meanings, feelings, and mechanism are the same in all human beings, because the soul is the same in all human beings. Love is a precious essence that keeps our soul healthy and happy. Some feel that they have enough, and some fear it. Some never find it and lead empty, loveless lives with an empty part of their soul, which remains unhealthy and devoid of ecstatic feelings of love. This magnetic force of our soul draws us together and keeps the relationship strong and healthy. Love is a deep-seated, magnetic force in our soul. When it thinks of it, there is a physiological reaction and pleasant feelings. Love is not only between two individuals. It is anything our soul perceives as pleasant. I love to work out, to develop a healthy body. I love to play golf. What ecstatic feelings after I walk! I love my kitchen garden and roses. I am elated; my soul is tranquil and disarms the hate. Some like bird watching and travel thousands of miles to take pictures of rare birds. What a joy for them when they take a picture and brag about it. In a nutshell, everyone has passion and love for something, which is part of their magnetic soul. Upon accomplishment, it gives them great happiness and highly satisfied feelings. Love and the memory of love create connections between our dendrites of the neurons in our brain. The connections that are reinforced become stronger and remain with us for our lifetimes. Some connections, if not reinforced, die down. I will explain this while I discuss the synaptic plasticity (regeneration and degeneration of our synapses in the brain).

According to the ancient Hindu philosophy of chakras, when we open the fourth chakra, there is energy sent to our soul, which reinforces the love of (soul) magnetic energy, the binding theory of the brain (the combination of all the functions of our five senses and the brain) by which thoughts and actions action take place. Thus, we love ourselves and invite love from others. We offer them our love first and invite their love for us. We all need this, and we gravitate toward those who reciprocate by the magnetic energy of their soul. It could be a verbal compliment, empathy, nurturing, caring, sincerity, a welcoming expression of our emotions, feelings, and acknowledgment of them for who they are, thus rejecting any judgment. There is the start of incipient love, which may last or disappear along with the neuronal connections of our brains. This gets reinforced by trust and mutual respect. If none of the above happens, it is nonexistent love. Our soul does not waste its energy in that case. Undue attachment to one object reduces the flow of energy from the soul of others. In the case of couples where there is an intense attachment and love, some psychologists use the term *oral incorporation*. In these cases, if there is a loss of the object, the grieving process is delayed to the point that the person can dip into severe depression and psychosis, with no desire to live. It may cause death, which we call the "heartbroken state." These individuals are unable to incorporate another soul's love energy into theirs. In these cases, the synapses are shattered and their neurons fail to develop new connections with other dendrites. To understand further, please refer to the chapter on the anatomy of the primary soul. Culturally, there is more bonding and sharing among those of the same color, religious, and ethnic backgrounds; age groups; sexual orientation; and so on. But true magnetic soul interaction and blending the love energy of the magnetic soul breaks all the rules and barriers so the people can share the glory of their mutual love energy. Love does not have one side. It is just like a coin, which has two sides, with inscriptions on both. I have not yet seen a coin with inscriptions on one side and blank on the other. If it does occur, usually this coin is not accepted for its value.

I have a good friend who is a high-powered attorney; he has been divorced for the last twenty years. He has dated many women but never felt there was any love. I met him last year for a dinner. He seemed happy, calm, reasonable, sweet, comfortable, pleasing, respectful, elated, and giving.

Normally before, I used to call him a type-A personality, which meant he was self-gratifying, short-tempered, irritable, and unfocused. He was a my-way-or-the-highway-type of guy, but we had and have mutual respect for each other. My psychiatric bulb went on, blink-blink, when I saw him in such a state of tranquility. I asked myself, *What has happened to this man? It's a night-and-day difference.* I used to tell him, "Calm down! Otherwise, you will have a heart attack." Sure enough, he had one (some sort of heart problem). Once, he shared his death experience while he was under the heart treatment procedure.

I could not keep quiet. I asked him, "What happened to you? I feel there is something different and unusual. You are very calm."

That was it. He described falling in love with a young lady, much younger than he. He spent half of the time describing her. Then he paused.

I asked, "How do you feel about it?" Wow. There he went nonstop until the end of our dinner.

He said, "I feel lighter. I have never been so happy in my life, I have attained the sense of spirituality. I am connected with an angel. I sleep, eat well, exercise, jog, and my heart is healthy. I have lost weight. I feel as if I am on ecstasy [high on drugs]. I work less and feel like going home at five because someone is waiting for me [love]. I feel touched, moved, and inspired to the heights beyond any normal limits. I do not feel mundane but sacred. I have a purpose to live happily. My soul feels connected to a force beyond my imagination. I do not feel angry. Passion flows through my body. I do not use antidepressants anymore. My blood pressure is normal. Sex life is great. I feel proud of caring and sharing with someone, my soul mate. My thoughts and memory are clear. I feel it is a mysterious force in me full of unexplained mysteries. All my sensations are pleasurable. They were dull and numb before. It seems to be as if there are two forceful magnets pulling each other closer and closer. Life is balanced, and there is equilibrium." He described his feelings in brief: "Love is beauty, and beauty is love. I smile more and worry less. My desire of life is fulfilled. There is an end to my wants in the area of love, which I have been wanting for a long time. My belief and imaginations always dictated that I would never feel the feelings I am having. I guess my beliefs and imagination were wrong. This is a gift that belonged to someone else. How could it happen that I got it, without deserving it? This is just like a chemical reaction of the two elements becoming one compound, as it happens in chemistry. At times, I question, is it a coincidence, or is it meant to be? Why me?"

Paramahansa Yogananda writes in his book *The Divine Romance* (1940), "Love is a golden mansion in which the king of eternity homes the entire family of creation. Like a river, love flows continuously through the humble, sincere soul, but it bypasses the rock of egotistic, selfish sense thwarts souls, because it cannot pass through them. Love is an omnipresent spring with countless fruits of the holy spirits of love which sparkle in true souls" (295). Do not limit your love to one being, however; be lovable to the exclusion of all else. Rather with the love you feel for the one you love most, love all beings and all things, including the one you love. When you try to imprison omnipresent love in the form of one soul, it will escape and play hide-and-seek with you until you find it in every soul. Love may exist in the presence of passion, which is often mistaken for love. It can fly away. Passion and love together are a bittersweet mixed drink that produces some joy but sometimes an after-sorrow. But when pure love is ignored, the taste for passion loses itself in the sweetness of true feelings. Love is wonderfully blind, for it dwells not on the flaws of the beloved but loves unconditionally through eternity. When dear ones are parted by death, the mortal memory may fail to recall the pledges of love they made, but true love never forgets; nor does it die. Grieve not for lost love, whether it is through death or the fickle fluctuation of human nature. Love itself is never lost but just plays hide-and-seek with you in many hearts, that in pursuing it, you might find its ever great manifestations. It will keep hiding from you and disappointing you until you have quested long enough to find its abode in the one who resides in the deepest recesses of your own soul and in the heart of everything. I see life on earth as only a scenic backdrop behind which my loved ones hide at death as I love them when they are before my eyes, so does my love follow them with my ever-watching mental gaze when they move elsewhere, behind the death screen. Those whom I have loved I could never hate, even though they grow uninteresting through ugly behavior. In my museum of recollections, I can still behold those traits that caused me to love them. Beneath the temporary mental masks of those whose behavior I dislike, I see the perfect love of my great beloved, even as I see it and dislike it in those worthy whom I love. I shall truly love every being, every race or color, animate or inanimate, until my breath is alive and my heart is breathing under the guidance of my soul.

Self-acceptance is our first chance to have unconditional love. Our magnetic soul has not only attraction to the opposite sex, but it could be for those who share our feelings and views. Another magnetic soul has the same feelings of love. Then and there is mutual sharing of love. Understanding each other is essential for initiating and the continuance of mutual love. There are magnetic vibrations, which are felt by each other. If we do not feel such magnetic vibrations, there are no feelings of vibrations and feelings of love. At times, people's self-perceptions are negative in terms of low self-esteem. Such individuals have difficulty initiating love vibrations from the soul. Love is not a one-sided game. This is the game of two mutual winners. Some of us have an avoidant personality; in such cases, we avoid others and prefer to be aloof. We radiate love because we have created a coherent center within ourselves, which in turn harmonizes the surrounding circumstances. James W. Prescott, PhD, formulated the brain behavior theory of emotional-social regulation to explain the pathological depression and violence that result from maternal social deprivation or the social isolation of rearing infant animals. This theory involved the cerebrum-limbic-frontal lobe complex. He proposed that the cerebrum has a major role in the sensory-limbic (emotional) brain activity, which also integrates this activity with higher brain processes (the frontal-lobe cortex). According to Prescott, a lack of "mother's love" results in developmental disorders. This could explain a person's lack of empathy or lack of love and connectivity to others. Mirror neurons in modern science are the brain's pearls, and through them we receive love from others and share with others. Deprivation of the senses, like vision, hearing, smell, taste, and touch, could cause lack of development of love and caring in an animal's offspring, which could be explained even in human infant development. Due to lack of a mother's love, there is a high incidence of depression and even pathological violence.

The triangular theory of love was a theory developed by Robert Sternberg, in which he describes the love theory to have three components:

- Intimacy, which means feelings of attachment and closeness
- Passion, which means drives connected to infatuation, obsession, and sexual attraction
- Commitment, which encompasses, in the short term, the decision to remain with another, and in the long term plans made with that other

Passionate love and compassionate love forms are interconnected. Passionate love is associated with strong feelings of love for a specific person. This love is full of excitement and newness. Passionate love is important in the beginning of the relationship. There is a chemical component to the passionate love (92). There is an intense urge involved in the stage of passionate love. Constant thinking about the person causes anxiety and restlessness. There is a constant urge to text or to talk to or see the individual. Parents notice changes in the behavior of their teenagers and question what is going on. These are tender stages of the development of the identity of sexuality—like male, female, and homosexual behavior. Different cultures and families deal with the stage of passionate love differently. In open societies, it is fine for a young girl or a boy to go on a date, while societies where sexuality is treated as very close, it unacceptable for young girls or boys to date until they are married. Things happen, secrets dominate, and truth does not prevail in some families. Denial is a major factor in such families. It all depends on the parent-child relationship and the norms and rules of the family. Open discussion with your children is essential for their sexual growth and for their identity.

I remember my older son had an infatuation with a young girl at the age of thirteen, and he asked my wife to buy a gift for the young girl. My wife argued with me about this because she thought he was too young for that. She asked me to talk to my son because I was a male figure. I reassured her and explained to her how good it is, because he is learning what it feels like to be a male, and when he grows up, it will be very healthy for him to know how to deal with and respect a female. He needed to learn how women think and how to share his feelings with the opposite sex. My wife was calm and happy after that explanation. Though this stage is dominated by the hormones, there is more going on in the brain and the soul. As our brain develops and grows, so does the magnetic field of our brain, which gets stronger and shares the appropriate energy with the opposite sex's soul. Some call it chemistry. I call it an intersoul merger of some parts of the magnetic field energy. That's how we like each other and develop feelings and passion for each other. Though passion starts with the thought of a person and then grows into feelings and infatuation, passionate love is not only limited to sexual relationships. Couples feel physically attracted to each other. Couples express feelings of nurturing, dominance, submission, and self-actualization (93). Couples have strong sexual arousal between them, but it grows weaker as we get older. There is no definite time limit. It all depends on their life events, like children and creativity. Compassionate love follows the passionate love. It is a state of mutual understanding and caring for each other. Intimacy remains bonded in this part of love. Trust is built among them, and there is a frequent interchange of magnetic energy of the soul. Both consult each other, and their opinions are well respected. Decisions are made together. Arguments are not pathological. Dominance is strengthened. Each one of them is free to express thoughts and feelings, Independent roles are taken over. Males do male things, like work, earning, and yard work. Females take over female-dominant roles, like raising children, shopping, cooking, and so on. Pleasure is derived by doing things together, like vacationing and sharing hobbies. It is an arena in which individuals nurture each other and care for each other. Some individuals use physical intimacy to deepen their emotional intimacy. They laugh with each other. Their sexual interactions are sacred to them, and they are sacred to each other. Sexual intimacy satisfies a need to reduce tension built up in our excessive, unwanted magnetic field. Thus, the release of sexual energy gives pleasurable relief to our souls. Studies have shown that there is an excessive violence and anger in humans and animals where there is a lack of sexual intimacy. Thus, sexual intimacy is not only a relief of excessive magnetic energy; it also is meant for keeping the species alive by the reproduction of offspring.

Oxytocin is secreted by the pituitary gland and plays an important role in females for passion, romance, and love. Sexual desire is not only hormonal but also neurophysiologic. There is sharing of the energy of souls during the sexual act, which enhances the mutual sharing of feelings and thus reduces any anxiety, anger, or stress.

What is the definition of love? According to the *Merriam-Webster* Dictionary since 1828, it is "a feeling of strong and constant affection, for a person that includes sexual desire; the strong affection felt by people who have a romantic relationship." This is a simple definition, but there is more to the definition of love: strong affection for another out of kinship ties (maternal love for a child); affection based on sexual desires; affection and tenderness felt by lovers; affection based on admiration, benevolence, or common interest (a friend or old schoolmate); warm attachment, enthusiasm, or devotion; the object of attachment, devotion, or admiration (baseball was his first love); a beloved person (darling, often used as a term of endearment); unselfish, loyal, benevolent for the good of others as (a) the fatherly concern of God for humankind, (b) brotherly concern for others, and (c) a person's adoration of God; an amorous episode (love affair); and the sexual embrace (copulation).

Elain Mcstravick blogged about the question "What is love?" She summed it up that love is an action only possible when one operates in the spirit and one of the attributes of the fruits of the spirit, along with joy, peace, suffering, kindness, faithfulness, gentleness, and self-control. The spirit helps us to attain these attributes. Our best and only perfect example is the character of Jesus Christ.

Love, in my view, has multiple pathways in the brain and externally. The main seat of love is embedded in the soul (a form of magnetic energy), along with thoughts, desires, wishes, wants, feelings, beliefs, and purpose both consciously and unconsciously. Whenever a thought of love erupts in our soul out of nowhere, it sends an electric impulse to our brain and a feeling of love is generated by the neuronal stimulus, which creates a vast array of neurochemical and electric impulses, which are sent to our nervous system and endocrine gland to stimulate the hormones. After that, the electrical impulse is sent back to our brain and the magnetic energy of our soul feels the reaction created. It could be a positive or negative sensation. Thus our soul feels ecstatic and euphoric. Though from the outside, our sensory apparatus can stimulate some feelings (vision, hearing, smelling, touching, taste), when we see someone we love, there is a sensation sent to our brain and soul that triggers the feelings of love. The mechanism of love is described as follows:

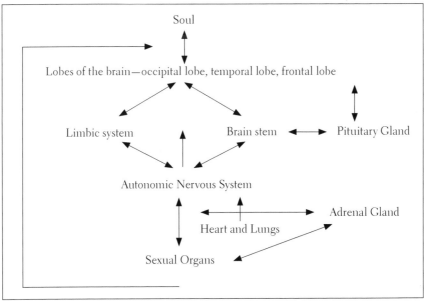

Mechanisms and pathways of love

The soul binds the entire process of love from all the neurological, neurochemical, and sensations produced by hormones. It is the thought of pleasure and the binding emotional senses that begin when an infant learns he or she is being loved or rejected. The smell of a mother's body and the suckling of breastfeeding create a sense of bonding and a perception of love. In the case of a blind and deaf infant or child, the sense of smell is the primary sensory information registered through the vestibulocerebellar connections (94). In such cases, a failure to register in the infant's developing brain the smell of the mother's body through breast-feeding inhibits bonding. It creates "basic trust," intimacy, and the stability of love and relationship. Prescott developed the theory of somatosensory affection deprivation (SAD) theory. He describes "maternal-social deprivation." This somaesthetic process (image of the body created by the brain from sensory input of touch, pressure, heat, and pain) and the vestibulocerebellar process (of movement) are two critical emotional senses that define the sensory neuropsychological foundation for maternal-infant affectionate bonding. According to Prescott and other neuroscientists, brain studies in monkeys reared separate from mothers (mother-infant separation) show structural and functional abnormalities in the limbic-fronto-cerebellar brain system (loss of mother's love), which are directly related as a causative process of the depression and pathological violence of these deprived monkeys (95, 96). Psychiatrists call it *failure-to-thrive syndrome.* In such developmental disorders, humans developed psychosocial dwarfism, separation anxiety, delinquency, academic problems, borderline intelligence, avoidant personality, and depressive disorder due to negative attachment experiences. Maternal care could be deficient due to mental illness of the mother, if a child is institutionalized for a long period of time, or if the primary object of attachment dies. Bowlby describes children separated from their mothers going through a process of protest by crying, calling out, searching for the lost person (mother), and succumbing to despair, in which case the child loses hope that the mother will return. There is a detachment in which the child emotionally separates himself or herself from the mother. The child develops ambivalent feelings toward the mother. The child both wants her and is angry with her for her desertion. Some children have affectionless personalities characterized by emotional withdrawal with little or no feelings and an inability to develop affectionate relationships (97).

When individuals are wounded and traumatized emotionally as children, the attempt to rehabilitate them is difficult. Love appears unsafe and at times threatening. This trauma shatters the energy of the soul to the point that as grown men or women, their souls cannot reattain the lost part of the love. Love starts in the womb of the mother after the fertilization of the egg with sperm. It is around the fourth week of gestation that a primitive brain starts dividing into various parts, like the forebrain, midbrain, and hind brain. By the fifth week, the cerebral cortex, thalamus, and basal ganglion start emerging as described in the book by Kaplan and Sadock, *Synopsis of Psychiatry*, There is fast growth of the brain and also death of some of the neurons, called *apotosis*, which is essential but too much apoptosis can cause numerous congenital abnormalities. I am of the view that this is the time when there is a generation of the "incipient soul," which gives rise to the infantile soul at birth. During this process, the brain and other parts of the infant are growing and differentiating from the fetus to an infant at birth. The fetus is connected with the uterus of the mother through the placenta and umbilical cord. All nutrients, blood, hormones, and other related chemicals are passed on from the mother to the fetus. Thus, the incipient soul is in constant touch with the maternal soul. Development of the soul depends on the physical and emotional status and health of the maternal soul. Any change in a maternal soul brings on changes in the health of the incipient soul.

Once the bond between the maternal and incipient soul is developed, it lays the foundation of love for the fetus and mother. This bond is so strong that it is inseparable, unless there is an abortion or a harmful event, like a decline in the health of the mother or a congenital abnormality of the fetus. Once all the sensory apparatuses of the fetus are developed, they directly relate to the sensory apparatus of the mother and the external world. There have been reports that a fetus in the womb of a mother can smile and twins fight and play with each other. The fetus can hear and feel startled by any noise. That is why we sing songs and melodies to a pregnant mother. At times, the fetus is angry, restless, and agitated, and there is excessive kicking. In normal cases, the soul of the mother is strengthened by the soul of the fetus and the process continues until the fetus is born after nine months. This mutual love of the souls creates a maternal instinct, which may be genetic in mothers. The mother's soul expands into joy and pleasure at the incipient soul through nine months of carrying a baby, which is not an easy task. Why do mothers crave various foods and have odd tastes at times? My view is that it is the fetus that contributes to such cravings by sending signals to brain and soul of the mother to look for such foods and tastes, which are carried to the fetus by the blood supply. In this day and age, an ultrasound can tell the mother about the excited heartbeat of the baby, the sex, and any abnormalities. This is the process in which the mother's soul experiences joy, pleasure, a sense of fulfillment, wishes, desires, future plans, emotions, feelings, love, wants, hopes, patience, passion, and the sense of responsibility. In some cases, there is a resolution of emptiness, aloofness, and depression. Mothers feel much better and remain depression free, especially during the last trimester of their pregnancy.

My view is that love starts from the womb of the mother (uterus) and continues until the death of the individual. It still exists and remains an integral part of the soul, even after the death of an individual. Love is a strong magnetic energy, which is strengthened by the five sensory apparatuses and biochemical and electric currents registered in our brain (limbic system, frontal lobe, and autonomic nervous system). It is ecstatic memory registered in our brain with constant interaction with our soul. Some believe it is a mystic force. But for me, it is a real physiological, anatomical, and psychological process. There is a constant interaction of the photons of our soul, which give feedback to our primary soul (nervous system). This creates a sense of elation, happiness, joy, laughter, humor, and well-being; a heightened mood; pleasure; intent; the courage to pursue happiness and self-confidence; and the desire to achieve one's utmost. These are feelings beyond the feelings. Lack of such feelings can lead to lovelessness, sadness, depression, and emotionlessness.bell hooks in her book *All about Love*, writes, "At the time, recently separated from a partner of almost fifteen years, I was often overwhelmed by grief so profound it seemed as though an immense sea of pain was washing my heart and soul away." Scientists almost totally avoid the study of joy, laughter, humor, and happiness and their relationship to human well-being—let alone the soul, which is the supreme power that runs the human life.

The soul of a pregnant woman who is looking forward to being a mother goes through enormous changes, both physically and emotionally, which we attribute to the enormous change in hormones both in the body of the woman and secreted by the placenta of the fetus. There is a constant exchange and flow to the fetus and back to the pregnant woman via blood and the nerves in the umbilical cord attached to the fetus. Under normal circumstances, there is fatigue or morning sickness, moodiness, happiness, and anxiety at the unknown consequences of the pregnancy.

As the pregnancy progresses, there is an improvement of the moodiness and morning sickness. There are planning and changes in life upon the birth of the baby. There is anxiety about childbirth and the health status of the baby in spite of the fact that we are well advanced in diagnosing any abnormalities of the fetus, as well as the sex of the baby. Modern medicine has helped us to induce normal labor and take care of the mother and baby during the nine months of the mother's pregnancy and the birth. There are numerous experiences; some people are surprised at learning they are pregnant or that they are having twins. There are feelings of happiness in spite of the physical discomforts. Anger is a factor in unplanned pregnancy and in other unpleasant fearful experiences, like rape or any sexual assault. Love, including affection, intimacy, and physical desire are strongly connected with the hormone oxytocin, which has been called the "hormone of love." Oxytocin increases the contractions of the uterine muscle, thus helping in the delivery of the baby. In current studies, oxytocin levels have been related to passion and sexual desire in females. It is essential in sexual desire and the orgasmic stage of sexual activity for females, causing contraction and dilatation of the uterus and vagina during the sexual act. Sadness and even depression are related to the sickness or death of the baby. There could be postpartum depression and in some cases postpartum psychosis. At times, there is violent behavior in pregnancy and some changes in the feelings of the mother.

In the case of the baby, there is an intense and fast growth of the neurons, dendrites, and the connections. There is a constant interaction between the mother's soul and the infantile soul, which develops after birth. During this period of growth, the sensory apparatuses develop at a faster pace. Neurons grow and multiply (neurogenesis). There is an increased connectivity of the dendrites (synaptic plasticity). All the information created by the senses is retained in the neurons of the baby. This genetic mechanism is highly developed in animals and birds. That is how they recognize their offspring in a group of animals. Birds can recognize their chicks out of thousands of chicks. This is how love begins to grow as the soul grows. Is love inherited, and is it part of the genetic code? Yes, it is. For those who believe love is mysterious, I would tell them it is not mystical. It is a real form of energy stored in our growing souls. There is constant growth of this energy as our body grows and intimacy grows between the child and the mother. This is a small seedling of love that will grow to be an adult tree of love. The infantile soul absorbs this energy 30 to 40 percent faster than grown adults do. Any negative or faulty energy stored will produce a deformed tree of love from this deformed seedling. Besides genetic and inherited love, external factors play an integral and important role in the development of a healthy love versus unhealthy love (lovelessness, hatred, vengeance, anger, maladaptive behaviors and so on). Those who have not developed this seed of love will never know in their lifetime that how hard it becomes to continue to believe in love, which we all want and need. Few ever feel they have enough. Many live in fear of it. We all search for it and gauge our lives around it. When found, it has enormous power in our lives.

I do believe the truth of love is first and foremost the duty of humans to "know thyself." Know your strengths and weaknesses. Once you have achieve that goal, you can accept them. Cash in on your strengths and use them when needed. This will help you to achieve your goal. This process goes on throughout our entire life. We are learning machines with enormous power to correct ourselves; do not be shy of sharing with your trusted one because we learn from each other. We learn from our parents, teachers, gurus, and friends and from the entire environment around us. That is how you learn to love yourself. If you dwell on your weakness, you are shy of loving yourself. Your self-esteem is weak, and your own guilt takes over your strengths. You become self-critical and feel weak within yourself, which impedes your march toward your goal. Nobody is born perfect. We perfect ourselves when we accept and perceive perfection. Again, perfection is not absolute. It is relative. Your perfection may be imperfection for others, which does not matter because you know yourself better than anyone else. Pay attention to yourself first, and then others will come to you. In this competitive world, we feel overwhelmed when comparing ourselves to others. Learn from their successes and richness, and apply that to yourself. Then your self-love is enhanced, and you have plenty to give and share with others. Then others will come to you and learn from your self-love and apply it to themselves. Now you have given and you have received. Do not develop a syndrome I call lack of expression of love (LEL), which I learned from my own growing pains during the early stage of my life.

I learned something from Paramahansha Yogananda's book, *The Divine Romance*:

> I sought love in many lives. I shed bitter tears of separation
> and repentance to know what love is. I sacrificed everything,

all attachment and delusion, to learn that I am in love with love—with God—alone. Then drank love through all true hearts. Many souls wander wastefully, helplessly, why love feels from one heart to another, awakened souls realize that the heart is not fickle in loving different ones but is loving the one God, love that is present in all hearts. (445)

The Lord will ever-so-silently whisper to you, "I am love, but to experience the giving and the gift of love, I divide myself into three—love, lover, and loved. My love is beautiful, pure, and eternally joyous, and I taste it in many ways, through many forms. As a father, I drink reverential love from the spring of my child's heart. As a mother, I drink unconditional love from the soul-cup of my tiny baby (infantile soul). As a child, I imbibe the protecting love of the father's righteous reason. As an infant, I drink causeless love from the holy grail of maternal attraction and love of her feeding me sweet, healthy, and sacred milk, which comes from her soul and blood through her breasts. As a servant, I sip respectful love from the chalice of the disciple's all-surrendering devotion. As a friend, I drink from the bubbling fountain of spontaneous love. As a divine friend, I quaff crystal waters of cosmic love from the reservoir of God-adoring hearts. I am in love with love alone, but I allow myself to be deluded, when as a father or mother, I think and feel only for the child; when as lover, I care only for the beloved; when as a servant, I live only for the master. But because I love, love alone, I ultimately break this delusion of my myriad human selves. It is for this reason that I transfer the father into astral land when he forgets that it is my love, not his, that protects the child. I lift the baby from the mother's breast that she might learn it is my love she adored in him. So love plays hide-and-seek in all human hearts, that each might learn to discover and worship. Human beings implore one another, "Love me alone." Love the one, love all of us. To tell another, "I love you," is false until you realize the truth. The moon laughs at millions of well-meaning lovers who have unknowingly lied to their beloved ones. They can no longer use their breath to say, "I love you." They can neither remember nor redeem their promise to love each other forever.

Love is a unifying force; it attracts things together like a magnetic force. It allows us to grow independently but still keeps the union strong. It creates a sense of security and allows us to avoid insecure feelings of abandonment, anxiety, and depression. To offer loving energy, whether it is a verbal compliment, empathetic acknowledgment, or physical nurturing, invites similar energy in return. Just like with our children, approval of some gesture from our children is a building block of love and confidence. We always look forward to approval from our parents. A simple compliment and approval creates immense feelings of being loved. Undue attachment and love to one person reduces that flow of love from others. I use the terminology *pathological love* when there is a lack of boundaries. Jealousy reduces the flow of love to one who deserves it. Fear of rejection is a major factor in our lives. I may avoid expressing my love to my friend who may say, "Oh, well, thank you, but no, thank you. I love John." Fear of rejection creates negative vibes within ourselves. What a loss of love—love that is there but never expressed. More than anything, love is a spiritual connection, the sense of being touched, moved, and inspired to heights beyond our normal limits. Learning to love takes lot of energy on many levels. All of our five sensory apparatuses should feel it, see it, hear it, touch it, smell it, and taste it. Our sixth sense—the soul—should feel tranquil and soothed. It creates a sense of warmth, elation, lightness, and freedom of our soul.

According to Hindu philosophy, chakra four is the center of love. Gary Zukav calls it the fourth center, which points to "the heart." According to him, when energy leaves this center, love radiates warmth and passion you feel. Everyone becomes your relative. Plants, animals, birds, and insects also become your relatives, and you feel the pain and joy of others. You care for others. You are open and welcoming. When negative energy leaves the fourth chakra, you are cold and treat others with a cold shoulder, your heart aches, and you feel anxious, empty, and aloof. Others do not matter since there is no positive energy to give. You dwell in negative thoughts. Others recognize that you have no empathy and love. You are easily distracted by criticism, because of your sensitivity. Your self-esteem is low. Your relationships are very superficial. There is fear and doubt for no reason. You are unable to bind the energy from third and fifth chakras.

This is the Hindu philosophy of love. When you want to regain the love energy, sit quietly with your eyes closed and meditate for a while. During the process of meditation, say hello to yourself and focus on your body. Feel if any part of your body needs attention. Focus on that part and direct your energy to that part. Gradually, you will hear a hello back from your body. Keep practicing until you have a sensation for your body and yourself. This experience of loving yourself will radiate soul energy to others, and you get love back from others. You will feel joyful and delighted. Being one with self is the key to being one with others. Loving relationships are essential aspects of life for growth and good health. It is important that we broaden our understanding of loving relationships, like how they work and what they mean, what they mean to us, and what we believe about them before we enhance them or destroy them.

We have to be willing to spend time and energy to understand unsuccessful and successful relationships. A loving relationship cannot be taken lightly, unless we are looking for pain and tears from failure. Carl Rogers wrote about marriage, "Though modern marriage is a tremendous laboratory, its members are utterly without preparation for the partnership functions. How much agony and remorse and failure could have been avoided if there had been at least some rudimentary learning before they entered the relationship?" Most studies on love concur that security, joy, and success in life are directly correlated to our ability to relate to one another with some degree of commitment, depth, and love. Most of us have learned from experience that our inability to live in harmony with others is responsible for our greatest fears, anxieties, and feelings of isolation. It can even cause severe mental illness. In a primary relationship, you choose to relate on a regular basis and frequently. In a secondary relationship, you have some choice to relate to the other on a less regular basis. The intensity of love is based on your perceptions of love.

Leo F. Buscaglia, PhD, was my idol in the eighties. I would watch all his lectures about love on television. I was very impressed and moved by his depth of knowledge about love. His style was original and soothing for my soul. He writes in his book *Loving Each Other* that to nurture the primary love, we need the following ingredients:

- Communication
- Affection
- Compassion and forgiveness
- Honesty
- Acceptance
- Dependability
- Sense of humor
- Romance (Including sex)
- Patience
- Freedom
- Love of God

For those who believe in God, their love for God is unshakable, unquestionable, and undeniable. Their love of God is love beyond the love. Love is integral part of the soul, which I call "spiritual love." They love God unconditionally, even in the pain and loss caused by natural calamities and even if they lose a loved one. They rationalize that it was the will of God that their loved one was taken away from them. Even if someone has a devastating disease, like cancer, they still believe it is the will of God. Loving God becomes an integral part of their genes. Depending upon the cultural norms and religious beliefs, the majority of us stick with the religious beliefs into which we are born and in which our upbringing takes place. This spiritual love of our soul has the ultimate goal of joining the super soul energy of God. Some religious spiritual leaders have abandoned their families and given up princely states, money, and the luxuries of life. There is no reasoning and no what-if or but for such dedicated love. The soul receives strong, soothing energy from the super soul, which gives it strength to overcome any difficulties, any pain, any sorrow, or any grief. Even in failures, their strength excels them in the successful path of life. I am very impressed and moved by the live sermons of Joel Osteen, who is an American preacher, televangelist, and author and the senior pastor of Lakewood Church. His religion is nondenominational Christianity. His sermons are seen by a million viewers in one hundred countries in one week. I call him an angel of God's love of the modern age. His power of positive thinking and love of God are pure and infinite. His soul has the unification and blessing of the super soul (God). I strongly recommend his book *Your Best Life Now*.

Guru Nanak and Buddha gave up everything for the love of God. For those who are lonely and grow up alone, the love of God gives them hope to live and a sense that there is someone, an angel, around them to protect them, increasing their sense of security. In grief and depression, the sense of the presence of God's love gives them hope to heal and be strong.

Erich Fromm defines love as "the will to extend oneself for the purpose of nurturing one's own and for others' spiritual growth." Love is as love does. Love is an act of will—namely, both an action and intention. We do not have to love. We choose to love. Since the choice must be made to nurture growth, in my view, love is an instinct. It has a memory component. We remember how we were loved and how we loved. It is a learned phenomenon for children but unless and until we have an attraction of our magnetic soul with another magnetic soul, love is weak and may not even take place. All our five senses are involved.

I met a pretty young lady and was attracted to her, but when I talked to her and heard what she had to say, there was immediate repulsion. In another case, there was immediate attraction for both. If I give love attraction and do not receive back, or vice versa, love is not initiated in the initial form of infatuation.

The current concept of love or loving is changed with the invention of smartphones, social media like Facebook and LinkedIn, chat rooms, Google, dating websites, blogs, and pornography websites. The concept is more of an electronic love. We post our pictures; we text our messages and are more expressive without any fear. We are more open and less fearful of rejection. We do something and express our feelings, including anger, as we feel. We fall in love via communications and express our compliments on Facebook, liking the pictures of people. We even don't know if they are real, male or female, or age appropriate. We have to redefine the concept of love in this electronic age. Some are real people, and some don't exist in a real sense. There are case reports. Though these mechanisms have brought us together, I can fall in love with a lady from Russia, not knowing who she is. If she is real, we may meet. By then, most of the barriers to the love process are resolved. We know about each other, and the process is enhanced. There must be disappointments, and I am sure there must also be happy reunions. Is there some electronic soul attraction or rejection on Facebook or dating sites?

There was a case report of a basketball player who was in love with someone for years but found out it was not all true. This neologism is growing every day at a fast pace. Compassion and passion are resolved before the couple even meets each other. No matter how we feel, there are millions who fulfill their fantasies of love and sex. Those who are unable to give and receive love are in the ecstatic fantasy of a full life. They fulfill their impulses, desires, and needs with the mere click of a button. One feels secure while texting from a distance. The flip side of the coin is there are rapes, child sexual abuse, and criminal acts involved at their peak. This neolove is going to evolve further, and time will tell how far we will go.

As explained by yoga practice, thoughts are packets of potential energy that grow more solid when favorable conditions are present and obstacles are removed. They become desires, and desires become habits and then ways of living with physical consequences. Thoughts can produce effects of the same nature. Kindness to others is just like kindness to oneself. As described in the Bhagavad Gita, when a wandering *sadhu* (a wandering man in quest of love to attain liberation of his soul and attain moksha), or a holy man, was asked, "What is your purpose in life?" he answered, "I am a farmer. This body of mine is a field. I sow good thoughts and actions in my body, and I reap the reward by generating good thoughts and actions in return."

The Buddha explained, "All that we are is the result of what we have in our thoughts. It is founded in our thoughts, what we are made of. What we think, that is what we become." Ralph Waldo Emerson explained further. He added that the ancestor of every action is a thought. Thus, our thoughts, taken together, bear fruit in our actions, decisions, and desires, which shape our lives. In part, the body bears the fruit of what we think, in so far as our way of thinking affects our health and safety. Thoughts are pillars of our karma. For example, the global environment is shaped by the sum of what its inhabitants do, which in turn is shaped by how they think. The relationship of countries and policies are made based what we think of each other. Wars have been fought for what we think of our enemies. "Those who strive resolutely on the path of yoga see the self within. The paranas could be explained as the energy of an electric current sent to our neurons through our sensations and magnetic energy generated by our organs (heart). Or they are the energy (electric current) that leads to the generation of the final magnetic field called ataman (the soul). Thus, thoughts are generated in the form of a magnetic field, a form of energy that stimulates our neurons to create and process our thinking until we come to a conclusion and then take action. Thoughts are the motor of every invention, action, emotion, and feeling. Everything in the magnetic part of our soul starts with a thought, which becomes thoughts. Everything we do starts with the mighty thought.

The key to love is communication—how you talk to someone, how you feel, and what you mean. Say it clearly, listen to what others say, and make sure that you are hearing accurately. This skill is most important for creating and maintaining a loving relationship. Nonverbal communication is just like a mirror in which you see yourself. Love is reflection like a mirror. You see yourself, and the same is a reflection of the other's love, which is felt and perceived by the soul. We use facial expressions. In psychiatry, we use the term *affect*. We can see what exactly it is. Is it a flat affect, a restricted affect, a sad affect, an elated affect? Your eyes will see all that and send a message to your neurons to work out what exactly it is. How comfortable do you feel when love is returned to you? Physical gestures will give you an enormous amount of information about the depth and the truth of love. Is it warm, real, and genuine or superficial? Honesty is the hallmark of true love, while dishonesty is one of the prime determinants of a failed relationship. It has caused families to separate and lovers to physically harm one another or even kill each other. This is what we call a "crime of passion."

Love needs courage, and courage needs reciprocated love. There can be no relationship and love in weakness, timidity, uncertainty, and fear of risk. They prevent us from coming together. A relationship requires us to be bold and assertive, to commit. Problems in human interaction are inevitable. There is no such thing as a perfect relationship, one that is utterly secure, happy, and binding. By the nature of the relationship, this cannot be. How can we expect that the others will desire to be with us always? How can we expect that someone else will always find happiness in the same things in which we find happiness or care about the same people, have the same interests, or want to be doing the same activities at the same time? There will always be difference, since we all are wired up differently in our brains. We have our own childhood experiences and memories, conflicts, beliefs, and cultural differences. When we form a relationship, we must give up the desire of the perfect resolution of any conflict. Disagreements and frustrations are inevitable. Some we resolve at that moment; some we will overcome in time. At times, there may not be a problem, but we think there is a problem. We speak the same language in a different way about the same problem. We have to have courage to face whatever needs to be done. Nothing lasts forever, and this is true of love. It will not last forever. Pain, pleasure, and life do not live forever. Deal with it here and now. Dwelling in the past is useless, because we cannot bring the past back. The future is unknown, so why not focus on the here and now. Love is not static, like a stationary train on the track. It is dynamic and moves with us as we move and grow. Love changes as we change. It follows our experiences, like a shadow.

Relationships and love are instincts, since we are social animals. We must accept the fact that our instinct is to reach out to others. Dependence can be traced to our infancy. As we grow, we become aware of our needs and greeds. Some of us never learn and dissolve our feelings in loneliness. Loneliness is a devastating feeling of depression and anxiety; it can lead to psychotic disorders and drug and alcohol dependence. I had a patient who stated, "I would rather make love to a bottle of whisky than any women in my life." How can he develop a loving, caring relationship when his self-gratifying narcissistic adaptation to life is dominated by addiction? Loneliness could be a genetic disorder or due to psychiatric disorders, especially in depression. The person's soul does not have enough magnetic strength to attract and be attracted by others. Aloneness is a somewhat healthy defense mechanism. I have a few friends who have lived alone for twenty to thirty years without any psychotic breakdown. Aloneness is a satisfying behavior for them. They seem content and satisfied with their life events. They are well-to-do financially and are afraid to share with anyone else. The question of whether to love or not to love does not bother them. Are they contend with their lives?

I asked my friend, "Don't you feel lonely?"

He was very unconcerned. "Sometimes," he replied, "but I keep a schedule and stick to that. I am a self-disciplined man." He smiled.

I think some of them have a syndrome that I call "lack of expression of love" (LEL). At times, as a matter of fact, placing ourselves in the hands of love has proven to be more of a problem than a solution. Having loved and lost, most of us become suspicious of love. My first diamond of love was lost at age five and a half when my mother died, and my second bright crystal of love was shattered when I lost my second love (a girlfriend). At times, it turns into pain when lost; most of us have been raised to believe that strength lies in independence. Society tells us that we must make our own way. We come to believe that only when we no longer depend upon others can we say we have reached full maturity. We fear commitment, which may destroy our individuality and our hard-attained artificial freedom. At times, this leaves us with a frustrated, empty life. It is true that we are all alone. In fact, we were brought into this world alone and we will die alone. In between, we will have to grow alone, make personal decisions alone, determine our choices for change, and grow alone.

Beach and Deutsch, in the book *Pairing*, write (426) cited by Leo Buscaglia (Loving eachother)

> Millions of men and women yearn for intimate love and
> cannot find it. Night after night, day after day, they stalk
> one another, at once both hunters and the hunted. They
> prowl the singles bars and clubs and hotels, and cruises

and weekend trips. Robed and groomed, scented for the rituals, the brasher ones reach out and the quiet ones watch and dream and wait. Then with rare exception everyone goes home, if not empty handed, at least empty hearted. Others have lives that are filled, even overcrowded with people or perhaps devoted to one important person they see regularly, sleep or live with. Yet most of them, too, have an inner sense of isolation. Why, they wonder, why do they feel alone?

The only hope is to know who we are and who the other is and what we need to keep our love alive and keep us together. We must respect the other person's relationships apart from us. If people are important to the one you care about, they should be important to you. Love is like an endless river of water flowing through life. Even if someone takes a dive into the river of love, it will never dry up. You do not give love; you share it. By sharing it, you ensure it will never vanish but be strengthened. This is the power of love. When you are alone, you are just one, but when you share your love, you are two, thus strengthening the power of life and the soul. Each one of us has a desire to love and be loved. Though it remains at the unconscious level.

Lead yourself to yourself, and bring the deep love you feel to your consciousness. You will find how powerful and joyful it is to find the urge to love and be loved. Some come across as macho, strong, and evil, but deep beneath their skin is a tender layer of love, ready to erupt. Don't keep your guard up. Whenever this urge comes, let it flow. You will find out how beautiful you are inside and how loved you feel outside. You have to unlock the inside box for the outside to appreciate how wonderful you are in the locked box of love. Love is learned and is a learning process, like fear, jealousy, hate, and prejudice. Once you unlock this box, they all vanish, and you feel free. You can smell it, like a rose. The putrid smell of anger, jealousy, and fear is gone. Your desire is free to achieve what it wants to achieve. Jealousy is out of comparison. We have been conditioned to compare ourselves to others and others to ourselves. Somebody has a better car than mine. Someone is prettier than I am. Someone has more money than I do. When comparison overpowers your reality, jealousy becomes the norm of thinking. Justifying oneself by saying that it is the other who is wrong is a by-product of our own comparison. If you stop comparing, then jealousy drops and disappears. You simply know you are you and nobody else, and there is no need to compare. If you don't get over it, you may end up comparing yourself to a tall green tree full of fruit and blame God for not giving you fruit to bear. It is better you don't compare yourself to birds, mountains, or rivers. Thank God for that; otherwise, you would not be sane, and your jealousy would be out of your control. Comparison is a foolish attitude, because each person is unique and incomparable. You are your own self. Nobody has ever been like you, and nobody will be like you, so why compare? You are an original. There is no carbon copy of you.

The other countries in the world think dollars grow on trees in America. All you have to do is shake the tree, and dollars will fall on the ground. All they have to do is collect them and come home with bags full of dollars. My friends, reality will teach you the truth. Once you are here, you have to work harder than you are used to in your life. Perfection and honesty are rewarded. Competition is the song of everyday life. Jealousy creates defenses like generalization and rationalization, which remind me of a story.

Ramu, who was an old farmer, lived in a village. One day, Niku told him, "Your house is burned to ashes."

Ramu asked, "What about Jesse's, Bill's, and Dave's houses?"

Niku replied to him that a flood had washed away all of those houses. "Good," replied Ramu.

Niku was surprised to hear that. "Why do you say so?" asked Niku.

"Well, my house was the smallest of all of them, so it is good that they lost their houses."

Niku learned the lesson of jealousy. If everybody is in misery, it feels good; if everybody is losing, it feels good. To a jealous man, if everybody is happy and prosperous, it tastes bitter. This is especially true of those who are ignorant of themselves. They have not known themselves, and they have not allowed themselves to blossom, so the moral of the story is to know thyself and live with thyself. Because of jealousy, you will constantly suffer; you become mean to others and pretend and cover up your weaknesses for no reason.

If you stop comparing, your negative feelings, which keep you a slave, will be gone. You will accept yourself for who you are. Your conscience will be clear; you will imbibe love from outside. Your soul attracts other souls with its positive magnetic energy. Do not ever kid yourself. You know if your actions are good or bad, harmful, or full of jealousy. Accept them, and know them well. Once the hidden inner dark box of love is opened, you will feel positive and self-confident. We all have different wiring in our primary soul. That is what makes us different, with different thoughts, desires, and wishes, but love is the same for all of us. There is nothing like white love, black love, or green love. It has no other name but "love." Love has vast boundaries within our soul. It is relative to what a giver gives and a receiver perceives. There is nothing called perfect "love." Love is held in a dark box by our defense mechanisms, like projection, displacement, and denial. We say, "He did it. It is his fault. I have no problem."

We need to recognize these defense mechanisms and shatter them with the bullet of love. Failure and success are two good friends. They go hand in hand. Sometimes, you fail, and sometimes, you succeed. We learn from both. The same holds true of love. Sometimes, we fail to receive, and sometimes, we fail to give, to recognize this is the key to the success of love. Sometimes, love is covered by the dark shadow of life, and sometimes, it shines like the brightness of our soul. The most liked word in English is *yes*, and the hated word is *no*. Yes keeps the options open for hope and positive results. No closes all the hopes and the options. We humans, right from childhood to the end of life, like to hear "Yes," but it is not always possible. The same holds true for love. There are times when we have to set limits and use the word *no*. If we say no to a child, it does not mean we do not love him or her. The mother stops breastfeeding a child at a certain age, depending on cultural norms. That does not mean the mother stops loving her child. I told my second son when he graduated from college, "You are on your own, Son."

I texted him the song by Paul Anka called "Papa." It does not mean I stopped loving him. Some call it tough love. Limit setting is an integral part of healthy love. I developed a limit setting theory of life after learning from my patients in my private practice of psychiatry and from my personal experiences of life.

Limit Setting Theory of Love

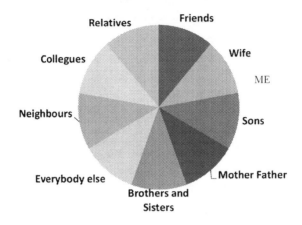

Figure I

Let us presume I am in the middle and I am connected with a rope to everyone else around me. I call it my outer world. The rope represents love, emotions, feelings, likes, dislikes, intercultural relationships, responsibilities, and day-to-day interactions. It is different for different people and depends on the individual. The strength of my rope depends on my relationship. I have a certain relationship with my wife that is different from the one I have with my sister or mother. The same hold true of the strength of the rope between my two sons and brothers. In brief, my love has its strengths and accommodations. This rope also represents free room to roam about in my circle, because you have to give space to others for their actions and behavior. You have to give something without getting anything. I call it breathing room. It allows people to move freely and do whatever they feel the need to do—to love or not love, to borrow money or a lawn mower. The list goes on. I will even accommodate mistakes or insults to me. Give everyone room to dance the way they want to; otherwise, you will choke your relationship and choke your emotions, worrying about every trivial thing. We all need room to dance the way we want, including me, in the circles of others. Each one of us has a circle. It differs from each individual. Bill Gates may have bigger circle to do bigger things and bigger responsibilities than I do. The diameter of the circle is different for each one of us, because we are all different and have different beliefs, cultures, and needs in life. Each one of us has a different lifestyle and different needs for the fabric of our emotions. Go ahead and draw an imaginary circle depending on your lifestyle and think about your emotional needs.

How do I use this circle? When my two boys were growing, if they did something wrong that was trivial, I ignored it one-quarter of the time. I pretended I did not see it a quarter of the time. I avoided saying anything, as long as they stayed in the circle. I would talk to them once they moved out of the circle. So I would speak one-quarter of the time. If I took action all the times, then it became like a boot camp. It became a choking relationship. We all need room to correct our mistakes. So at times, limit setting and limitations are an essential part of love. Good limits make good friends and neighbors and a healthy family structure. Boundary setting is a space. It determines how and where you start and where others start and end, according to the IPFW Parkview student assistant program. Think of it as a fence in your backyard. You are the gatekeeper and get to decide whom you let in and whom you keep out, whom you let into the whole backyard and whom you let just inside the gate. You may still be keeping a distance, but you are giving the people a chance to prove their trustworthiness, both physically and emotionally. The purpose of setting healthy boundaries is, of course, to protect and educate others in how to take care of you and themselves too.

Healthy boundaries do not always come naturally or easily. We learn to "be" in all kinds of relationships by modeling, by watching how others handle relationships. In early childhood, our examples are our parents, grandparents, aunts, uncles, babysitters, teachers, neighbors, media figures, and whoever there is around us on a regular basis. As we grow into adolescents, we rely less on our parents and more on other friends. We learn good and bad. Good is always good, but bad is always bad. We learn badly from bad, not to be bad or do bad things. As the saying goes, smart people learn from the mistakes of others. Schoolteachers and friends are an essential and integral part of the learning of boundary setting. This is the stage when our neurons grow rapidly and the synaptic connections between our dendrites are at the peak of development. Our brain grows at a faster pace until the age of twenty-five. There is a pruning of the dendrite connections. Those connections that remain dominant dictate our future interactions and relationships. Some connections remain dormant and become an unconscious part of our relationships. The connection that disappears will not register and become part of our memory; thus, we forget the major portion and remain unaware of those interactions and relationships.

If you grew up in a dysfunctional family or dysfunctional environment, like one filled with violence and drugs, you may not have learned how to develop relationships and set boundaries. It is possible that the connections of neurons and dendrites are abnormal. These people are prone to antisocial activities and ending up in jail. They develop abnormal personality disorders, like borderline, histrionic, narcissistic, avoidant, dependent, and obsessive-compulsive personality disorder and so on. Though there is a genetic factor predisposing people to these disorders, the bottom line is relatedness to others and the self is chaotic and inappropriate. A man or woman who is self-aware of his or her personality refers to all of the characteristics that adapt in a unique way to ever-changing internal and external environments. Personality disorders are common and chronic. They occur in 10 to 20 percent of the general population. About 50 percent of all psychiatric patients have a personality disorder, which predisposes them to drug abuse, suicide, depression, and episodic mania or impulse-control disorders. People with personality disorders are far more likely to refuse psychiatric help and deny their problems, while those with depression or anxiety are willing to seek help. Generally, personality-disorder symptoms are acceptable to the ego of the person (ego syntonic, compared to ego dystonic, which refers to symptoms that are unacceptable to the ego). People with personality disorders do not feel anxiety for their maladaptive behaviors because they do not routinely acknowledge pain from what others perceive as their symptoms. They often seem disinterested in treatment or are resistant to any treatment and recovery. They develop an ego syntonic soul, which uses defense mechanisms to rationalize their behavior. Their ego-syntonic soul is maladaptive and justifies their malfunctioning and behaviors, which are not acceptable in social norms or sometimes even legal norms. For example, for them, it is okay to rob a bank because they need money. It is okay to steal and prey on weak people. It is okay to rape or assault a female without remorse or guilt. The ego dystonic soul accepts its faults and wrongdoings and feels guilt or shame, which prevents him or her from acting out or committing a crime. Analysts will call it having a super-ego, which is a healthy part of the ego dystonic soul. It does not matter whether they are professionals or nonprofessionals, some people use their intelligence to be con artists and run Ponzi schemes. They lure innocent people into investing or take advantage of vulnerable people who lack the skills to recognize a fraud. Bernie Madoff is an example. If you want to learn about those people, then watch *American Greed* on CNBC. You will find out for yourself the number of people who play these tricks for self-gratification without guilt or remorse. Their soul is corrupted with greed and need.

I met a middle-aged broker from California who was charming and very knowledgeable. Every time I met him, he would talk of business and different deals. I would listen to him. I learned from his friends that he had conned his brother and mother and whoever came his way, his so-called friends. I knew almost everything about him. He would present me these billion-dollar deals and talk about his relationship with billionaires in real estate deals and other deals beyond my imagination. Being a psychiatrist, I understood and wanted to know more.

"How much do you want, John?" I asked. He gave me a number of $200,000 for a billion-dollar deal. I asked, "How you can do a billion-dollar deal for $200,000. It is too little."

He would give examples and show me charts and the names of other investors. Long story short, he believed in his lies and had a fixed belief that he would be a billionaire. I never interacted with him again and never returned his phone calls. He suffered from a syndrome we call pseudologia-fantastica; his factual material and belief were mixed with extensive and colorful outcomes. It is distorted truth. These people may give conflicting and false accounts about other areas of life. At times, they lie about the deaths of their parents and make other sympathy-seeking statements. At times, they claim to be war heroes and decorated high officials without any merit. This is a fixed belief for such individuals, and they do not acknowledge that they are lying. This is a malfunction of the soul in which energy is sent back to the neurons, thus creating such thoughts and behaviors. It is very important for readers to recognize such individuals with repeated questions and delaying any action they suggest. Go ahead and set limits by refusing to be sucked into their pathological circle. Close the door of the fence. You'll be better off and not lose. You do not need such people in your life anyway, but the sad truth is that there is someone else waiting to be sucked into their system because of their charm and convincing, remorseless behavior.

Limit setting is very essential in your life in dealing with people who have the personality disorders (PD), which I'm going to describe briefly, since there are volumes of books written about these disorders with different theories. It is very hard for a layperson to recognize these individuals. After reading about these personalities, you should suggest your family members, loved ones, and friends who exhibit these behaviors to seek psychological and psychiatric help for therapy and appropriate treatment. If you feel they have PDs, know that you cannot save the world but can avoid the ones in your circle who interact with you. According to the fifth edition of the *Diagnostic and Statistical Manual of Mental Disorders* (DSM-5), a general personality disorder is an enduring pattern of behavior and inner experiences that deviates significantly from the individual's cultural standards. It is rigidly pervasive, has an onset in adolescence or early adulthood, is stable through time, leads to unhappiness and impairment, and manifests in at least two of the following four areas: cognition, affectivity (mood and changes in mood), interpersonal functions, and impulse control. When personality traits are rigid and maladaptive and produce functional impairment or subjective distress, a personality disorder (PD) may be diagnosed or recognized. We are all wired up differently and have different personalities, which helps us to understand why we have different approaches to love and why we receive and react differently to love for ourselves and for others. I will describe a few causes.

1. Genetic factors

This comes from an investigation of more than 15,000 pairs of twins in the United States. The concordance of personality disorders was more in monozygotic twins than among dizygotic twins. Moreover, according to one study, monozygotic twins reared apart are about as similar as monozygotic twins reared together.

2. Biological factors

People who have impulsive traits often show high levels of testosterone, 17-estrodiol, and estrogen. Dexamethasone suppression tests (DST) show abnormal results in depressive borderline personality.

3. Psychoanalytic factors

Freud suggested that personality traits are related to fixations at the psychosexual stage of development. Those with anal characteristics are stubborn and cheap or miserly, closed fisted, and highly conscientious because of the struggle over toilet training during the anal period. Those with oral characteristics are passive and dependent on others for food. This is just a theory but may not hold its footing in modern science. Does that mean that in such individuals a connection of dendrites, axons, and neurons is stuck at that phase of life, that there is no further growth or connection of dendrites? If that is true, then what about the growth of the dendrites, axons, and neurons in other areas of life? Wilhelm Reich coined the term as *character armor* to describe people's characteristic defensive style for protecting themselves from internal impulses and from interpersonal anxiety in significant relationships. He attributed these developmental characteristics to defense mechanisms. I would like to describe each personality in brief because volumes are written about these. Those who want to learn more can read *DSM-5*, which is written for the professional in the field of mental health treatment.

The following are a several personality disorders.

1. Paranoid personality

These people are highly suspicious of others, preoccupied with unjustified doubts and the loyalty of friends or loved ones. Some doubt the fidelity of their spouse without any basis or truth. They do not confide in others. They usually read hidden meanings into benign remarks or events. They refuse responsibility for their own feelings and assign responsibility to others. They have intense jealousy, beyond the norms of day-to-day life. They are highly litigious and persistently bear grudges.

2. Schizoid personality

These individuals are socially withdrawn. Others perceive them as eccentric. They lack a desire for a close relationship and pleasurable activities. They are emotionally cold and aloof. They prefer solitary activities. We call them at times introverts. Usually, these individuals lack interest in sexual activities. Many prefer to work night shifts or where there are not many social activities.

3. Schizotypal personality

They appear odd or peculiar to average individuals. They have odd and bizarre thinking and ideas and lack close family and friends. Social anxiety dominates their day-to-day life. They usually believe in telepathy. They have odd speech and are suspicious and paranoid at times.

4 Antisocial personality

The twelve-month prevalence rate is around 0.2 percent to 3 percent. These individuals have a failure to conform to social norms with respect to lawful behavior, as indicated by repeatedly performing acts that are grounds for arrest. These are deceitful people, repeatedly lying and conning. They tend to profit from others and are highly impulsive. They fail to plan for the future. They express irritability and aggressive behavior, engage in frequent physical fights and assaults, and are reckless with disregard for others. They have job-related problems and family problems with an inability to sustain relationships. They lack remorse and guilt. Some of them are charming, well integrated, and at times friendly and very convincing. They lack anxiety and depression. They con others and are always focused on creating new schemes. Drug and alcohol abuse is common, as are child abuse and spousal abuse. Once this personality develops, it turns into a chronic phase, starting from late adolescence. Some may grow out of it once they grow older. Most of them end up in jails. The prison population may range up to 75 percent and those with alcoholism up to 70 percent. There is a high prevalence of attention deficit/hyperactivity disorder.

5. Borderline personality

It may have a prevalence of 1 to 2 percent, twice as common in women as men. These individuals almost all the time are in crisis, with mood swings from depression to elation. The behavior of these individuals is highly unpredictable. They have tumultuous interpersonal relationships. We use the phrase "all good and all bad." You could be the best today and loved, but tomorrow, you are an evil person and hated the most. You wonder what happened. They have difficulty dealing with loneliness and are always looking for a relationship, which results in promiscuity. They have intense and inappropriate anger, beyond its normal course, with difficulty dealing with abandonment. In addition, they have recurrent suicidal gestures, chronic feelings of emptiness, and identity disturbances with an unstable self-image or sense of self. At times, under stress, they may go through a micropsychotic episode with depression and paranoia. These individuals use primitive defenses, like projection (138).

6. Histrionic personality disorder

These individuals, when in relationship, consider the relationship to be more intimate than it actually is. They show self-dramatization with exaggerated expression of emotions. They exhibit very extroverted behavior and are seductive in nature. They have difficulty in maintaining lasting relationships. It is more common in women than men. They are dependent, which makes them trusting and gullible.

7. Narcissistic personality

They have a grandiose sense of self-importance. They usually color their achievements beyond the proportion of reality. Their fantasies of success are beyond the norms of life, and they have an unrealistic desire to be recognized by high-positioned people. They fish for excessive admiration, have a sense of entitlement, and tend to exploit others. There is lack of empathy for others; all that matters is how and how much self-gratification they can get. They are usually arrogant and feel others are envious of them. Deep down, their self-esteem is very low, and they compensate by belittling others. They cannot deal with healthy criticism. Their attitude is my way or the highway. They usually feign sympathy to get what they want, due to which their interpersonal relationships are difficult. At times, they can slip into depression if their demands are not met. In layman's terms, we call them selfish, self-centered, and arrogant people. They have difficulty dealing with stress and create stress for others while working in an organization or in their respective environment. Though they may have success, they are not well-liked individuals (142).

8. Avoidant personality

These individuals live socially isolated lives, since they are sensitive to rejection. They have difficulty developing a relationship, wanting to avoid any ridicule or insult. They view their lives as inadequate and therefore avoid any unworthy comments by others. They remain tense and have difficulty dealing with minor stresses of day-to-day life. They remain preoccupied with any rejection or criticism in a social setting. Their best defense is to avoid any contact or situation that could be confrontational in a normal setting. Usually, they avoid any interviews or occupations that require interpersonal contact. They perceive any comment made by others very critically. They have difficulty engaging in public speaking. Any time their request is not met, it leads them to withdraw and have feelings of being hurt. Usually, they don't have close friends or confidants (139).

9. Dependent personality

These individuals have to have their needs met by others, whom they expect to assume their responsibilities in major areas of their lives. They develop clinging behavior due to a fear of separation. They lack the skills to make decisions and always look for reassurance. Besides needing others to assume their responsibilities, they lack the initiative to start any new project or make a decision. There is a constant urge for nurturance from others; they feel helpless when left alone. Usually, there is an urgent need to look for another relationship when one fails, as they had depended on it and have an unrealistic fear of being left alone. They are pessimistic, self-doubting, and passive. Some have difficulty expressing their aggression or sexual feelings. These individuals usually tolerate abusive relationships or alcoholism of a spouse to avoid disturbing the sense of attachment.

10. Obsessive-compulsive personality

These people usually exhibit stiff, formal, and rigid behavior. They have a preoccupation with details, rules, lists, and orders to the point that activity is lost. They have minimal leisure time; more productivity is the main focus. Such individuals are highly inflexible and overconscious, beyond the norms of normal day-to-day values. At times, they hold on to useless objects that they do not need. They have difficulty accepting tasks assigned to others, unless they are perfect and exactly the way they want. Usually, they are perceived by others as stubborn. They are formal, serious, and lack a sense of humor. They are afraid to make any mistakes and are indecisive. They ruminate about making decisions. They stick to the rituals imposed upon them. There is a struggle between "doing and undoing." Usually, they live a miserable life and hold on to money as much as they can. In some cases, the severity is such that they are unable to function in their occupation and in social settings. There is excessive anxiety, and they could even suffer from depression; it affects their relationships with peers or even spouses. The defense mechanisms are strong and include rationalization, isolation, intellectualization, reaction formation, and undoing. They may indulge in rituals like washing their hands repeatedly because of a fear of germs.

11. Passive-aggressive personality

These individuals find any reason to delay and find faults with those on whom they depend, due to a lack of self-assertiveness. They are not direct about their wishes or desires and fail to ask needed questions. These individuals have a lack of self-confidence and mostly are pessimistic. They express their anger passively, by not performing to their best capabilities. They may leave work halfway through, at times doing something wrong just to punish others. They may show up late at work, just to annoy others.

12. Depressive personality

These individuals feel little joy. They are gloomy, submissive, pessimistic, self-derogatory, hopeless, and helpless and believe in doom and gloom. They are often perfectionists, overly responsible, and easily discouraged about new conditions. They feel malcontented and always have a gloomy outlook even with their successes. They are highly insecure and feel inadequate in spite of their achievements. They are indifferent to praise or compliments and usually brood about the past. The present is unsatisfactory, and the future looks full of gloom and doom.

13. Sadistic personality

These individuals exhibit cruelty and demeaning and aggressive behavior toward others without secondary gains. Their goal is not to steal or rob someone; they are fascinated by violence, weapons, and injuring or torturing others. Some develop sexual sadism and indulge in rape and sexual mutilation of others to get their sexual arousal.

14. Sadomasochistic personality

Some develop sadism in which they have a desire to cause pain to others and are sexually, physically, and psychologically abusive. Masochism is achieved by sexual gratification by inflicting pain to oneself. They suffer guilt and remorse, which makes them inflict injury to themselves in order to deal with the guilt and shame. Both can exist in one person.

15. Know-it-all personality

Some have a distorted image of themselves. They feel superior to everyone. They pretend and pose to others about their knowledge and impressive behavior. They thrive on approval from others; this exists in most of the well-educated individuals. Google and other sources of information have created a new breed of individuals, know-it-all personalities. They constantly search on the Internet and do gain knowledge about different subjects. An attorney friend of mine had read some articles on mental illness and was imposing all his knowledge on me in a friendly social gathering. He went on to the subject of mental illness. All around me were very impressed and astonished to learn about his knowledge. I listened for a while, and some of my friends asked me, "What do you think?" After a pause, I said, "A few articles don't make you a psychiatrist, but thirty-five years of experience does." I added, "Reading a few articles about law does not make an attorney, but thirty years of experience makes an attorney." There were a few laughs, but my attorney friend did not like that. His looks told me all. These days, I use two words, common words, like *maybe* and *possibly*. This keeps me out of trouble. People can go and check on their phones and Google it and tell you facts and figures right then and there.

16. Perfect personality

There is nothing called the perfect personality. While I was writing this book and researching, I never came across this term. We all have some traits from one or more than one personality. As long as it does not impair your day-to-day functioning, it is fine and great to have a healthy soul. Personality disorders are only diagnosed by professionals when a patient is unable to function from day-to-day life; otherwise, we all have to live with something. It is surprising to know that in the United States, the prevalence of personality disorder is 10 to 20 percent, which means out of 350 million people, there are 35 to 40 million people, one or two in a family of 10, with a PD. We all swim in the ocean of life together. We work together and live together. Why? I wrote about personalities to discuss how we can set limits in this vast environment. Sometimes, it is impossible to set limits. We must use the trial-and-error method. Sometimes you succeed, and sometimes you fail. It is okay. There is a whole population of Canada's worth of people in America with personality disorders. Hence, the limit setting and love is different with different relationships. Fifty percent of all the mental illnesses are due to personality disorders. We have to keep that in mind while defining love and limit setting with others. I usually set limits when someone moves out of my circle of limit setting. Now let us look at how you can deal when others around you step out of your circle and you are not able to fix it.

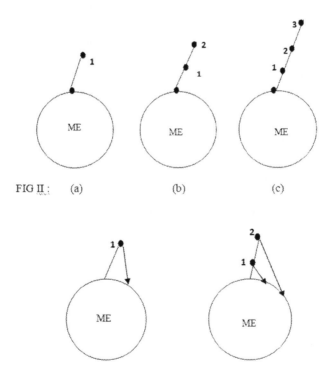

FIG II : (a) (b) (c)

Fig III

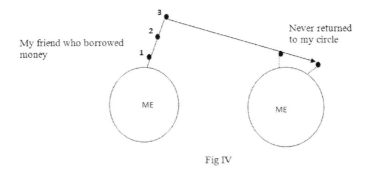

Fig IV

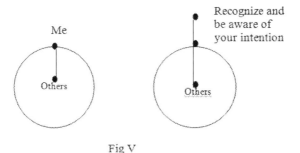

Fig V

Let us look at the first figure, where someone went out of my circle. I realized but the other person did not realize what he did or he did it knowingly and purposefully, for example. My neighbor borrowed a lawn mower from me and brought it back with an empty gas tank. I was tolerant and did not say anything. The second time he borrowed my lawn mower again and brought it back with the gas tank empty, I told him, "Well, John, the least you can do is return the lawn mower with gas in it."

He replied, "Sorry, I will never do it again. Thanks!" He never borrowed my lawn mower again. I brought him back to my circle. He remained my good neighbor. But some never realize and continue using you until and unless you speak out and say, "Sorry, I cannot lend you the lawn mower. Sorry for that. Figures II, III, and IV show some people continuing to moving out of the circle. If you set limits and say no, either they cut the relationship with you off or you let them go. Both ways, you lose a relationship, and the other person loses you as a friend or relative. I had a friend whom I really trusted and liked. He borrowed some money he needed to buy goods for his family. The second time, he was running short on his mortgage and I loaned him the money. After a few months, he asked for more. My answer was simple, "Pay me the money you owe first before I even think of anything." I never heard from him. I called him a few times, but he would not return my calls. Well, it was my fault for lending him money the second time. The moral of the story is he lost me and I lost a friend. Well, we lose some and gain some. Life goes on. We all have come across such events in our lives.

Let us look at figure V. If I have a limit-setting circle, others do too, and I am at the line of the circle. I have to act rationally and appropriately. If I feel someone took advantage of me, I have to be cognizant of the fact that others can feel the same way I feel or felt. Thus, it is a learning curve for me as well as for others. Let me give a simple example. I borrowed a wheelbarrow from my neighbor. It broke. The wheel came off. I bought a new one and took it to his house. He thanked me and said, "You did not have to do that."

"Yes, I had to do that," I answered.

We remain good friends. If I need his help, he is there for me. This is the way we not only develop a relationship that is healthy, but we also teach each others who we are and how we live our lives. We also learn how others feel and act. This is a dynamic process, not a static one. We have to adjust and modify our approach in how we continue a healthy relationship and love. Those who grow up in dysfunctional and unhealthy environments have difficulty learning how to develop healthy limit setting. We all have different experiences of life. I described various personality disorders. It is very hard to set limits and create love in such PDs. Sometimes, we have to let people go and learn to live a loving and anxiety-free life. The personalities described earlier are chaotic and will disrupt your life. I usually stay away and let those people go out of my life. Humans with personality disorders are everywhere, sometimes in our families, at workplaces, and in our neighborhoods. You're better off avoiding such individuals. We may be in a dysfunctional, dependent relationship and not recognize the signs or ignore such dysfunctional behavior. It is important to recognize the status of the relationship. Having a relationship and love for the people with personality disorders is always chaotic. As mentioned in an article in the IPFW Parkview Student Assistance Program (Life Stream.org/Wellness/

Wellnessboundaries.html), the characteristics of healthy boundaries are as follows:

- Feeling like your own person
- Feeling responsible for your own happiness
- Being together and separateness are balanced
- Having friendships outside of the relationship
- Focusing on the best quality of both persons and others
- Achieving intimacy without using chemicals
- Maintaining open, honest, and assertive communications
- Committing to a partner
- Accepting changes in the relationship as we grow with time and situations
- Asking honestly for what you want
- Accepting the ending

Unhealthy characteristics include the following:

- Feeling inadequate without a partner, usually in dependent personality disorder
- Relying on your partner for your happiness too much or there is too little togetherness, usually in dependent personality versus schizoid personality
- Being unable to establish friendship with others, usually present in borderline personality
- Focusing on the worst qualities of the partner, usually in narcissistic personality
- Using alcohol or drugs to reduce inhibitions, which create a false sense of intimacy, usually present in antisocial personality
- Playing games, being unwilling to listen, and exhibiting manipulative behavior, usually in an antisocial personality disorder.
- Having jealousy, a relationship addiction, or lack of commitment, usually present in borderline personality disorder
- Feeling the relationship should always be the same, usually independent PD
- Being Unable to express feelings, including anger, appropriately, characteristic of borderline personality disorder

Limit setting is useless when we threaten or blame and do not take any action when the time comes. It gives the other person permission to continue the behavior, which they usually do.

In this digital era, we have to set limits with ourselves. Once you send a photo or express intimate feelings or even bad language, it is everywhere. Who knows who else is going to know about what you sent or whatever your loving partner sent you? That is how nude pictures go viral on the Internet.

Many writers have expressed that love is blind. Yes, it is bind, since our sensation of vision and hearing are ignored by our soul. Though our neuronal mechanism stays intact, we still don't perceive and hear the reality. All we feel is love. Our mind is blind to all the input from our love, since it does not exist. Memories of our love remain registered in our soul. Pleasant sensations and even the pain of love remain integral parts of our soul's magnetic energy. Any thought from thousands of miles triggers the feelings of love in our body and soul. Love to a mother's soul is blind, no matter what her children do and how they behave. Mitochondria in all fetuses come from the mother's egg. The children are so conditioned that the mother's love paralyzes our will. After thirty-seven years, my first love still haunts me, even now. I still think of love lost in a vast storm of my life. In my view, love is an immortal part of an immortal soul. The mind is a transitory function of the neurons, which fades away once the strong magnetic energy of our soul gets a foothold in our body. The mind is a figment of our imaginations, created by philosophers without its existence. It is what it is; it is not what it is not. It does not exist if it does not have existence.

CHAPTER 6

CONSCIOUSNESS AND THE SOUL

My soul was born in the womb of my mother at a stage when my brain was developing and was able to conduct electric current between different parts of my body. The exact time and stage of development is unknown to me. The first stage of the soul I call the "insapient soul." This gradually grew into the "infantile soul" as time went on. My "infantile soul" gave rise to primitive consciousness and the primitive self, since I was able to swim around in the amniotic fluid like a fish swims in the deep water of the ocean. As my sensory system developed (hearing, vision, sense of touch, and so on), I was able to feel the cozy temperature of the amniotic fluid. I was blind and alone in the dark shadow of my life. The normal physiology and health of my mother was the only hope for me to continue my survival. I felt the twitching of my muscles and heard bizarre noises both from my mother's organs and from outside. Sometimes, I would kick my mom's womb and wanted to scream. I do not know whether she was able to hear my screams or laughter, but I would feel her hands on her abdomen to comfort me, since she felt my kicks. I was able to hear whenever she ate or drank, watched TV, listened to music, or talked to someone I never knew. I was frightened whenever she went to see the fireworks and heard the noise coming from an airplane flying in the air.

My heart would beat faster and faster. It would calm down when there was no noise or any threatening event.

As my cerebral cortex developed, I did feel energy flowing through my body. I could think but was unable to comprehend or express my feelings. All I could do was swim around and around with the hope of reaching my destination in the outside world. I could feel there was something outside. *What is it?* I could not decipher. Once the action potential developed, my nerves were developed, and the neurons started shaping and functioning, there was a regular flow of electric current through my nervous system, and the magnetic energy of my soul got stronger and stronger. My neurons, axons, and the connections between my dendrites kept growing at a faster pace than I could handle. My primitive consciousness started having more and more strength. Thanks to my God or my destiny and my mother, I did not have any congenital abnormalities. Finally the day came when the order came from the contraction of my mother's uterus. My head bones were shrunk and squeezed against each other to avoid any injury to my brain and to my mother's birth canal. The journey was painful and traumatic to me and my mother. It was the slap on my back that made me gasp, and I took the first breath. I opened my eyes and looked around. What is that all about? I had altogether different feelings. My infantile soul and primitive consciousness started to grow every day and night. Thanks to the genetic code in my DNA, which was normal. Thanks to my mom and dad. I showed emotions by yelling, smiling, and crying. I would feel the touch of my mother and others who wanted to hold me and express their love to me. I could sense others and their intentions and emotions soon after. Though I had not developed language and speech, I was still was able to comprehend. I was attracted to the speech of others, which started developing sooner than I could think.

Dehaene and Lambertz tested two-month-old babies by using MRI while the babies were listening to the speech of their mothers. They found the activation in the brain was diffuse and not restricted to the primary auditory area. On the contrary, an entire network of cortical regions were lit up and were traced to the language area at exactly the same place as in the adult brain (the left hemisphere's temporal lobe and the frontal language areas). Even Broca's area was activated. Is it possible that the infants recognized their mothers' speech after birth?

Stanislas Dehaene and his wife did extensive work on two-month-old babies, and their tests showed that in infants, the latency of the brain responses are dramatically slower. They seemed to take more time. The baby's brain needs one-third of a second before the frontal lobe responded. A full second was needed before their prefrontal cortex reacted, about three to four times the delay in adults. In their work, the babies scored high on tests of consciousness (192), because of the gradual myelination of long nerve fibers. The fetal soul and infantile soul grow as our nervous system grows and interacts with the environment and the external stimuli, which generated and registered new experiences and memories. New theories in neuroscience suggest consciousness is an intrinsic property of everything, just like gravity. Christof Koch and Giulio Tononi developed a theory called integrated information theory (IIT), which claims that consciousness appears in the physical system, which contains many different and highly interconnected pieces of information. Based on that hypothesis, consciousness can be measured as a theoretical quantity, which the researchers call phi. Tononi says that human consciousness is similar to ringing a bell; scientists send a magnetic pulse into the human brain and watch the pulse reverberate through the neurons—back and forth, side to side. The longer and clearer the reverberation, the higher the subject's amount of consciousness. Using that test, Koch and Tononi can tell whether a patient is awake, asleep, or anesthetized. Doctors and scientists could use this knowledge to tell if a person is in a vegetative state or is dead; it could even tell us how much awareness a person with dementia has. The same could be assessed in a newborn. We could also determine when a fetus develops consciousness (390). This supports my theory of magnetic energy to initiate and sustain consciousness.

The Swedish pediatrician Hugo Lagrererantz and the French neurobiologist Jean Pierre Changeux concurred with my view that birth would coincide with the first access to consciousness (193). They argue that the fetus in the womb is sedated because of "neurosteroid anesthetics pregnanlone and prostaglandin D2 secreted by [the] placenta." At birth, there is a surge of stress hormones and stimulating neurotransmitters, like catecholamine, which makes the baby alert, awake, and energized after a few hours, having a conscious soul. Consciousness and soul go hand in hand. Though it is the birth of the soul that gives birth to consciousness and the concept of self, consciousness gives enormous magnetic energy to the soul. The soul perceives and recognizes the consciousness. We spend most of our time being conscious, which is due to the constant firing of neurons, like the beating of heart muscles. The rest of the body's movements and activities, which cause an enormous electrical current (ibid), provide a constant source of energy to the soul for our survival. In order to remain conscious, we need a constant source of energy and a resting period for our neurons and the rest of the body (secondary soul, tertiary soul) as described. Sleep is a source of rest for our soul and consciousness. Some claim sleep is a part of unconsciousness, in spite of the fact that our neurons still function and generate energy. Sleep gives rest to our sensory system. Usually, our metabolic rate is low during the sleep period; there is also low consumption of oxygen and a low heart rate. The soul never sleeps, since electric current has to be there to continue the functioning of the body and our organs.

We need to look at our cousin animals that have not developed speech and written language. They do possess a soul and consciousness. They have developed a verbal language of their own. We could watch a herd of elephants, where the grandmother takes the role of leader and guides the whole herd to green pastures and watering holes. They are conscious of each other and follow the rules and regulations to keep the herd in a cohesive state. They show love for each other and even discipline for the young or rebellious ones. They talk to each other. They fight the predators together. They grieve their dead members. They have the same sensations as humans. As a matter of fact, their senses are far superior, which replaces our development of language and technology. They can smell, hear, and see for miles. Our sensation is primitive compared to animals'. Don't you think an elephant can find water underground and dig a hole? They find minerals they need from miles away and travel to unknown regions. I call that an invention that involves consciousness and cognition. It is encoded in their DNA and RNA, like in humans. Their emotions are stronger than ours in certain cases. A female elephant can adopt an orphan elephant baby and give him or her the same love that the mother would have given to that elephant baby. Though we have developed night-vision goggles, they already have night vision. They communicate with each other and other species of different shapes, sizes, and languages.

Language is learned process. If I do not know Chinese, how can I communicate with a Chinese speaker? If a Chinese person does not understand Russian, Hindi, or English, then how could he or she communicate with those people? How do we like and hate each other? My neighbor was a sweet old Spanish lady. I did not understand a word of Spanish, and she could not speak English. Believe it or not, we used to communicate and understand each other most of the time. It was our soul's communication. The same holds true of the animal kingdom. I learned this while sitting on the porch of my house in Virginia Beach. There were foxes with babies wandering in my backyard. The crows in the trees always made certain noises, which were understood by the squirrels and rabbits. They would run, climb the trees, and hide in bushes with certain warning calls. I watched that for years. How is it possible that crows would produce the same noise to signal the threat to other animals? This happens every second in wildlife. Animals are conscious and aware of their surroundings and have a sense of self and others. This has happened since the inception of life on earth.

We human beings are gifted to learn different languages to promote trade, invent, and share our knowledge of science for our future growth. In the same way, animals learn from different species to survive. Evolution has taught living beings how to communicate just to adapt and survive. It boils down to neurons, axons, and dendrites of the brain. I find carnivorous animals are more aggressive than herbivorous animals. Is it the hippocampus of carnivorous animals that is more developed or the limbic system in herbivorous animals? If that is true, then we humans can learn from this evolutionary process and adopt healthy ways of living our lives. We can solve obesity and related illnesses. This holds true in many high-functioning animals like dolphins, monkeys, lions, and crows. Monkeys can invent tools. Who knows? As evolution continues, in millions of years, they may be able to developed language or be able to function at higher levels like us. What happens to humans in millions of years? As we invent new things, our brain may evolve into new species. We may live on the moon, on Mars, and under the ocean. The pace at which our intelligence is growing, our brain may evolve into an amazing cortex and limbic system. I do predict change. What kind? I do not know.

I was impressed to watch on YouTube a documentary about animal odd couples, which gave me great insight into the soul and consciousness. I really recommend it to all readers. There exists a relationship between animals of different species. Usually, when they are abandoned and join together in captivity, they bond with each other to avoid the stress of loneliness. Some think that animals develop friendships, thinking that they have a pet. Some call it unconditional love. Food for lions became a symbol of love and companionship. I saw on a video a lioness adopting a baby gazelle, and instead of eating it, she loved and protected baby gazelle. A lioness in South Africa adopted a baby gazelle in the wild.

Unfortunately, other lions ate that baby gazelle. She adopted six baby gazelles and unfortunately lost all six to other lions.

The most touching story occurred in captivity. There was a farm where all the orphan animals were protected and lived together. There was a blind horse and a goat. They lived like two wonderful friends. Every morning, the goat would wake the blind horse, and both would graze and rest in the shade. She would take the horse to the water stream and bring him back to the barn where they spent their night. They communicated through their sense of smell but would talk with different sounds produced for different activities. How could they understand each other's language? It is like a Chinese speaker speaking to a Russian speaker. Their empathy for each other was extreme. If the horse got tired, the goat would stop and rest with him. Both were conscious of the other's presence and needs. They communicated with each other through their magnetic souls. There was an automatic exchange of thoughts, wishes, desires, and the magnetic energy of their souls. The goat knew what the horse needed, and the blind horse knew what the goat wanted. They lived their life with love and feeling for each other.

One day, the blind horse died, and it was a devastating event for the goat. She would sit and not care about grazing the grass or drinking water. The goat never got attached to any other animal and died sad and heartbroken. Even events of mating between different male and female animals have been reported. Does this explain how in the wild world evolutionary changes may have taken place or are taking place right now? Thanks to the Internet, there is a wide range of information coming out, which someday may give us insight into the process (194). Attributing consciousness to an animal should not be based solely on their anatomical structure or shape. We have studied monkeys and their responses to simulation; their cortex shows selective responses to stimuli. They possess a form of subliminal perception (195). Functional MRI (fMRI) shows the monkeys' prefrontal cortex lights up like humans' do when stimulus is provided to the visual or auditory sensory system.

According to Hindu philosophy, "the Soul (atman) is spiritual in all creatures, their real innermost essential being" (2, 38, 39). It is eternal, ageless. It is at the deepest level of one's existence. Though atman is the soul, some wrote in these texts that pranas are the primal energy, thus pranas could be used as an atman. Pranas represent the "vital signs of life" (living energy) by which we identify the presence of life. In the Upanishad books, sages defined the capacity of a body to direct, conserve, and employ energy at a high level of complexity. They taught us various functions in the body, which we call thought and consciousness. Pranas are the composite energy of all the senses of our body. For example, if sight leaves our body, we become blind. We can still live (secondary soul, ibid). However, when pranas leave the body, it is death of the body. When Pranas come back to the body, we call it life. If sight returns, we can see again, which adds to our conscious state. We can relate the inner feelings to the exterior existence. The sages testify that they have confirmed all this by direct observation, but that observation need a highly trained observer. It requires extensive training and meditation to become aware of pranas (soul) and what lies beyond that. I was amazed to learn how Hindu Rishis knew about human anatomy and physiology, explaining the conscious and unconscious soul and pranas, without studying human anatomy and human physiology thousands of years ago. Was it their imagination or spirituality? Did they have existing knowledge that we are not aware of? They did not have MRI, EEG, ECG, and the rest of the advanced tools that we have. I have no answer for how they could have explained consciousness, the soul, and the self.

The Bhagavad Gita explains that pleasure mainly comes from transitory experiences of the senses and is limited. Joy comes from being in harmony with creative forces of the universe and one's own destiny and is everlasting. The self is the source of abiding joy. Our hearts are filled with joy upon seeing it enriched in the depth of consciousness. If the self was not there, who would breathe, who would live? It is the one who fills every heart with joy. When one realizes the self in whom all life is one, changeless, nameless, and formless, then one fears no more. Until we realize the unity of life, we live in fear. For a scholar who does not know the self, his separateness becomes fear itself (2, 225–240).

J. C. Chatterjee describes Vedic thinking. The soul exists between birth and the death of the self (body) continues to exist even after the death of the body. The self-identity and continuity is maintained by the soul, even when it is not connected with the body. It floats between life and death. In the same way, a piece of music broadcasted into space maintains its self-identity and individuality, even when rushing through the electromagnetic field, so that it can be reproduced as the same music by means of a suitable receiver. The soul, in the same sense, maintains its self-identity and is born and dies again and again until it reaches a stage of purusha, the ultimate being, and then the final stage of total freedom (moksha). This belief is based on the theory of reincarnation in Hindu philosophy (199). In Christian belief, it is called resurrection. In the real scientific world, we still have a lot of work to do in order to reach such conclusions. My view is the soul persists in the form of electromagnetic energy outside of our body and exists as long as the energy exists. What happens to such energy thereafter, I do not have a clear vision of that. Energy cannot be created or destroyed. If that is true, then we should have some answers.

There were many philosophers and saints who took on the subject of consciousness and the soul. Thomas Aquinas wrote about the soul. Eastern Hindu Rishis wrote about consciousness, unconsciousness, and the self thousands of years ago. I presume they had great influence on Western philosophers, who attempted to explain the soul and consciousness. There are different definitions given by different researchers. Some say it is a state or quality of awareness or of being aware of an external object or something within oneself (200, 201), one's ability to experience or feel wakefulness, having a sense of selfhood and an executive control system of the mind (202). Most ancient philosophers have been discussed in chapter 1. But I would like to mention Freud, who described the topographical model of the mind in his publication *Interpretation of Dreams*. He explained the mind has three parts: conscious, preconscious, and unconscious.

THE CONSCIOUS

The perceptions come from outside of the body or from inside of the body, by which our mind is brought into awareness. Consciousness, in contrast, is a subjective phenomenon whose contents can be communicated only by language or behavior. Consciousness used a psychic energy, which Freud called "attention cathexis," whereby a person is aware of a particular idea and feelings as a result of investing the discrete amount of psychic energy in the idea or feelings.

THE PRECONSCIOUS

It is composed of mental events, processes, and contents that can be brought into conscious awareness by the act of focusing attention. This attention involves memory. For example, if we forget the name of a friend, we pay attention and focus so we may recall his or her name. It interacts with both the conscious and unconscious. To reach to conscious awareness, the contents of the unconscious must be linked to the word and thus become preconscious. The preconscious system also serves to maintain the repressive barrier and to censor unacceptable wishes and desires.

THE UNCONSCIOUS

In this, the mental contents and processes are kept from conscious awareness through forces of censorship or repression. They are closely related to instinctual drives. In Freud's theory, unconsciousness was thought to contain primarily the mental representation and derivatives of sexual instincts. The unconsciousness system is "primary process thinking," which is aimed at wishful fulfillment and instinctual discharge. It is based on the pleasure principle and disregards logical connections. Memory in the unconscious is dissolved. Thus, when analysts treat the patient's verbal recathexis, it allows the memory to reach consciousness again. This is only possible by passing through precociousness. When censors are overpowered, the elements can enter the consciousness (31, 131–132).

Freud put forward the theories without having many of the tools that neuroscientist have now. Neuroscience has come a long way since the 1900s. Though his theory has lost its momentum, we still use the pearls like primary and secondary thought processes, wish fulfillment, and the existence of dynamic unconscious.

Freud used the term *psychic energy*. What kind of energy is it? What exactly is it? Is it what I call the electric current, action potential, or magnetic energy, or is it a biochemical reaction that produces energy for the functioning of the body and brain? We understand the neuroscience, that whenever we have a stimulus like the prick of a needle, there is an electric current that travels through our nervous system, and we feel pain in the sensory center of the brain. We use our sensory system (vision, hearing, and so on). There is a firing of the neurons, which generates an enormous amount of neurotransmitters and electric current to achieve the desired goal, thought, emotion, behavior, and desire. The list goes on and on. Freud failed to explain such events in spite of the fact he himself was a neurologist. On the bases of neurobiological advances in science, Freud's theories lost their luster.

As described by the Hindu Upanishad and Bhagavad Gita, pranas are the energy that travels to the highest centers through the nerves, which we call electric current. These pranas generate enormous electric current, which leads to generation of a magnetic energy called atama, the "soul." The soul is part and parcel of our body and brain. Being conscious of itself causes firing of the neurons that generate the energy (magnetic) that is consumed for all the actions, thoughts, emotions, and so on. They are all seated in our soul, and each unit of energy is used for each functional unit of our body and soul.

The self-conscious soul (an energy form) reads from a multitude of active centers in the brain while we are conscious and engaged in a multitude of activities. Our soul, which is conscious, selects the interests or attention and integrates them into a unity to give us a conscious experience from moment to moment. It also acts backup storage for neuronal centers. Thus, it is my view that the soul acts and exercises a superior interpretive and controlling role upon the neural events by virtue of two-way interaction between them. The unity of conscious experience does not come from the ultimate synthesis in the neural machinery but the integrated action of the conscious soul on what it reads out from the immense diversity of neural activities in the liaison brain. Karl R. Popper and John C. Eccles in *Self and Its Brain* propose the theory of three worlds (207, 359).

World 1 is physical objects and states, which include inorganic matter and the energy of the cosmos; biology, the structure and action of all living beings, human and animal; and artifacts of human creativity—tools, machines, books, works of art, and music.

World 2 is the state of consciousness, including subjective knowledge and experiences, like perceptions, thinking, emotions, dispositional intentions, memories, dreams, and creative imaginings.

World 3 is knowledge in the objective sense, like cultural heritage, which includes philosophy, theology, science, history, literature, art, technology, theoretical systems, scientific problems, and critical arguments.

If we look at these worlds of humans, we can see that they interact with each other in whatever situation, time frame, or events. Sir John Eccles and Karl R. Popper proposed that it is the self-conscious mind that interacts with the neuronal machinery of the brain and the neuronal machinery interacts with the conscious mind to unify the actions and results of all three worlds. For example, books, pictures, machines, houses, children, noise, and music can only be consciously perceived when our sensory system projects to our brain by appropriate pathways. Thus, world 2 can reciprocally bring changes, like muscle movement, to complete the desired action. This raises several questions: What exactly is the mind? Is it a form of energy generated by our brain? Or is there a special center of our neurons that we neuroscientists have yet to find that combines all the sensory apparatuses? Is it the same thing, a chemical or electromagnetic field that thinks and acts as commander in chief? My view is that it is the magnetic energy of the soul that interacts with our neuronal machine both ways. The mind does not exist. It is an imaginary name given to our day-to-day functions as a unit. Both Popper and Eccles mention the brain and mind interaction through our outer senses and inner senses as they send back and forth information that interacts in the middle with the following (203 Page 261) functional units: ego, self, soul, and will.

They concluded that the self-conscious mind is scanning the modular activities in the liaison area of the cerebral cortex, where the self-conscious mind is located. This remains an unanswerable question in principle. In an article published by the Edger Cast Network on the Human Consciousness Project in 2016, which is conducted by the International Consortium of Multidisciplinary Scientists and doctors, Eccles wrote, "Today most scientists have adopted a traditionally monist view of the mind-brain problems, arguing that the human mind, consciousness and self are no more than a byproduct of electrochemical activity within the brain.

In recent years, a number of scientific studies conducted by independent researchers, have found that as many as 10 to 20 percent of individuals who undergo cardiac arrest report lucid, well-structured thought processes, reasoning, memories, and sometimes detailed recall of their cardiac arrest. What makes these experiences remarkable is that while studies of the brain during cardiac arrest have consistently shown that there is no brain activity during this period, these individuals have reported details and perceptions that appear to indicate the presence of a higher level of consciousness in the absence of measurable brain activity. Moreover, these studies appear to suggest that the human mind and consciousness may in fact function at the time when the clinical criteria of death are fully present and the brain has ceased to function. What a thought-provoking question and argument raised in this article! It goes to my theory of the magnetic soul. In my view, the mind does not exist. It is the magnetic soul energy that exists in these cases, for minutes to hours or for a long period of time. The soul's magnetic energy is generated. It has clear memories, perceptions, thought processes, reasoning, and detailed recall. These events do not exist in thin air. These are processes and forms of magnetic energy. Even if the brain may not be active, this energy exists within our skulls and the rest of the body. As explained earlier in the chapters describing life after life, Dr. Parnia has done a lot of research on near-death experiences during cardiac arrest and has explained his findings in his book extensively. He is still working in Cornell University. Most of the patients went through a similar experience. They felt very serene and had the sensation of meeting their dead relatives. Some felt calm, comfortable, and peaceful. Some felt like they were watching their bodies from above. They even described listening to doctors and nurses. Dr. Parnia has collected five hundred case histories of near-death experiences. Those who had near-death experiences felt as if they were near God. Such occurrences have been reported from all over the world in cardiac arrest patients. He postulated that it could be due to a chemical event that can cause hallucination or may have transcendental or spiritual feelings. In the case of cardiac arrest, the heart stops beating and blood flow to the heart and the rest of the body is stopped.

The definition of death is no heartbeat, no respiration, and death of the brain. When the pupils do not respond to light, it indicates the death of the brain stem (and that is the death of the patient). These days, research indicates reversing death from one hour to several hours after the cardiac arrest may be possible, as described by Dr. Parnia. My view is though there is death, our body has cells that take time to die by a chemical process. The magnetic energy is still present and has stored all the sensory experiences and memory for unknown hours. They spread above, and the patient experiences the events described by Dr. Parnia. If patients are resuscitated, the magnetic soul rejoins the cellular structures and revives the patient. I am sure someday Dr. Parnia will develop mechanisms to revive cardiac arrest patients based on the principle of the magnetic soul, which is a strong form of magnetic energy accumulated during our lifetime. As explained, the magnetic soul has the property of sending strong electric current to the neurons to cause connections of the dendrites in seconds. Therefore, my view supports this concept of the revival of dead patients. Different patients had different experiences during near death and after death experiences due to their belief system, which could be from religious beliefs and lifetime experiences stored in the cloud-computing file of their magnetic soul.

In an interesting article in the *New York Timeon march 21ˢᵗ 1995* by Sandra Blakeslee (204) who candidly describes the process. Consider this. It is a beautiful spring day, and you are walking down a country lane, absorbed in thought. Birds are chirping, roses are in full bloom, and the sun feels warm on your face. Suddenly, you hear a dog barking, so you switch your attention to see if the dog means to bite. It is all due to stimulation of our sensory systems, which carry the message down different pathways and then are unified, in order to react to the stimuli in a cohesive way, as one unit. Sandra interviewed many neuroscientists. Dr. Koch described the basic idea as follows: cells involved in forming a perception will fire simultaneously, thus binding together in time rather than space. Every perception would be based on the temporary activation of an ensemble of neurons. When a new perception is formed, the previous ensemble falls away and a new grouping of neurons fires, forming a new perception. A single neuron can participate in the representation of many things, depending on the ensembles they joined in any one instant. According to Dr. Charles Gray, who recorded the electric activity of brain cells in different parts of the monkey's visual system, cells in the brain fire in synchrony. Nobody knows how and when. Dr. Gyorgy Buzsaki, a neuroscientist at Rutgers University in Newark, New Jersey, has found a class of cells called inhibitory interneurons, which have an inherent tendency to fire in a wave-like pattern. These neurons could perform a binding function. A convincing piece of information was given by Dr. Rodolfo Llinas, a professor of neuroscience at New York University. He describes the brain stem as containing the nucleus of cells that burst at a rate of ten cycles per second. These cells are in the inferior olivary nucleus. Neurons send long fibers up to the cerebellum, where they make dense connections, thus amplifying their signals. Information flowing into the cerebellum is regulated by these bursting cells, making sure that the movements only occur ten times a second. This oscillation literally binds commands with muscle movements. Dr. Llinas added that the same kind of binding mechanism may exist for the entire brain at a faster frequency of forty cycles per second. Dr. Llinas and his colleague Dr. Urs Ribary, also at New York University, have measured such signals in human brains, using a machine that detects the magnetic field on the scalp. The forty cycles per second continuously sweep the brain from front to back every 12.5 thousandths of a second. This could be the binding signal that links information from the parts of the cortex that handle auditory, visual, motor, and other sensory signals. Dr. Llinas believes that the forty-cycle-per-second waves serve to connect the structures in the cortex, where advanced information processing occurs, and the thalamus, a lower brain region where complex relay and integrative functions are carried out.

In walking down the sunny path, absorbed in thought, a person would be generating regular forty-cycle-per-second rhythms while constructing internal images of the external world, which agree with each other. The brain keeps updating the scene with a steady rhythm. But when the dog barks, posing a threat, the forty-cycle-per-second signal is abruptly reset so as to incorporate the novel stimulus into the overall scene so that the new information can be dealt with. According to Dr. Llinas, consciousness is the dialogue between the thalamus and the cerebral cortex. Dr. Llinas's theory rests on his measurements of various electrical rhythms in the brain as well as on the observations that when the intralaminar nucleus is damaged, people fall into a deep coma. Many neuroscientists have replicated the theory of Dr. Llinas.

Dr. Mirces Steriade from the Laval University School of Medicine in Quebec has measured forty-cycle-per-second rhythms, which "exist spontaneously when animals are in the active state of vigilance." Dr. David Hubel from Harvard Medical School raises a valid question. There are two hundred possible areas in the brain. Very few have been explored in detail. He adds it is possible that there could be as-yet-undiscovered, highly specific areas in the brain where information comes together and is bound into a unitary experience (204).

If Dr. Llinas and others are correct and their theories are viable, then it helps my view of the magnetic energy called soul, which binds all the sensory stimuli in the hypothalamus and cortex with forty cycles per second. It adds to the piece of the puzzle of the solution of mindless body and endless soul. We spend most of our lives being conscious and less time in an unconscious state (like when we are asleep). When we are awake and vigilant, there is constant generation of electrical energy of the soul. Thus, it is the magnetic energy of the soul that gives rise to consciousness. Some may argue that it is the other way around, that consciousness gives rise to the magnetic energy of the soul. I can live with both arguments. Our brain is active during sleep and works at the unconscious level. It uses less energy, but it still generates electrical energy as seen in EEG. The waves are weaker, but they still exist. That gives us an insight that the soul energy still exists and is produced during sleep, as recorded in EEG.

Idris Zamuri, in an article published in the *Journal of Biomedical Science and Engineering* in 2014 has argued in a detailed article, "Anatomical Origin and Applications of Brain Waves," that the seat of the soul lies in the great limbic system (the origin of brain waves). He, along with his colleagues, argues that this is also the spiritual area of the brain since all the signals arising from human activities are concentrated, modulated, and processed here. According to his work, the great limbic system and cortical network seem crucial in generating brain waves. These systems cover the whole part of the brain and therefore are important in inducing various functions of the brain via oscillations or brain rhythms. These brain waves were studied in terms of epilepsy, brain mapping, and brain networking and even in pursuit of soul searching. Brain waves are a kind of traceable neurophysiologic energy in the living brain. They are invisible to the human eye. They are only detectable using electroencephalography (EGG), electrocorticography (ECOG), and magnetoencephalography (MEG). Oscillation with synchronization does exist inside and outside of our brain. These are classified as the following:

1. Microscale oscillations (activity of a single neuron)
2. Mesoscale oscillations (activity of a group of neurons)
3. Macroscale oscillations (activity of different parts of the brain and nervous system, including all the sensory systems)

I will describe the waves in brief:

1. Gamma (above 30 Hz)
2. Beta (13 to 30 Hz)
3. Alpha (8 to 13 Hz)
4. Theta (4 to 8 Hz)
5. Delta (0.5 to 4 Hz) (205)

The amplitude of the brain wave is measured by using microvolts (mv). These are classified in the following way:

1. Low amplitude (less than 20 microvolts)
2. Medium (between 20 and 50 microvolts)
3. High amplitude (more than 50 microvolts)

When we are conscious, alert, active, thinking, and actively paying attention, they are found at the frontal and central part of the brain (206). It appears as consciousness slips toward drowsiness; theta waves are associated with sleep, deep meditation, creative inspiration, and unconsciousness. New thinkers reported kappa waves (10 Hz) are associated with thinking. Surface or scalp EEG has low signal resolution due to the scalp, bone, and dura matter covering the brain. MEG is based on magnetic field changes that accompany neuronal activity. MEG has two main uses in the future. Evoked fields are commonly used for motor, sensory, visual, and auditory mapping, while the event-related field is used for cognitive tasks and resting-state activity. Spontaneous activity is mainly used for detecting seizure activity and for studying brain maturity, consciousness, and brain networks (37). This confirms my view that there is an existing magnetic field in our body that needs extensive research and attention to understand the concept of the soul and consciousness.

Our soul has both components of the conscious and unconscious, regardless of sleep-wake periods. Let me discuss sleep first, and then we'll go from there. Sleep is the most significant human need. We humans spent almost one-third of our lives asleep and three-quarters of the time in wakeful consciousness. This is a universal behavior in all living creatures. Our brain and the rest of the body require proper and adequate sleep to function in day-to-day life. Some need more sleep; some need less. The range is six to nine hours. Newborns and infants up to four months need sixteen hours of sleep on average (208). It has both quantitative and qualitative properties. Prolonged sleep deprivation leads to severe physical and cognitive impairment. Most of the psychiatric and psychological disorders have some sort of sleep disorder. Sleep is made of two physiological states: nonrapid eye movement (NREM) and rapid eye movement (REM). NREM is 75 percent of our sleep and has four stages. They vary in time span as below:

NREM

- Stage 1: 5%
- Stage 2: 45%
- Stage 3: 12%
- Stage4: 13%

REM is 25 percent of our sleep. In NREM, most physiological functions are markedly lower than in wakefulness. While in REM, there is a high level of brain activity and physiological activity, similar to what they are in wakefulness. After ninety minutes of NREM sleep, we get into the REM stage of sleep. In normal humans, NREM sleep is a peaceful state relative to waking. The pulse rate is five to ten beats lower. Respiration, blood pressure, and action potential in muscles are lower. Blood flow to the brain and rest of the body is somewhat lower. The deepest portions of NREM sleep are stages 3 and 4. If a person is aroused in these stages, he or she shows disorganization and a brief state of confusion. Nightmares and night terrors are common in this phase of sleep (207). EEG studies during REM sleep show the following:

- Irregular patterns, sometimes close to aroused waking patterns
- Pulse, respiration, and blood pressure higher than in NREM
- Brain oxygen use higher than in NREM
- Decreased CO_2
- Thermoregulation altered; possible increase in body temperature.
- In men, partial or full penile erection (This study is used to evaluate the causes of impotence in men.)
- Near or total paralysis of muscles
- First period short, around ten minutes, and increases to fifteen to forty minutes each episode after sixty to ninety minutes of NREM
- Most REM periods occurring in the last third of the night

In depressed patients, there is increased REM sleep, and the time between NREM (sixty to ninety minutes) is decreased. Antidepressants reduce REM sleep. In dementia and Alzheimer's patients, there is reduced REM sleep as well.

The neurotransmitters involved in the sleep process are the following:

1. Serotonin
2. L-tryptophan
3. norepinephrine
4. acetylcholine
5. melatonin

In order to explain the relationship between unconsciousness,

consciousness, and the soul, I am going to focus on sleep terrors and nightmares.

SLEEP TERRORS

Sleep terrors occur in NREM (stages 3 to 4). There is a sudden arousal with intense fearfulness. These individuals may cry, scream, and have intense anxiety. At times, it may appear like a panic attack. When they wake from this event, they may be confused or incoherent. Usually, there is no memory of the episode. They at times may have a faint memory of the episode. It is called pavor nocturnes and is most often present in children. In adults, there is usually a history of traumatic experience or a psychiatric disorder (209).

NIGHTMARES

Nightmares occur in the REM stage of sleep. Usually, they evolve from a long, complicated dream that becomes increasingly frightening. Individuals, when they wake up, usually remember the dream. Drug and alcohol abuse are highly associated with nightmares (210). Freud described his in his publication (1900) *The Interpretation of Dreams*. He describes dreams as a conscious expression of unconscious fantasies or wishes, not readily acceptable to the conscious, waking experience. The dream images represented unconscious wishes or thoughts, distinguished through the process of symbolization and other distorted mechanisms. Freud added that there is a censor between the unconscious and preconscious. The censor functions to exclude unconscious wishes during the conscious state, but during the regressive relaxation of sleep, it allows certain unconscious contents to pass the border but only after transformation of these unconscious wishes into disguised forms experienced in the manifest dream contents by the sleeping subject. Unconscious thoughts and wishes include sensory stimuli (pain, hunger, thirst, urinary urgency) and day residue (thoughts and ideas and preoccupation during waking life). In addition, it allows repressed, unacceptable impulses that are blocked by the sleep state; the dream enables partial but limited gratification of the repressed impulse that gives rise to the dream.

Human babies have billions of unconnected neurons. By the age of two, synapses, dendrites, and neurons begin connecting extremely rapidly as they take in sensory information. As many as two million new connections or synapses are formed in the human infant every second. By the age of two, children have more than one hundred trillion synapses, which is double the number of an adult (35, 8). By age three, almost 90 percent of our brain is developed, as our axons, neurons, dendrites, and synapses grow at a fast and furious pace. That is why pruning starts, which means we have to lose the connections to have normal growth. Look at a three- to four-year-old child. Once language develops, there are common questions asked by children: Why? How? A child consciously becomes very curious and tries to learn everything as soon as possible. Sight, hearing, and other sensations constantly look for exploration of the environment.

I was travelling from New York to Virginia Beach with my nephew. On the way, he asked me a number of questions. I tried my best to answer them. He was around four. One question made me somewhat annoyed. We were on Verrazano Bridge. His question was, "Why is there a bridge?"

I answered, "Because we cannot drive through the river. That is why there is a bridge. We can drive our car over it. Otherwise, we would have to swim or use a boat or fly over it."

This answer was not sufficient or convincing.

"All right, when you grow up in a few years, you will have the right answer."

Why was that? His neurons and dendrites were growing so fast. They argued within him that there was something else? This issue is resolved by the pruning of our dendrons and axons as we mature. Almost 50 percent of our synapses are pared back. Some remain dormant and may be used in the future, and some are lost; we never use them. But connections keep developing as we learn from our environment. Our (soul) magnetic energy keeps pace with such changes. Some of the synapses that are dormant and retain energy and memory are those that give birth to the unconsciousness of the soul. Those that retain full function give birth to the consciousness of our brain. These mechanisms explain the neuroanatomical and neurophysiologic aspects of unconsciousness and consciousness. These are exclusively my thoughts and hypothesis to explain the basic origin of unconsciousness and consciousness. I would welcome any suggestions or thoughts to improve upon this hypothesis.

Let's look a child born in India who comes to America. His language is Hindi, and he goes to school and learns English. For a short period of time, he will translate English into Hindi in his brain and then respond in English, until he masters the English language and Hindi starts fading away. These are neuronal mechanisms. He has to develop a new connection of dendrites and synapses to register the new language (English). Throughout our childhood, our environment refines our brain, taking numerous unrefined and unpredictable possibilities and shaping them back to correspond to what we were exposed to. Our brain keeps forming fewer but stronger connections. This process goes on as long as we are alive and keep learning. Those synapses that go away and die down, we never know about their contents, thoughts, or experiences. Those that are dormant and are used periodically become an unconscious part of adulthood. Whenever they are triggered, either by our thoughts, symbolic representations, and dreams, they can erupt into our conscious energy and thus we recall the events that did not exist in our day-to-day consciousness.

A couple of decades ago, it was thought that brain development was mostly complete by the end of childhood. But now we know that the process of building a human being takes up to twenty-five years. In adulthood, our brains continue to change; they can be shaped and can hold that shape. This is called *plasticity*. Imagine yourself going to medical school or becoming a scientist, artist, athlete, or anything else you would like to be. It is all due to neuroplasticity. Different areas of the brain will become activated and have strong and powerful connections, which once stimulated, create the desired and effective results. This contributes to our consciousness and awareness, which leads to such effective results. All these changes tell us who we are as a self, which I would discuss in details. Some neuroscientists argue that we at times run our activities automatically throughout our lives. Our brain rewrites them to build dedicated circuitry for the mission, and we practice the activity, like walking, talking, swimming, or driving. This is attained by using energy to wire dedicated circuitry in the hardware of the brain. Once this circuitry is established, we are able to do such actions without thinking (without conscious effort). You lose access to the sophisticated programs running in the brain. So you do not know precisely how you do what you do. When you are ready to go to bed, you may hear a conversation from your wife or friend, but you have no idea how your body balances its numerous actions. You climb the stairs and walk up to the bed. You may verbalize some words. You go straight to bed. You become unconsciously motivated to reach the bed. I used to drive to and from my office, park the car, and walk to or from the hospital, without being aware of what happened while I was doing the activity. We all have such routines in our lives. I have lived in my house for eleven years, and I do not know how many steps there are between my bedroom and the hallway. I asked this question to my wife: "How many steps there are between our hallway and the bedroom?" She laughed and ran to count the steps. Now how do we explain that?

Yes, we are hardwired for day-to-day routines. When I drove to my work, I was not attentive but remained conscious. It is my soul's magnetic energy that takes over my sensations, muscular mobility, and thinking, guiding me to my destination. It could be some part of my soul's unconscious or inattentive part. If my soul were not conscious, I could have hit other cars or an electric pole. My soul directed all my regular functions without disruption to attain my desired goal. I wake up and get ready, and I know I have to go to my office to see my patients. I am aware of that and am conscious of that. Unconsciousness is due to lack of attention. Both unconsciousness and consciousness need energy to sustain them. This energy is in the form of electrochemical or electromagnetic energy. This raises questions. Does unconsciousness have energy? Or is it there but remains dormant? Or is there no energy involved at all? In my view, even in dreams, while we are unconscious, our brain produces an enormous amount of electrochemical energy and electromagnetic energy, as mentioned earlier. This is our soul energy, which is produced by electric activity and the firing of neurons even in sleep. At times, in REM sleep, energy use is as high as it is while we are awake. Thus the theory that unconsciousness does not have and does not need energy is unjustifiable.

In 1965, psychologist Eckhart Hess designed an experiment. Eckhart asked men to look at the women and asked their opinion about the pictures presented to them.

- How attractive are they on a scale of one to ten?
- Mean or kind?
- Friendly or unfriendly?

Men found the women with dilated pupils to be more attractive. Men were unconsciously steered toward the women with the dilated eyes, finding them to be more beautiful, happier, kinder, and friendlier (213). This does not explain unconsciousness. Geoffrey Mill, a psychologist, found that women during their regular menstruation cycle and ovulation (fertile) appeared more attractive. It is not an unconscious mechanism. During these periods, women are more approachable and by instinct want to seduce men, due to their physiological changes and increased estrogen and oxytocin, the passion hormone (214). During this time, women are very fertile and ready to mate for reproduction. Their magnetic energy of soul is elevated to attract male souls for procreation. It is the same mechanism in animals when a female is in heat. They are seductive because of their instincts and the desires of their bodies to mate. These are conscious magnetic energies of the souls to attract opposite souls. If the opposite soul has an attractive magnetic energy, that results in mating. It is the vibrations of the souls that attract opposites. At times, this can result in a one-night stand, a temporary relationship or love, what we call a soul mate. In my experience, I have seen obese couples as soul mates, interracial couples as soul mates, and beautiful couples as soul mates.

Look, colors, race, casts, or creeds have nothing to do with unconscious events. It is integration of the soul's magnetic energy that attracts the other. They then blend in a soul mate state, which is the conscious aspect of our lives. An extensive study done at B.M. Science Center in Finland, translated into English by Dmitry Skarin, concludes my view of thinking.

> Understanding human consciousness requires the description of the law of the immediately underlying neural collective phenomena the nested hierarchy of spatiotemporal pattern of 3D electromagnetic field produced by neuronal assemblies. Their analysis has shown that the structure, organization, dynamics and casual relationship of such nested hierarchy of operational architectonics of brain activity and guided by the universal physical law such as criticality, self-organization, and emergence. The proposed architectonics framework depicting the mechanism and dynamics of consciousness allows us to literally "see" how the phenomenal (subjective) care is instantiated in the brain. According to this framework, if the operational level of brain organization (as a whole) is taken away world ceases to exist. (215)

CONSCIOUSNESS

Consciousness is not well understood or defined. It is well expected that it exists. Consciousness is the state or quality of awareness or of being aware of an external object or something within oneself (216–217). Some define it as sentience, subjectivity, the ability to feel, wakefulness, awareness of having a sense of selfhood, the ability to experience, and an executive control system of the mind (219). Dehaene argues that in order to understand consciousness, it is essential to understand conscious access. What does that mean? At any given time, we have a massive flow of sensory stimulation by our sensory apparatus that reaches our brain. Only a few of these sensory stimuli reach our consciousness. For example, I am writing this book, and there are numerous objects I see. My hands are writing. I look at beautiful roses in my backyard. I am sitting in a chair with a glass of water in front of me. There are several other objects around me, but my full attention is on writing the book. If I make a blunder, I become self-conscious, which means that my emotions, strategies, errors, and regrets will enter in my mind. Thus a thought or a few thoughts become part of my consciousness. So I have to withdraw from these thoughts to make room for other thoughts or events to be perceived, but previous thoughts lie dormant in my unconsciousness. I have to be attentive to retain this thought in my brain. Our brain ruthlessly discards the irrelevant information and ultimately isolates a single conscious object, based on its relevance and importance to us. This stimulus then becomes important and directs our behavior. Vigilance is also called "intransitive consciousness." For example, we may have a headache or bellyache. We become aware and conscious of the same from within ourselves rather than outside stimuli. We may not feel such events if we are in a coma or under anesthesia.

Many scientists and philosophers interpret consciousness as related to the sense of self, the "I." How can we ever understand conscious perceptions without first figuring out who is the perceiver? Cognitive scientists call it metacognition (thinking about oneself). Many studies done on patients with brain lesions or injuries suggest that unconsciousness is hidden in the basement of the brain, in the amygdala. Its functions are to receive and react to fear with fight or flight mechanisms. When a dog attacks you, the response is instantaneously to fight or flee. It happens before the stimuli are registered at the conscious cortical level. According to Ledoux (1996), such emotional appraisals are made extraordinarily quickly and unconsciously, mediated by the circuitry of the amygdala. It is well documented in the neuroscience literature. Swiss neurologist Ediuard Claparede demonstrated an unconscious emotional memory; while he was shaking the hand of an amnesia patient, he pricked her with a pin. The next day, her amnesia was improved and the doctor tried to shake her hand. She refused to shake his hand. Such events prove that there is a complex emotional operation that may unfold below the level of awareness. They may arise from subcortical nuclei specialized for emotional processing. This activation has been studied by fMRI in the superior colliculus nuclei (219).

Dehaene Stanislas, in his book, recites the example of a patient with a lesion of the inferior parietal lobe of the right side of the brain. She would miss all the food on the left side of the plate and eat all the food on the right side of the plate. At times, the patient complained of not having enough food. Her visual sensation was intact. Still, somehow, a higher-level lesion prevented her from attending to the left side of the plate by preventing registration at a conscious level. The question raised by him was "Is the unattended information totally lost?" The answer is no. The cortex still processes the neglected information but at an unconscious level. He called it "spatial neglect." Another interesting experiment, done by John Marshall and Peter Halligan, demonstrated an interesting finding. They showed a spatial neglect patient pictures of two houses, one with a fire, which was on the left side, and another without a fire on the right side. Upon asking the patient, "What is the difference between the two houses?" the patient denied any difference between the two. Upon asking which one he would prefer to live in, he consistently avoided the house on fire, which indicates that his brain was processing the visual information deeply enough that it could categorize the fire as a danger to be avoided. The fMRI showed later that in the spatial neglect patient, an unseen stimulus could still activate the regions of the ventral visual cortex that respond to the houses and faces. Even the meaning of neglected words and numbers invisibly made its way into the patient's brain. The most interesting aspect of this writing, which intrigues me, is that the "invisible made its way to a higher level of the brain," according to Sackur Naccache and his colleagues (220). The invisible is invisible under normal circumstances. It is not due to invisible imagination but a scientific one. Our soul's magnetic energy is still generated by the electromagnetic firing of the rest of the healthy parts of the brain. This is the unconscious magnetic energy of our soul, which is stored from either memories or experiences. The notion of the house on fire exists in our rational soul energy. Thus, patients will exhibit a rational approach to living in a fire-free house. This evidence and experiment supports my view of the magnetic soul, which operates by sending information or electric current to the healthy parts of the neuronal brain. This creates a rational approach even if it is unconscious because of a lesion in some part of the brain. It creates a conscious approach to the solution of choosing a house without fire. Is it the cognitive part of our magnetic soul, which already has stored memories and experiences that reasons it through to choose the house without fire? As explained earlier, the axons and dendrites that are dormant or partially functional (unconscious) dictate the choice of a house without fire.

Our brain is a large institution with a staff of a hundred billion neurons and trillions of connecting dendrites and synapses. Our brain relies on a familiar briefing mechanism. The function of consciousness and soul may be to simplify perceptions by drafting a summary of the current environment before voicing it out loud, in a coherent manner, to all the other areas of our brain involved in memory, decisions, actions, emotions, and behaviors. The brain's conscious briefing must be stable, sound, and integrative. It is just like in a nationwide crisis; it would be pointless for the CIA or Secret Service to send the president thousands of successive messages, each holding a little bit of truth and let him figure out for himself. In the same way, the brain cannot stick to a low-level flux of incoming data; it must contain an interpretation of the environment written in a "language of thoughts" that is abstract enough to interface with the mechanisms of intentions, presentations, actions, and decision making. Daniel Dennett, in 1911, wrote, "The improvements we install in our brain when we learn our language which permits us to review, rehearse, redesign our own activities, turning our own brains into echo chambers of [a] sort, in which otherwise evanescent (fleeting) can hang round and become objects in their own right. Those which persist the longest, acquiring influence we call our conscious thoughts."

It is quite obvious that the consciousness came first followed by unconsciousness thereafter both grow up together and complement each other. The chances of solving complicated problem are better when two conscious heads work on it, and then common ground is reached through a single consciousness. The head can solve a complicated problem, but two conscious heads are always better than one. Judgments and confidence occupy central locations in our consciousness. In order to be useful to us and others, each of our conscious thoughts must be earmarked with confidence. Not only do we know that we know or that we do not know, but whenever we are conscious of a piece of information, we can ascribe to it a precise degree of certainty or uncertainty (221).

Our conscious should use same decision rule making, which we apply to our own thoughts and to those that we receive from others. In both cases, optimal decision making demands that each source of information, whether internal or external, should be weighted as accurately as possible by an estimate of reliability, before all the information is brought together into a single decision space. Many centers in our brain are activated when we think about ourselves and others. We use the same database to encode our self-knowledge and accumulate information about others, having spent our life monitoring our behavior as well as that of others. Our analytic brain constantly draws inferences about what it observes (222).

Dehaene has raised some intriguing questions about consciousness. He questions why they occur and what it means. He precisely describes how the discovery of signatures of consciousness is a major advance, but these brain waves and neuronal spikes still do not explain what consciousness is or why it occurs. Why should late neuronal firing, cortical ignition, and brain scale synchrony ever create a subjective state of mind? How do these brain events, however complex, elicit a mental experience? Why should the firing of neurons in the brain area V4 elicit a perception of color and those of area V5 a sense of motion? (192). He explains candidly that when we say that we are aware of a certain piece of information, that we mean the information has entered into a specific storage space that makes it available to the rest of the brain. Among millions of mental representations that constantly crisscross our brain in an unconscious manner, one is selected because of its relevance to our present goals. Consciousness makes it globally available to all our higher-level decision-making systems. Dehaene and his colleagues propose that we possess a mental router, an evolved architecture for extracting relevant information and dispatching it. Psychologist Bernard Baars calls it the "global workplace" (223).

This is an internal system, detached from the outside world, that allows us to freely entertain our private mental images and to spread them across the mind in a vast array of specialized processors. According to this theory, consciousness is just brain-wide information sharing. Whenever we become conscious, we can hold it in our mind long after the corresponding stimulation has disappeared from the outside world.

Ned Block suggested two types of consciousness: raw, p-consciousness, and access A-consciousness.

P-consciousness is simply raw experience (224). It is moving color forms, sounds, sensations, emotions, and feelings. Without bodies and responses at the center, these experiences are considered independent of any impact on behavior called *qualia*. A-consciousness, in contrast, is a phenomenon whereby information in our minds is accessible for verbal report, reasoning, and the control of behavior. So when we perceive information, it is the access to consciousness.

On July 7, 2012, eminent scientists from different faculties and theories gathered at the University of Cambridge to celebrate the Francis Crick Memorial Conference, which deals with consciousness in humans and prelinguistic consciousness in nonhuman animals. After the conference, they signed, in the presence of Stephen Hawking, the Cambridge Declaration on Consciousness, which summarizes the most important finding of the survey. It reads as "We decide to reach a consensus and make a statement directed to public that is not scientific. It is obvious to everyone in this room that animals have the consciousness, but it is not obvious to the rest of the world. It is not obvious to the rest of the western world or the Far East. It is not obvious to the society" (225).

In addition, there were further remarks during that conference.

"Convergent evidence indicates that non-human animals, including all mammals and birds, and other creatures have the necessary neural substrates of consciousness and the capacity to exhibit intentional behaviors" (226).

I am very excited to learn that there are ongoing studies, which will improve with the advancement in diagnostic tools, to find more about the future functional role of such techniques in the field of consciousness studies, including the *Journal of Consciousness*.

A number of studies have shown that activity in primary sensory areas of the brain is not sufficient to produce consciousness; it is possible for subjects to report a lack of awareness even when areas such as the primary visual cortex show a clear electrical response to stimuli (227). Higher brain areas are seen as more promising, especially the prefrontal cortex of the cerebrum, which is involved in a range of higher cognitive functions collectively known as executive functions. There is substantial evidence that a "top-down" flow of neural activity (which means activity propagated from the frontal cortex to the sensory area) is more predictive of conscious awareness than a "bottom-up" flow of activity (228). The prefrontal cortex is not the only area.

In 2011, Graziano and Kastner proposed attention schema, the "theory of awareness." In this theory, the superior temporal sulcus and the temporal-parietal junctions are responsible for awareness. The same cortical mechanism is also used to attribute awareness of self; damage to these areas of the brain leads to deficits in consciousness, such as hemispatial neglect (229).

The most intriguing evidence was produced by Adenauer G. Casali in 2013. He and his colleagues proposed the perturbation complexity index (PCI). It is a measure of the algorithmic complexity of the electrophysiological response to transcranial magnetic stimulation. This measure was shown to be higher in individuals who are awake in REM sleep than in those who are in deep sleep or in a vegetative state, making it potentially useful and as a quantitative assessment of the consciousness state (230). Several studies have been conducted by neuroscientists in epilepsy. Patients who suffer from partial epileptic seizures experience an altered state of consciousness. Consciousness may be altered or lost. After seizure, they have difficulty focusing and shifting attention (231, 232). In addition, alcohol and drugs, like marijuana, LSD, and psychedelics, can cause an alteration in consciousness and even perceptions. Some individuals experience hallucinations; some users even experience mystical or spiritual feelings (233). There is an altered consciousness reported by researchers during meditation by the yogis (234).

For us who are in the medical field, treating patients' day in and day out, consciousness is whether a patient is oriented to date, time, person, and place. In patients where there is head trauma, brain disease, and damage due toxins and drugs, our goal is to find the cause and treat the cause. The medical focus is on the amount of consciousness a patient has. The level ranges from coma and brain death at one side and full alertness and purposeful responsiveness at other end (235). This gives us information to assess for administration of anesthesia or inducing medical coma (as in Joan Rivers's case). Any medical condition or conditions that inhibit consciousness are considered disorders of consciousness. Let me name a few of the disorders.

LOCKED-IN SYNDROME

The patient has awareness and meaningful response but has quadriplegia and pseudo-bulbar palsy. Brain stem death is irreversible, and there is a loss of integrative functions at some point in the dying process. This follows the loss of self-consciousness and personhood, self, or sense.

In a persistent vegetative state (PVS), there is a clinical manifestation of the higher brain structures, like the cerebral cortex, and possible damage to the hippocampus and thalamus. In such cases, their body and soul are alive because there is enough electric current and magnetic field (soul) generated by the rest of the nervous system, body, and body organs, but the magnetic energy of the soul is weak and cannot combine all the sensory input to give rise to consciousness. I would propose that if hearing connections or any other sensory connections are spared, these patients may be able to hear or see things around them without being able to communicate because of motor deficit. Is it possible that there may be neuroplasticity (generation of the connections of dendrites and axons) at a certain point and time? These patients may be able to revive and regain their soul's strength and attain individuality. It may be possible that with advancement in neurogeneration and stem-cell research, we may someday replace or regenerate neurons and thus give life to such people. But my view is clear that the soul does exist around their nervous system and body and can have life and death experiences, as reported in many cases and written about in books like "life after life." Cases mentioned in the literature that have drawn lot of attention are Karen Ann Quinlan (March 29, 1954 to June 11, 1985) and Tony Bland (September 21, 1970 to March 3, 1993).

Both cases lacked mental activity, like consciousness, dreams, thinking, or experience of sensations. This is due to the lower functioning of the brain working upon the death of the higher functioning of the brain (36). Brain death is usually pronounced when both higher (cortex) and lower (brain stem) are dead. The heart has its own brain, like the SA node and the AV node, but it still is connected to our brain through the autonomic nervous system (sympathetic and parasympathetic nervous system) to the cardiac center in the medulla oblongata and pons. The heartbeat produces a constant electric current and magnetic field energy twenty-four/seven, while we are wake or asleep. In the same way, our neurons have an innate property to constantly keep firing electric current, which is created by constant consciousness and sensory apparatus input. It is constantly modifying and recreating actions, thoughts, emotions, and the magnetic field and consciousness. Being conscious, we produce enough electric current to create magnetic fields that acts as a backup file for all the memories, impulses, and desires. In order to be conscious, we need energy. To have energy, it needs to be created. So who creates the energy? It is the constant firing of the neurons, like the cells of our heart. This is electric energy (like ECG and EEG), measured by an electrocardiogram (ECG) and electroencephalogram, in living human beings and animals.

Firing of the neurons	
Electrochemical energy	↑ ↓
Magnetic energy of the soul	↑ ↓
Consciousness and unconsciousness	↑ ↓
Self	↑ ↓

Stapas Bhattacharya, in his book *The Brain Stem: Brain Waves of Atman-Brahman*, recites the words of Michael Hancon (page 192):

> Few modern people believe that the brain is pervaded by some sort of mysterious "soul"; but how the neurons and synapses of the mind can generate subjective experiences of color, hate, fear and love is an utter mystery. In fact, many scientists believe it is the greatest mystery of all.

In order to prove my theory of magnetic soul, please pay attention to modern techniques and tests used in neuroscience, which with further advancement in the future, will be the source of improvement in my current existing theory. I will explain the most important ones and the easiest to understand.

CHAPTER 7

ELECTRICAL AND ELECTROMAGNETIC ASSESSMENTS OF THE BRAIN AND THE SOUL

With recent advancements and understanding of the brain functions, we have been able to diagnose neurological and mental illness better than we could a decade ago. There are many tools for us to investigate the functions of our nervous system. There is a long list of such tools and tests with long names, which appear to be beyond the comprehension of a nonscientific person. Long names and medical terminology is intimidating and cumbersome for nonmedical persons. So it is boring and not worth the while to venture out to understand. My main goal is to simplify them and make them understandable to a layperson. Don't let the long names scare you. You don't have to remember them. Just understand them, because my hypothesis about the soul is based on these scientific investigations, since I have claimed the soul to be based on electromagnetic mechanisms, which are described here.

ELECTROENCEPHALOGRAPHY (EEG)

This simple test has given us an enormous amount of information about the electrical impulses generated by our brain. It is primarily used to evaluate seizures. The latest version is called quantitative electroencephalography (QEEE) and cerebral evoke potential (EPs). We commonly use them for sleep studies and many other disorders as ordered by doctors and neuroscientists. Electrodes are applied to the scalp, and electrical waves are recorded by the computer. Reports are printed and read by the doctor. Why am I mentioning this? It provides scientific proof that the brain has electrical activity, which gives rise to the electromagnetic field, which I call the soul.

FUNCTIONAL MAGNETIC RESONANCE IMAGING (FMRI)

It measures brain activity by detecting changes associated with blood flow and neuronal activity. Blood flow to the brain is coupled with neuronal activity. Diffused MRI uses the change in magnetization between oxygen-rich and oxygen-poor blood as its basic measure. It was first invented by a Japanese neuroscientist. Why is this long name and complicated procedure even mentioned? Well, I have to mention it to support my hypothesis about the magnetic soul. In simple terms, I wrote that free iron increases the magnetic energy of the soul, while oxyhemoglobin does not affect the magnetic energy of the brain. It is my view that healthy blood flow to the brain produces enough magnetic energy to support the magnetic field created by billions of neurons. By this additional energy, our soul is strengthened.

CHRONIC THERAPEUTIC BRAIN STIMULATION

The exact mechanism of action of brain stimulation remains unknown. There is now sufficient evidence to suggest that brain stimulation exerts its effects via a number of different but interrelated mechanisms that come into play depending on the site being stimulated, the disease entity being treated, and the stimulation parameters used. The mechanisms of action can be classified into four categories: 1) inhibition of the target,

2) activation of the target, 3) combined inhibition and activation, and 4) disruption of pathological oscillation (329).

DEEP BRAIN STIMULATION (DBS)

It is used to have a functional inhibition of the target (330). Electrodes are implanted in the patient's brain as approved by the FDA. This technique is used in Parkinson's disease, dystonia, chronic pain disorder, and in some cases, multiple sclerosis and obsessive-compulsive disorder (331). Wayne K. Goodman from the Department of Psychiatry of Mount Sinai Hospital reported his findings in an article in the fall of 2016 that DBS treatment yields positive results in patients with obsessive-compulsive disorder in refractory patients.The patients who did not respond to medicine and therapy have showen improvement to DBS according to him, more than 60 percent of participants had significant improvement (335).

DEEP BRAIN TRANSCRANIAL MAGNETIC STIMULATION (TMS)

This technique is approved by the FDA. It involves passing an electric current through a coil placed over the head. The rapidly changing current creates a magnetic field, which passes unimpeded through the scalp and the skull and induces an electrical field to the cortex of the brain. This electrical field changes neuronal activities at the site of stimulation and within the interconnected neuronal networks. Repeated application is referred to as rTMS. The maximum electric field generated is located at the brain surface (332). The H-coil is a novel rTMS tool, which enables direct stimulation of deeper and larger brain volumes, potentially affecting extensive neuronal pathways, including deeper cortical regions, without a significant increase of the electric field induced in the superficial cortical layers (333, 334). Overall, studies published indicate that the deep TMS is generally safe and well tolerated by the majority of subjects. TMS can directly activate deep neurons in the prefrontal cortex of the brain (336). Though the exact mechanism of action is still unclear, some researchers have claimed that TMS can induce neuroplasticity and alteration in synaptic efficacy. This is a new treatment modality in major depression, bipolar disorder (337), post-traumatic stress disorder, schizophrenia, autism spectrum disorder, chronic pain disorder, migraine headaches, blepharospasm, Parkinson's disease, and smoking cessation. These studies are pure scientific proof that our brain and body operate on the fundamental principle of the magnetic soul. It is the supreme form or energy in our body, which operates in our entire life. Without this energy, life would be impossible. A healthy level of magnetic field is created by our brain, thus preventing the diseases mentioned above. Our soul is a healer by itself under normal circumstances.

VAGUS AND TRIGEMINAL NERVE STIMULATION

This technique is used as an adjunct therapy for reducing the frequency of seizures in adults and adolescents over the age of twelve (338). This modality of treatment is not frequently used in spite of the fact that the FDA has approved it. The brain regulates the normal functions of our organs, especially the heart through the vagus nerve, via electric current regulation. The heart has its own electric current system, as evidenced by ECG. The vagus nerve branch to the heart, when stimulated, can cause a decrease in the frequency of the heartbeat. Heart pacemakers and defibrillators are based on electric stimulation or inhibition of heart rate to treat arrhythmias or heart blocks. Another important aspect that the cardiac pacemaker bypasses is heartrate variability (HRV). HRV is a noninvasive measure of the vagus-sympathetic modulation of the heart that can predict morbidity and mortality (heart disease, coronary artery disease, postinfarction, and sudden cardiac death) (339). The cardiac pacemaker is probably the most prevalent of present bioelectromagnetic treatment.

BIOPHYSICAL STIMULATION FOR BONE HEALING

Many doctors have found that electrical, magnetic, and mechanical stimulation can increase osteogenesis (growth of bone cells) (340). These methods are approved by the FDA. There are too many studies to mention here. In recent years, there has been a growing interest in treating cancer tumors by electrochemotherapy, using magnetic fields applied to cancer tumors. Studies show different tissues respond differently, depending on the structure of the tissue (341). Further research is in progress to study this field of science.

ELECTROPORATION AND ELECTROCHEMOTHERAPY (EP)

This is also known as electropermeablization. The basic principle is to increase the permeability of the cell membrane so that foreign DNA could be transferred to a cell for gene therapy. Even some drugs are delivered into cancer tumor cells. This is accomplished by exposing the cell membrane to electric fields of sufficient magnitude and for a certain time. EP has proven to be highly effective in increasing transmembrane flux by two to four orders of magnitude without significant side effects (342). I could postulate based on this technique that the magnetic field can cause such mechanisms to play on a natural basis, whenever the body and soul needs our body to function. This could explain mutation on a microlevel and evolution on a macrolevel. Our body produces enough electric and magnetic fields to create electroporation day in and day out when needed to prevent diseases or to incorporate foreign DNA into our cells, like that from bacteria or amyloidal bodies and viruses.

MAGNETOENCEPHALOGRAPHY (MEG)

The main use of MEG is to study the functioning of the brain by measuring magnetic fields. We use a magnetometer and gradiometer. There are two types of MEG recording brain waves: First is evoked or event-related fields. These are used for measuring motor, visual, auditory, and sensory fields and cognitive tasks. The second is resting state or spontaneous activity. It is used to study seizure activities, brain maturity, consciousness, and brain networks (255). The simple explanation is that these measure magnetic fields generated by the electric current generated by neuronal activities and by the actions of our body. Professor Abraham R. Liboff was the pioneer who introduced the importance of the extremely low frequency (ELF) magnetic field technique and its biological effects on human beings. He called it the electrobiomagnetic field (EMF). It is quite obvious that a living creature is an electromagnetic system and is able to respond to electric and magnetic stimuli based on the principles of physics. Based on this principle, I do acknowledge that we human beings are able to function by the magnetic fields generated by the entire brain and our body. I name this form of energy as the soul of our body.

ULTRASOUNDS AND DOPPLER SYSTEMS

These are frequently used for diagnostic and for investigative purposes to assess abdominal lesions and measure the blood flow in the arteries. Recent developments have shown that ultrasounds can penetrate the skull by using the focused ultrasound (mRgFus) (259).

ELECTROCONVULSIVE THERAPY

This is a very well-studied modality of treatment in psychiatric disorders; the name *convulsive therapy* is pretty scary. The Nobel laureate Paul Greengard suggested changing the name to *electrocortical* therapy. I absolutely agree and support his suggestion, to ovoid the bad concept of convulsion (seizure), which is frightening and creates doubt in some patients. Lucio Bini and Ugo Cerletti were able to use electricity to induce seizure. In 1938, they were able to treat a patient with delusions and an incoherent patient with ECT. The practice of ECT also benefitted from the controlled-trials methodology, which demonstrated its safety and efficacy, and from refinements made in diagnostic systems through the process of informed consent. Hungarian neuroscientist Ladislas von Eeduna made the observation that the brain of epileptics had greater than normal numbers of glial cells, where as those of schizophrenics had fewer, and he hypothesized that there might be a biological antagonism between convulsions and schizophrenia. Neurons maintain a resting potential across the plasma membrane and may propagate an action potential asynchronously. A seizure occurs when a large percentage of neurons fire action potential (electric current) in unison. Such rhythmical changes entertain neighboring neurons to propagate the seizure activity across the cortex and into deeper structures. It eventually engulfs the entire brain in high-voltage synchronous neuronal firing. There is increased blood flow and use of blood glucose and oxygen after ECT application to the patients, as shown in positron emission tomography (PET). ECT itself acts as an anticonvulsant because its administration increases the seizure threshold. The mechanism of action of ECT has focused on changes in neurotransmitter receptors and, recently, changes in the secondary messenger system. Virtually every neurotransmitter system is affected by ECT, but a series of ECTs result in down regulation of postsynaptic b-adrenergic receptors. The same mechanism takes place with all antidepressants. There are changes in serotonergic, muscarinic, cholinergic, and dopaminergic systems.This modality of treatment is used in patients with refractory response to medication in Psychotic depression and other psychotic disorders.

POSITRON-EMISSION TOMOGRAPHY (PET)

PET can detect the regional blood flow to the parts of the brain. Blood carries glucose, which brain cells thrive on. They consume more when they are active. Glucose metabolism increases with neuronal activity. By detecting greater blood flow, PET infers which regions are active and nonfunctional because of disease.

Recent studies have raised several questions about ECT in the treatment of psychiatric patients, such as microscopic changes in the brain structures. In animals, after application of ECT, there is synaptic plasticity in the hippocampus, the sprouting of mossy fibers, an increase of connectivity in prefrontal pathways, the promotion of neurogenesis, and the suppression of apoptosis, which happens in healthy human beings on a regular basis. ECT is indicated in major depression with or without psychosis, especially in treatment-resistant patients. Other indications include bipolar disorder with depression, catatonic schizophrenia, schizoaffective disorder, Parkinson's disease, neuroleptic malignant disorder (side effects of antipsychotic medication), atypical psychosis, women with pregnancy who do not respond to medication, and older patients who cannot tolerate medication. The procedure used to be performed by placing electrodes on the bifronto-temporal area of the skull. Now a day's electrodes are placed on the right side of the skull to prevent memory loss. The electric stimulus should be enough to produce seizure. Some readers of this book may wonder why I am writing all this. I am writing this is because man-made external electric current applied to the brain can treat patients with psychiatric illnesses. So what about normal individuals? In normal individuals, there is enough and appropriate electric current generated to function normally. All the changes mentioned are present in the neuronal system of our brain, which generates enough magnetic field when needed for our higher neuronal functions. It is available to our brain for normal functions and to bring on microscopic changes, as described above. I call this magnetic field a soul. It is present in our body until we die. This also gives a scientific proof to my hypothesis of the magnetic soul.

The list goes on and on. My interest will be to explain fMRI, ECOG, and MEG. Japanese researcher Seiji Ogawa and his colleagues invented functional magnetic resonance imaging (fMRI), a powerful and a harmless technique that does not require the use of any injection or medicine. It allows us to visualize the activity of the whole brain (237). It is based on the coupling between the brain cells and blood vessels. Whenever neuronal connections of dendrites and synapses increase their activities, glial cells, which surround the neurons, sense the surge in their activities. To complete this activity, there is a need for heightened energy. Thus, arteries open up, and blood flow is increased to the neurons. This means an increase in red blood cells, carrying hemoglobin. The fRMI detects the physical properties of the hemoglobin that conveys the oxygen. The hemoglobin without oxygen acts as a small magnet, while the oxyhemoglobin does not. Functional magnetic resonance machines are powerful magnets and are capable of picking up any change (even the smallest) in the magnetic field of the brain (neurons), which gives us information about the change in the magnetic field in relation to the internal or external stimulus. The activity of neurons is picked up by fMRI even at a millimeter resolution up to several times per second. The fRMI is not able to pick up precisely the time of the electric current at the synapses. For that, we use EEG, which gives us a digital recording of the brain's activity with millisecond resolution of the electric activity in the whole brain. These investigations give credit to my hypothesis that blood iron in the arteries and veins in between the neurons adds to the magnetic energy of the brain, in addition to providing nutrition and oxygen to our brain. Thus magnetic soul is strengthened to have higher functions of the brain as discussed earlier in the book (Ibid 238). EEG and fMRI are scientific proof of the magnetic energy of our soul. In addition to these tools, we still have magneto encephalography (MEG), which shows us ultraprecise recordings of the minuscule magnetic waves that accompany the discharge of currents in cortical neurons. Both EEG and MEG can be used together to measure the electric waves and magnetic waves by placing sensors on the scalp (skull) (192). These are noninvasive interventions. This procedure and mechanism adds to my hypothesis of the magnetic soul, which is the binding force for our all sensory stimuli to produce desired action by humans and other living souls (animals) around us.

The techniques used for brain imaging have led to a breakthrough in consciousness research, which gives me the opportunity to explain my views and strengthens the validity of the relationship of the soul and consciousness. Though I do admit a lot of research needs to be done to resolve the mystic notion of the soul, this will resolve the philosophical, religious, and mystic notions of the soul in the future. I am sure my critics will raise questions beyond my imagination, but I would love that because curiosity, criticism, caution, creation, and commitment. Neuroscientists should use the five C's, rather than give cold shoulder to old notions and beliefs.

I concur with the candid and scientific theories of consciousness and unconsciousness by Deheaene after using brain-imaging techniques and the techniques described earlier. He called it a "signature of consciousness." He describes a reliable marker that the stimulus can propagate deeply into the cortex; this brain activity is strongly amplified when the threshold for awareness is posed. It then invades many additional regions, leading to a sudden ignition of parietal and prefrontal circuits. In EEG, conscious access appears as a late slow wave, called a P3 wave. This event emerges as late as one-third of a second after the stimulus. Our consciousness lags behind the external world, as described by Benjamin Libet and John Daylon. Their extensive work also explains the delay in our actions and the plan of the action. Placing electrodes deep inside the brain, we see there is a late and sudden burst of high-frequency oscillation and synchronization of information exchanges across distant brain regions. All these events provide reliable indexes of conscious processing.

TRANSCRANIAL MAGNETIC STIMULUS

I would not close this chapter without describing transcranial magnetic stimulus (TMS). This is not the end of my proof of the magnetic soul in the brain. In fact, it is the start of the new theory of the magnetic soul. This discovery nails down my hypothesis that the electric current in the neurons generates a magnetic field, which is the soul, to explain the mysteries and myths of our brain's functions. In brief, we use the term *TMS*. TMS is a noninvasive, painless, and focused stimulation of the awake brain of the individuals (239) when repeated pulses are applied. (240). We can apply a maximum 50 Hz of magnetic pulse to our scalp, since there is the danger of seizure activity. TMS can focally stimulate the cortex by creating a dynamic magnetic field generated by brief but powerful electric current passed through an electromagnetic coil (241). This localized pulse magnetic field over the surface of the head depolarizes underlined superficial neurons (242), which then induces electric current in the brain. That is why at times we call it "electrodeless electric stimulation" (243). Magnetic fields produced by this are integral in transmitting energy across the skull close to the order of two tesla. This rapidly changing magnetic field then travels across the scalp and skull and induces an electric field within the brain. The new version if TMS is sTMS, synchronized TMS. It generates a fluctuation in the magnetic field. TMS only activates the magnetic field in the cortex; deeper parts of the brain are not activated. Because of the massive cortical neuronal mass, it is difficult to penetrate deeper into the brain. But neuroscientists in San Jose, California, and Israel have developed TMS that can reach deeper. Now, using other techniques like fMRI, PET scan, and SPECT, we have been able to activate the cortical-limbic loop (244). We still are not sure how these mechanisms work therapeutically. But there is evidence that TMS can increase the connectivity of axons and dendrites and plasticity (86, 171). Does that mean that the magnetic soul can cause an increase in dendrites and in the number of synapses under normal circumstances, whenever there is a learning process or during development of our brain? If so, this will be a remarkable discovery. If not, I think we neuroscientists must pay attention and increase research in this field, which is still in its infancy though it was pioneered by S. P. Thompson in 1910 and by C. E. Magnusson and H. C. Stevens in 1911 (192). Each individual needs a different strength of electric energy to produce the effect. TMS across different individuals is to determine each person's motor threshold (MT). MT is commonly defined as the minimum amount of electricity needed to produce movement in the contralateral thumb.

TMS was approved by the FDA for treatment of depression, which I will discuss in detail. It is important to understand the mechanism of action of TMS in order to validate our theory of the magnetic soul. It could be grouped according to the time effects: immediate, intermediate, and long term.

The immediate effects of TMS are thought to be from direct excitation of inhibitory or excitatory neurons. There is evidence that different frequencies, intensities, and coil angles can execute different elements (cell bodies) axons, interneurons, and neurons projecting to different parts of the brain. Epilepsy, which is caused by the sudden electric discharge from a group of neurons to the rest of the brain, can cause complex smells, sounds, and memories. For the intermediate effects of TMS (seconds to minutes), some suggest that there may be a transient change in gamma amino butyric acid (GABA) and glutamate. The exact mechanism is still unknown. T. Wu and M. Somme have suggested that chronic low-frequency stimulation of the motor center can produce inhibitory intermediate terms, while high-frequency stimulation can produce intermediate-term excitatory effects, lasting for several minutes (245). Current studies show that depressed patients treated with TMS have shown increased activity in the cingulate gyrus and limbic system (246). Though the exact mechanism of action of TMS remains incomplete and not well understood. Some claim it increases blood flow, as measured by fMRI (247) and causes the release of dopamine in the caudate nucleus (248).

As described in the book about Dr. Penfield, our cortical microcircuits contain a dormant record of the major and minor events of our lives, ready to be awakened by brain stimulation. Whether it could be done by TMS remains unanswered. Brain mapping suggests that each part of the brain and cortex holds its own specialized piece of knowledge. Stimulating the parietal lobe may cause a feeling of vertigo and even the bizarre out-of-body experience of levitating to the ceiling and looking down on one's own body (249). Michael Desmurget, in his neurosurgical procedures, demonstrated when he stimulated the promoter cortex at a relatively low threshold during surgery that the patient's arm moved, but the person denied anything had happened (she could not see her arm). When the patient had a conscious urge to move, she claimed her arm moved even though it was stationary. Deheaene explained that brain stimulation demonstrates a causal relationship between cortical activity and conscious experience (191). It appears that TMS at different frequencies has divergent effects on the brain activity compared to ECT. TMS has different mechanisms. ECT shuts off global and regional activity. TMS, used with fMRI, shows higher activity in the frontal lobe in depressed patients while using PET (PET scan). Studies conducted in Scotland and Australia show that changes take place in the lateral prefrontal cortex, cingulate gyrus, and limbic system (251, 251). As we progress in this area of research, there will be many other mechanisms and treatment potentials for TMS. My main thrust is that if TMS, which is a magnetic field applied to our brain, can cause and initiate stimulation of neurons and increase the electric activity, then the magnetic soul can cause electric discharge and activate the neurons in the brain to attain the normal function of human beings and other living creatures. It raises a burning question in my brain. Are all psychiatric and psychological disorders due to irregularities or malfunctioning in our magnetic soul, which in turn cause neuroelectric and neurochemical transmitters to malfunction, resulting in disturbed behavior? In brief, I will mention current uses of TMS in psychiatry among many of my colleagues:

- Depression (major depression)
- Addiction
- Obsessive-compulsive disorder (254)
- Tinnitus
- Stroke recovery
- Autism

(MEG) MAGNETOENCEPHALOGRAPHY

This technology is used to study the brain functions by measuring the magnetic field of the brain. Again, I do not want to get into details of this instrument or the mechanisms; my goal is to prove to my readers that this is another feather in our cap to say that our magnetic soul exists and is in full control of our life. Magnetometers and gradiometers are used in this technique. There are two types of MEG recording for brain waves.

1. Evoked or event-related fields. It is directly stimulation-related activity. These are commonly used for motor, sensory, visual, and auditory mapping. Event-related fields are commonly used for cognitive tasks.
2. Resting-state activity or spontaneous activity is used mainly in detecting seizure focus and studying brain maturity, consciousness, and brain networks (255). The basic function is to measure the electromagnetic field generated by the electric current produced by neuronal activities in our brain and in the rest of the body.

Professor Abraham R. Liboff was a pioneering American scientist who introduced the importance of the extremely low frequency (ELF) electromagnetic field and its biological effects in human beings. He called it bioelectromagnetism (256, 257). Liboff reached an inevitable conclusion: that living organisms react to imbalances produced by quasi-systemic electric changes, while also striving for their own well-being either by generating electromagnetic field (EMF) or through exposure to exogenous EMFs of extremely low frequency and intensity (ELF). Liboff introduced the concept that a living system is an electromagnetic system and as such is able to respond to electric and magnetic stimuli, according to the principles of physics.

I do acknowledge the fact that our soul is a purely biological magnetic system that controls our lives, behaviors, and actions. There are numerous techniques developed in modern neuroscience. I feel it is important to mention those that are based on electric stimulation, for example, deep brain stimulation (DBS), which is used in extreme cases of Parkinsonism with reasonable improvement. I met one of my relatives who had a devastating malfunctioning due to Parkinsonism. He had DBS treatment, and while he visited me, he was able to play cards, walk, talk, and comprehend everything we discussed. I tested him for his control of movement and found excellent coordination and power in his muscles. The shaking of his hands was minimal, It is an invasive procedure requiring surgical implantation of a device to the targeted area of the brain. DBS electrodes deliver high-frequency electric pulses to anatomically selected areas of the brain to within millimeter precision to influence neuronal function and signals. The ability to electrically stimulate the brain has provided significant benefits for neurological patients (258). In addition, we currently use ultrasound and Doppler for various investigations and diagnostic purposes, including various abdominal tumors, and to measure the blood flow from our arteries. Heyningen and colleagues (259) have developed a technique for precise targeting of focused ultrasound (mRgFus). The exact results are still not understood. One encouraging fact is that ultrasound can penetrate the skull with such precision. Research of such nature may be used in psychiatric disorders (260). There is evidence in this research project that there is mood elevation in depressed patients. The future will tell the tale of this research project. The brain is a highly specialized organ with electrochemical activity and connectivity. Brain functions can be altered in disease states because of disturbed neural functions of the brain network area. Neuromodulation is defined as the therapeutic modification of the brain activity by altering neurotransmission using magnetic or electric energy, as described in detail earlier (382).

Dr. Khurshid describes magnetic seizure therapy (MST). In MST, a high-frequency, magnetic pulse sufficient to induce seizure is used for resistant depression. These magnetic pulses are not affected by skull/scalp resistance. The electrical fields generated in the brain are more focal. MST has been shown to have no cognitive side effects (memory loss as in ECT) in preliminary studies (383). We need more studies in the future to formulate the treatment of mental illnesses.

MAGNETIC FIELD OF SOLAR, EARTH, AND LIVING BEINGS

Orthodox neuroscientists will discard any hypothesis or any theory created by scientists in the area of interaction between the magnetic field of living creatures and existing magnetic fields created by the solar system and Mother Earth. In spite of the fact that these neuroscientists bathe every second of their lives in this magnetic field of the earth and the solar system. Let us give them a chance to think and work on this aspect of living beings, including humans, animals, plants, and so on. There are numerous studies and lots of research done by various scientists. I will recommend a chapter in the book edited by Paul J. Rosch, MD, *Bioelectromagnetic and Subtle Energy Medicine*, chapter 37, written by Rollin McCarty and Annette Deyhle (86, 411). Most of the information is already published on www.heartmath.org, under the headlines of global coherence research. The science of interconnectivity theory is based on the principle of the existence of a global information field, connecting all living systems and contributing to all types of global consciousness. It is a fact and real that every cell in our body is bathed in an external and internal environment of fluctuating invisible magnetic forces that can affect virtually every cell and circuit in our biological system. Therefore, numerous physiological rhythms in humans and animals are global collective behaviors. They are not only synchronized with solar and geomagnetic activity, but disruption in these fields can create adverse effects on human health and behavior. These are between the human nervous system and resonance geomagnetic frequencies called Schumann resonances. This was first identified by Winfield Schumann, a German physicist, in 1952 (261).

The global coherence interconnectivity (GCI) hypothesis suggests that humans' and animals' health, cognitive functions, emotions, and behaviors are affected by planetary magnetic and energetic fields.

The earth's magnetic field is a carrier of biologically relevant information that connects all living systems. Thus, we can affect the global information field.

Large numbers of people creating a heart-centered state of care, love, and compassion will generate a more coherent field environment that can benefit others and help offset the current planetary-wide discord and incoherence.

As described in this hypothesis, human emotions and consciousness interact with each other, and information is encoded into the magnetic field, which is distributed globally. GCI promotes a belief that there is a feedback loop between human beings and the earth's energy and magnetic systems. It is suggested that this encoded information is communicated nonverbally between people at a subconscious level, which links all living beings. Magnetic fields act as a carrier wave for this information, which can influence all living systems, positively or negativity, within the field environment as well as in our collective consciousness.

If this belief is correct, then the magnetic soul should communicate with the global magnetic field and share information both ways, which means our magnetic soul is able to receive information and give information back to the global magnetic field of other humans and nonhumans. I have already described how we love each other and understand each other without verbal communication with animals and human beings. It raises questions.

1. If information already exists in the form of the global magnetic field and the individual magnetic soul, then should we be able to anticipate at times what is going to happen next?

2. Do some of us humans have highly developed magnetic fields in our brains or bodies, which help us to invent and create new things? Like science or a new business?

3. Are these brains able to tap into the existing knowledge and put it into action? Can I support this logic?

Newton did not invent gravity; it existed before he found it. Did $E=mc^2$ exist before Albert Einstein stumbled onto it and found it to put it into practice? The knowledge and information on Google existed and inventors put it together on search engines. Money existed way before Warren Buffett became a billionaire; he found how to get rich and did not invent or print the dollars. Did we learn from birds how to fly and then build airplanes? Light existed way before we found it; we did not invent it. Did language exist before we found it, created the alphabets to write it, and learned to speak it? Math existed way before we found it and learned it. The universe existed way before we realized it does exist. Music, the sound waves, existed before we stumbled on it. Did religions exist way before? All we did is put this in perspective for believers and followers. Old Hindu Rishis and yogis attested to that. They believed the Upanishads existed way before they were written and presented to human beings, though they did not claim them to be a magnetic global energy; they existed in the cosmos. The list can go on and on. My hypothesis or theory of the magnetic soul does concur with the findings of GCI.

The Institute of Heart Math (IHM) has identified a psychophysiological state that they call *heart coherence* (262, 263). The human body is designed to adapt to daily and seasonal climatic and geomagnetic variations. Disruption in solar and geomagnetic fields can cause adverse effects on human health and behavior, like a decrease in serotonin and melatonin levels, which affects many physiological functions. Some scientists claim that there is a melatonin and serotonin imbalance during increased solar and geomagnetic activity, which affects many physiological functions, for example, blood pressure, breathing, the immune system, cardiac and neurological processes (266), heart rate, and neurological, cardiopulmonary, and reproductive functions (267). Geomagnetic storms are also related to EEG changes in our brain, hormone responses, and even death. Increased solar activity can disturb the biological rhythm of humans and exacerbate existing diseases. There is an increase in heart attacks and death (268). There is an increase of 30 to 80 percent in hospital admissions for cardiovascular diseases and a higher rate of admission in hospitals for depression, mental disorders, and psychiatric conditions; higher suicide and homicide rates; and more traffic accidents. The birth rate drops and mortality increases. Migraine headaches increase in frequency (269). A study carried out in India on animals and humans (PC) (270) showed changes in the electrophysiology and neurochemical and biochemical parameters. The subjects experienced uneasiness, confusion, and restlessness and a lack of a sense of well-being when subjected to the pulsating fields. Some complained of headache (270). In an article about global coherence research, it is noted that, historically, many cultures believed their collective behavior could be affected by the sun and other external cycles and influences. Their belief has proven to be true. On a large social scale, increased violence, crime rate, social unrest, revolution, and frequency of terrorist attacks have been linked to the solar cycles and the resulting disturbances in the geomagnetic field (261, 4–5).

The first evidence of this was provided by Alexander Tchijevsky, a Russian scientist who noticed that more severe battles in World War I occurred during peak sunspot periods. Solar activity has not only been associated with social unrest; it has also been related to the periods of greatest flourishing, with definitive spurts in architecture, arts, and science and positive social change. Such positive changes can affect political, economic, medical, and educational systems, as well as people's relationships in their workplaces, homes, and communities. The question I have is how is it possible? It does not happen out of nothing. There is a sender and a receiver. My view is there is a clear interaction between the magnetic soul of living creatures (humans and animals) and the external magnetic field of the solar and earth's magnetic field. It could have a reinforcing force for our brain, which can influence our behavior, thinking, emotions, feelings, and consciousness. McCarty has shown in his laboratory that the heart's electromagnetic field can be detected by nearby animals or the nervous systems of other people (271). Our magnetic emotional energy has an enormous ability to affect other subjects without even communicating with them. This is radiated from the human heart and the magnetic soul. When we are in a coherent state, we are more sensitive to detecting the information in the field radiated by others (271). This has been explained in the chapter on the secondary soul, the heart. Kemper and Shaltout found significant changes in receiver's autonomic nervous system (272). There is growing evidence that a magnetic energy field forms in a group of people who communicate among each other. This energy connects all the members of the group. We have a body of evidence; for example, all the followers of any religion have a cohesive force that brings them together for a common belief or a common cause.

1. Christians attending a Sunday church service are more cohesive and have an understanding of each other compared to those who do not.
2. Hindus going on pilgrimage and bathing in the Ganges share more common understandings and a liking for each other.

3. Muslims attending the prayers in mosques have more common understanding and liking for each other. There is a cohesiveness of the magnetic soul of the brain. They are more tolerant and compassionate to each other.
4. A peaceful march of Dr. Mather Luther King Jr. created a common energy and solution to the common cause of African Americans.
5. Mahatma Gandhi's peaceful march of people caused a forceful magnetic energy for the freedom of India from British rule. This common and forceful magnetic energy created a collective magnetic force that led to the freedom of India.
6. The inauguration of the president of the United States of America in Washington, DC, creates an enormous magnetic force, which becomes a common force for those who attend when the president delivers the inaugural speech.

This makes me believe that when there is a strike against authorities or by terrorists, the same common magnetic energy creates the destructive behavior, belief, or emotions, resulting in mass killing and destruction. The tragedy of 9/11 could be explained by twenty-one hijackers with common, collective, cohesive magnetic soul energy to create destruction and the deaths of innocent people in the United States of America.

Michael Persinger, in his studies, examined the effect of the magnetic field on brain function and information transfer in humans. His claim indicates that applying an external field can induce an altered state of consciousness. His theory suggests that the space occupied by the geomagnetic field can store information related to brain activity and that this information can be accessed by the human brain (273). He added that the earth's magnetic field can act as a carrier for information between individuals, which could be shared and decoded. It has been further suggested that the human brain and heart frequencies overlap the earth's magnetic resonance, which is a receiver of biologically relevant information. They can also couple with earth's magnetic fields and thus feed information into the global field environment. This information creates curiosity in my soul. Does it mean that when we die, our magnetic soul becomes part of the earth's magnetic field? Then does it justify the Hindu philosophy that our soul becomes part of the super soul and thus attains moksha (freedom)? Does it also explain the Hindu belief of reincarnation and the resurrection of Christian philosophy? Being a scientific person, I do not believe that there is reincarnation, but the union of our magnetic soul with the super soul (geomagnetic field) is a possible event after death. What purpose does it serve? I do not know. Does it support my view of a "mindless body and endless soul"? Yes it does but, I would leave this question to be answered by the future scientists and my readers.

The geomagnetic field is influenced by the sun's and moon's rotations, solar flares, and possibly by interplanetary influences. Animals and birds can detect the earth's magnetic field and use it to navigate during migration. It has been shown that cows and deer, when grazing, tend to align their bodies north to south in response to the earth's magnetic field.

I assume, as we progress, there will be acknowledgment of our magnetic soul, which functions as a supreme commander in chief to regulate and combine all stimuli, both from inside and outside of our bodies.

Sodi (275, 276), who reported that the electromagnetic field could remarkably increase the growth of plants, suggested that his was another way to stimulate ATP synthesis. Sodi investigated this by preparing two small tumblers in which he put five dried beans and a fistful of soil. One was exposed to a pulsating electromagnetic field for five days. Highly reputable fertilizer was added to the other tumbler, according to the prescribed instructions. He was surprised to find that the stem of the plant subjected to the electromagnetic field increased much more than the fertilized plant's. Long-term studies showed that the fertilizer was effective in promoting increased growth but not to the extent achieved with pulsating electromagnetic fields. This experiment supports the theory that plants and trees do respond to the electromagnetic fields of the earth and solar system like humans and animals do (277).

Western scientists have rejected the notion of subtle energy in the living body, while Eastern philosophers and scientists believe in subtle energy in the living bodies. Hindus call it paranas and China's sage Lao Tsu called it qi (chi) energy. He was known as the father of Taoism. He describes this energy as follows:

- Look. It cannot be seen. It is beyond form.
- Listen. It cannot be heard. It is beyond sound.
- Grasp. It cannot be held. It is intangible.

NOTES

1. Saraswati, Chandrasekharendra. The Vedas. Bombay: Bharatiya Vida Haven, Havana's Book University, 2014, 400–407.

2. Eknath, Easwaran, and Michael N. Nagler. The Upanishads. Petaluma, CA: Nilgiri Press, 1987. Introduced and translated by Blue Mountain Center of Meditation, 2007.

3. Eknath, Easwaran. The Bhagavad Gita. Petaluma, CA: Nilgiri Press. Introduced and translated by Blue Mountain Center of Meditation, 2007.

4. Https. /Wikipedia. Foundation.org/wiki/Resolution "Encyclopedia of Soul." Wikimedia Foundation. Accessed April 5, 2016.

5. http://www.yoga-philosophy.com/2003.

6. Chopra, Deepak. How to Know God: The Soul's Journey into the Mystery of Mysteries. New York: Crown, 2000, 275–288.

7. Susan D. Gillespie, PhD, RPA, professor of anthropology, University of Florida, Gainesville.

8. Utley, Robert M., and Ellen Nanney. The Story of the West: A History of the American West and Its People. London: DK Pub., 2003.

9. Carlson, Paul Howard. The Plains Indians. Library of Congress Cataloging Publication Data, 1940.

10. Carlson, Paul Howard. The Plains Indians. College Station: Texas A & M UP, 1998.

11. Villoldo, Alberto. One Spirit Medicine: Ancient Ways to Ultimate Wellness. Hay House, 2015, 122.

12. Esposito, John L. The Oxford History of Islam. New York, NY: Oxford UP, 1999.

13. Esposito, John L. Islam: *The Straight Path*. 3rd ed. New York: Oxford UP, 1998, print, 73, 74, 12.

14. "Soul in Islamic Philosophy." Soul in Islamic Philosophy. Web.

15. www.itonline.org/shen/chapl.htm.

16. Wong, Eva. *Taoism: An Essential Guide*. Boston: Shambhala, 2011, print.

17. Ingerman, Sandra, and Henry Barnard Wesselman. *Awakening to the Spirit World: The Shamanic Path of Direct Revelation*. Boulder, CO: Sounds True, 2010.

18. "Rev. Criss Ittermann, Life Facilitator / Liberated Life Coaching." Rev. Criss Ittermann, Life Facilitator / Liberated Life Coaching. Web.

19. Sethi, Atul. "Rise of the Shamans." *Times of India*. N.P. Aug. 21, 2011. Web.

20. Theo, Peter. "A Brief Guide to Shamanism." petertheoaeffcu.org.

21. Judith, Anodea. *Wheels of Life: A User's Guide to the Chakra System*. St. Paul, MN: Llewellyn Publications, 1987.

22. Zack, Naomi. *The Handy Philosophy Answer Book*. Detroit: Visible Ink, 2010.

23. Pickren, Wade E., and Philip G. Zimbardo. *The Psychology Book: From Shamanism to Cutting-edge Neuroscience: 250 Milestones in the History of Psychology*. New York, NY: Sterling, 2014, 28, 38, 42, 44, 54, 80.

24. Stroll, Avrum. *Did My Genes Make Me Do It? And Other Philosophical Dilemmas*. Oxford: One World, 2004, 41–79.

25. Percival, Harold W. Thinking and Destiny: Being the Science of Man. Library of Congress, 47–1811 with printing, 1981, 22.

26. Martin, Raymond, and John Barresi. *The Rise and Fall of Soul and Self: An Intellectual History of Personal Identity*. New York: Columbia UP, 2006.

27. Goetz, Stewart, and Charles Taliaferro. A *Brief History of the Soul*. Malden, MA: Wiley-Blackwell, 2011.

28. Cottingham, John. *Descartes*. New York: Routledge, 1999.

29. *Descartes: Selected Philosophical Writings*. New York, NY: Cambridge UP, 1988, 218–230.

30. Shorto, Russell. *Descartes' Bones: A Skeletal History of the Conflict between Faith and Reason*. New York, NY: Doubleday Group, 2008.

31. Shaddock, Benjamin J., Harold I. Kaplan, and Virginia A. Shaddock. *Kaplan and Shaddock's Synopsis of Psychiatry: Behavioral*

Sciences / Clinical Psychiatry. 11th ed. Philadelphia: Wolter Kluwer / Lippincott Williams & Wilkins, 2007. Print, 535.

32. Stock, Brian. *Augustine the Reader.* N.P.: Harvard UP, 1998. Print, 10, 11, 15, 16.

33. Ley, D. Forbes. *The Best Seller.* Newport Beach, CA: Sales Success, 1990, 53.

34. Zukav, Gary, and Simon Schuster. *The Seat of the Soul.* N.P.: Fireside Book, 1990. Print, 30, 31.

35. Eagleman, David. *The Brain: The Story of You.* New York, NY: Pantheon Book, 2015.

36. Jeeves, Malcolm A. *From Cells to Souls, and Beyond: Changing Portraits of Human Nature.* Grand Rapids, MI: W. B. Erdmans, 2004. Print, 17.

37. Idris, Zamzuri, Mustapha Muzaimi, Rahman Izaini Ghani, Badrisyah Idris, Regunath Kandasamy, and Jafri M. Abdullah. "Principles, Anatomical Origin and Applications of Brainwaves: A Review, Our Experience and Hypothesis Related to Microgravity and the Question on Soul." *Journal of Biomedical Science and Engineering* 7 no. 8 (2014): 435–45.

38. Woods, Tiger. *How I Play Golf.* New York: Warner, 2001. Print.

39. Carpenter, R. H. S., and Benjamin Redid. *Neurophysiology: A Conceptual Approach.* London: Hodder Arnold, 2012. Print.

40. Waxman, Stephen G. *Clinical Neuroanatomy.* 27th ed. New York: Lange Medical / McGraw-Hill, Medical Pub. Division, 2013. Print.

41. Penfield, Wilder. *The Mystery of the Mind: A Critical Study of Consciousness and the Human Brain.* Princeton, NJ: Princeton UP, 1978. Print.

42. Eccles, John. *Brain, Speech and Consciousness: The Understanding of the Brain.* N.P.: McGraw Hill Book, 1973. Print, 189.

43. Jones, W. H. S., and E. Withington, Eds. *The Sacred Disease.* 4th ed. Vol. 2. N.P.: Loeb Classical Library. Cambridge: Harvard UP, n.d. Print, 127–185.

44. Jackson, J. H. *On the Anatomical, Physiological, and Pathological Investigation of Epilepsies.* Rep. N.3 p. 315 n. p. 339, 1873. West Lunatic Asylum Medical Report. Web.

45. Magoun, H. W. "An Ascending Reticular Activating System in the Brain Stem." A Res. Nervous and Mental Disease Proceeding 3 (1950): 480–92.

46. Moruzzi, Giuseppe, and Horace Winchell Magoun. "Brain Stem Reticular Formation and Activation of the EEG Electroenceph." *Clin. Neurophysiology.* S.l.: S.n., 1949. Print, 1: 455–473.

47. Pavlov, I. P. *An Investigation of the Physiological Activity of the Cerebral Cortex.* London: Oxford UP, 1960. Print.

48. Fleming, G. W. T. H. "Diencephalic Autonomic Epilepsy." *Arch. of Neur. and Psychiatric.* (August 1929). Penfield, W. *British Journal of Psychiatry* 76, no. 312 (1930): 358–74.

49. Jasper, H. H. *Epilepsy, Neurophysiology, and Some Brain Mechanisms.* 1969. Print.

50. Penfield, Wilder, and Joseph Evans. "The Frontal Lobe in Man: A Clinical Study of Maximum Removals." Brain 58.1 (1935): 115–38.

51. Sherrington, Charles Scott. "Man on His Nature." Cambridge U, 1940. The Gifford Lectures 1937–1938, 74.

52. E. Hamilton, and H. Cairns. Translated by W. K. C. Cuthrie Phaedo. Translated by H. Trednnick Phaedrus. Translated by Hackforth. Theatetus translated by F. M. Conford. Timaeus translated by B. Jowett. Princeton: Princeton University Press, 1961.

53. Brann, E., P. Kalkavage, and E. Salem. Translated. Plato: Phaedo. Newbury Port, MA: Focus, 1998.

54. Lawson, Hugh. *Aristotle De Anima.* Translated. New York, NY: Penguin, 1986.

55. G. Zilboorg, C. L. Temkin, G. Rosen, H. E. Sigerest. "Paracelsus— Diseases That Deprive Man of His Reason, 1567. Such as St. Vitus Dance, Falling Sickness; Melancholy and Insanity and Their Correct Treatment." Trans. Baltimore, MD: John Hopkins University Press, 1996.

56. Bruno, Giordano, and Arthur D. Imerti. "The Expulsion of the Triumphant Beast, New Brunswick." New Jersey: Rutgers UP, 1964. Print.

57. Edited and Translated by Curley, Edwin. "The Collected Works of Spinoza." Volume I. Benedictus De Spinoza. First ed. Vol. 1. New Jersey: Princeton UP, 1985. Print.

58. Dennett, D. C. "Kinds of Minds: Toward an Understanding of Consciousness." New York, NY: Basic, 2006. Print.

59. MacDonald, Patrick E., and Patrik Rorsman. "Oscillations, Intercellular Coupling, and Insulin Secretion in Pancreatic ß Cells." Plops Biology. Plops Boil, 49th ser. 4.2 (February 2006). Web.

60. St. Augustine. "The City of God." Translated by Marcus Dods. New York: Modern Library, 1993. Print.

61. St. Augustine. "The Trinity." Translated by Edmund Hill. Hyde Park, NY: New City, 1991.

62. St. Augustine. "On Genesis." Translated by Edmund Hill. Hyde Park, NY: New City, 2002.

63. Barnett, M. W., and P. M. Larkman. "The Action Potential." 192-7 7.3 (June 2007).

64. Junge, Douglas. "Nerve and Muscle Excitation." 2nd ed. Sunderland, MA: Sinauer Associates, 1981, 115–132.

65. Bullock, Theodore Holmes, Richard Orkand, and Alan Grinnell. "Introduction to Nervous Systems." San Francisco: W. H. Freeman, 1977. Print, 478–480.

66. Bullock, Theodore Holmes, and G. Adrian Horridge. "Structure and Function in the Nervous Systems of Invertebrates." San Francisco: W. H. Freeman, 1965. A Ser. of Books in Biology.

67. Martin, Raymond, and John Barresi. "Hazlitt on the Future of the Self." *Journal of the History of Ideas* 56 no. 3 (1995): 463–81.

68. Reid, Thomas, James Walker, and William Hamilton. *Essays on the Intellectual Power of Man*, 1785. Philadelphia: Butler, 1895, 1: 213–508.

69. Clarke, Samuel, and Anthony Collins. "A Letter to Mr. Dodwall and Etc.—In the work of Samual Clark." 1 vol. 1738 no. 3: 720–913. Reprint. New York: Garland, 1978.

70. Hume, David, L. A. Selby-Bigge, and P. H. Nidditch. *A Treatise of Human Nature*. Oxford: Clarendon, 1988. Print.

71. Hazlitt, William. "An Essay on the Principles of Human Action, and Some Remarks on the Systems of Hartley and Helvetius." Gainesville, FL: Scholars' Facsimiles and Reprints, 1969. Print.

72. Coleridge, Samuel Taylor. *Coleridge*. New York, NY: Dell Pub., 1772–1834. Print, 183–184.

73. Fichte, Johann Gottlieb, and Daniel Breazeale. *Foundations of Transcendental Philosophy: (Wissenschaftslehre) Nova Methodo (1798–99)*. London: Cornell UP, 1992. Print.

74. http:/www.ecomaill.com/greenshopping/otusa.htm 11/26/2015 3.26p (1–5).

75. Dr. Pawluk. "About Dr. Pawluk–Dr. Pawluk." Web. www.drpawluk. com/education/about dr_pawluk.

76. McFadden, Johnjoe. "Conscious Electromagnetic (CEMI) Field Theory." *Neuro Quant* Logy 5 no. 3 (September 2007): 262–70.

77. Hegel, Georg Wilhelm Friedrich, Arnold V. Miller, and J. N. Findlay. *Phenomenology of Spirit*. Oxford: Clarendon, 1977. Print.

78. Pierre, Cabins, and Jean Georges. "The Relationship of the Physical and the Moral in Man." 1802. Ed.George Mora. Marggaret Duggan Saidi; Baltimore Md, John Hopkins University Press 1981.

79. Marx,Karl and Friedrich Eagles.Capital:A Critique of Political Economy.New York International.1975.

80. Mill, James, A. Findlater, and G. Grote. *Analysis of the Phenomena of the Human Mind*. Vol. 2. London: Longman's Green Reader and Dyer, 1869.

81. Stronk, G. "Principles of Magnetism." In Williamson, Samuel J., *Advances in Biomagnetism*. New York: Plenum, 1999, 47–57.

82. Schwartz, G. E. "Energy Cardiology: A Dynamical Energy Systems Approach for Integrating Conventional and Alternative Medicine." *Advances in Mind-Body Medicine* 12 no. 4 (1996): 4–24.

83. Kleiner, R., D. Koelle, F. Ludwig, and J. Clarke. "Superconducting Quantum Interference Devices: State of the Art and Applications." *Proceedings of the IEEE*. Proc. IEEE 92 no. 10 (2004): 1534–548. Web.

84. Isselbacher, Kurt J., Eugene Braunwald, Jean D. Wilson, Joseph B. Martin, Anthony S. Fauci, and Dennis L. Kasper. *Harrison's Principles of Internal Medicine*. 13th ed. New York: McGraw-Hill, 1994. Print.

85. Sherwood, Laura Lee. *Human Physiology: From Cells to Systems*. Australia: Thomson/Brooks/Cole, 2007. Accessed from Cengage Learning, 2008.

86. Rosch, Paul J. *Bioelectromagnetic and Subtle Energy Medicine*. 2nd ed. New York: CRC Taylor and Francis Group, 2015.

87. "Your Heart's Electrical System." National Heart, Lung, and Blood Institute, NIH. Web. Updated November 17, 2011.

88. Rama, Rudolph Ballentine, and Alan Hymes. *Science of Breath: A Practical Guide*. Honesdale, PA: Himalayan International Institute of Yoga Science and Philosophy, 1979. p59

89. Chardin, Pierre Teilhard De. *Let Me Explain*. New York: Harper and Row, 1972. Print, 66.

90. Yogananda, Paramahansa. *The Divine Romance*. Los Angeles, CA: Self-Realization Fellowship, 1986.

91. Prescott, James W., PhD. "The Origins of Human Love and Violence." *Pre and Perinatal Psychology Journal* 10 no.3 (Spring 1996). Web.

92. Rabbin, Robert. *Igniting the Soul at Work: A Mandate for Mystics.* Charlottesville, VA: Hampton Roads Pub., 2002. Print.

93. Sternberg, Robert, J. "Triangulating Love." In Oord, T. J. *Altruism Reader's Selection from Writings on Love, Religion, and Science.* West Conshohoken: Templeton Foundation, 332.

94. Acker, M., and M. H. Davis. "Intimacy, Passion, and Commitment in Adult Romantic Relationships: A Test of the Triangular Theory of Love." *Journal of Social and Personal Relationships* 9 no. 1 (1992): 21–50. Web.

95. Prescott, J. W. "Somatosensory Deprivation and Its Relationship to the Blind." In *The Effects of Blindness and Other Impairments on Early Development*, edited by Z. S. Jastrembke. New York: American Foundation for the Blind (1976), 65–121.

96. Prescott, J.W. "Early Somatosensory Deprivation as an Ontogenetic Process in the Abnormal Development of the Brain and Behavior." In *Medical Primatology* 1970, edited by I. E. Goldsmith and J. Moor-Jankowski. New York: S. Karger, Basel, 1971.

97. Prescott, J.W. "Sensory Deprivation Versus Sensory Stimulation during Early Development: A Comment on Berkowitz's Study." *Journal of Psychology* 77 (1971): 189–191.

98. Meissuer, W. W. "Theories of Personality in Psychotherapy." In Kaplan and Shaddocks Comprehensive Textbook of Psychiatry. 9th ed. Vol. I. edited by B. J. Saddock and V. A. Shaddock. Philadelphia: Lippincott Williams and Wilkins, 2009, 788.

99. Thompson, Richard F., and Michael M. Patterson. *Bioelectric Recording Techniques: Receptor and Effecter Processes.* New York: Academic, 1973. Print.

100. Brodal, Alf. *Neurological Anatomy.* New York: Oxford UP, 1998. Print.

101. Kenshalo, D. R. "Correlates of Temperature Sensitivity in Man and Monkey: A First Approximation." In Sensory Functions of the Skin in Primates, edited by Y. Zotterman. Oxford: Oxford University Press, 1976.

102. Nolte, J. *The Human Brain.* St. Luis Mosby, 1999.

103. Penfield, Wilder, and Theodore Rasmussen. *The Cerebral Cortex of Man: A Clinical Study of Localization of Function.* New York: Macmillan, 1950. Print.

104. Baker, D. "The Innervations of the Muscle Spindle." *Quarterly Journal of Microscopic Science* 89, (1948): 143–186.

105. Dodson, R. S., and J. H. King. "A Determination of the

Normal Threshold of Hearing and Its Relation to the Standardization of Audiometers." *Journal of Laryngology and Otology J. Laryngol. Otol.* 66 no. 8 (1952): 366–78. Web.

106. De Reuck, Anthony V.S., and Julie Knight. *Hearing Mechanisms in Vertebrates.* London: J. and A. Churchill, 1968. Print.

107. Békésy, Georg Von., and Ernest Glen Wever. *Experiments in Hearing.* New York: McGraw-Hill, 1960. Print.

108. Yasuji, Katsuki. "Neural Mechanism of Auditory Sensation in Cats." *Sensory Communication* (1961): 561–83. Web.

109. Carpenter, Malcolm B., and J. Sutin. *Human Neuroanatomy.* Baltimore: Williams & Wilkins, 1983. Print.

110. Aguilar, M., and W. S. Stiles. "Saturation of the Rod Mechanism of the Retina at High Levels of Stimulation." *Optica Acta: International Journal of Optics* 1 no. 1 (1954): 59–65. Web.

111. Moncrieff, R. W. *The Chemical Senses.* London: Hill, 1967. Print.

112. Firestein, S., and F. Warbling. "Ionic Mechanism Underlying the Olfactory Response." *Science* 244 (1989): 79–82.

113. Tanabe, T., M. Iino, and S. F. Takagi. "Discrimination of Odors in Olfactory Bulb, Pyriform-Amygdaloid Areas, and Orbitofrontal Cortex of the Monkey." *Journal of Neurophysiology* 38 no. 5 (September 1975): 1284–1296.

114. Amoore, J. E. "Stereochemical Theory of Olfaction." *Nature* 198 no. 4877 (1963): 271–72. Web.

115. Watkins, Herman A. "Perception of Body Position and of the Position of the Visual Field." Washington: American Psychological Association, 1949. Psychological Monographs 302 no. 3: 1–46.

116. Fitzgerald, M.J.T. *Neuroanatomy, Basic, and Applied.* London: Baillière Tindall, 1985. Print.

117. Llinas, R. R. "Bursting of Thalamic Neurons and States of Vigilance." *Journal of Neurophysiology* 95 no. 6 (2006): 3297–308. Web.

118. Steriade, Mircea, and Robert W. McCarley. *Brainstem Control of Wakefulness and Sleep.* New York: Plenum, 1990. Print.

119. Richter-Levin, Gal. "The Amygdala, the Hippocampus, and Emotional Modulation of Memory." *Neuroscientist* 10 no. 1 (2004): 31–39. Web.

120. O'Keefe, J.I. "The Hippocampus as a Cognitive Map." *Neuroscience* 4 no. 6 (1978): 863. Web.

121. Koenig, M., and J. Grafman. "Posttraumatic Stress Disorder: The

Role of Medial Prefrontal Cortex and Amygdala." *Neuroscientist* 15 no. 5 (2009): 540–48. Web.

122. Bostock, Elizabeth, Robert U. Muller, and John L. Kubie. "Experience-Dependent Modifications of Hippocampal Place Cell Firing." *Hippocampus* 1 no. 2 (1991): 193–205. Web.

123. Warner-Schmidt, Jennifer L., and Ronald S. Duman. "Hippocampal Neurogenesis: Opposing Effects of Stress and Antidepressant Treatment." *Hippocampus* 16 no. 3 (2006): 239–49. Web.

124. Gibbins, Ian. "Peripheral Autonomic Pathways." *Human Nervous System* (2004): 134–89. Web.

125. Talman, W. T., and E. E. Benarroch. "Neural Control of Cardiac Functions." In *Peripheral Neuropathy.* 3rd ed., edited by P. J. Dyck, P. K. Thomas, J. W. Griffin, et al. WB Saunders, 1993.

126. Jänig, Wilfrid. *Integrative Action of the Autonomic Nervous System.* Cambridge University Press, 2006.

127. Goyal, R., and I. Hirano. "The Entire Nervous System." *N. Engl, J. Med* 334 (1994): 1106.

128. Renaud, Leo P., and Charles W. Bourquet. "Neurophysiology and Neuropharmacology of Hypothalamic Magnocellular Neurons Secreting Vasopressin and Oxytocin." *Progress in Neurobiology* 36 no. 2 (1991): 131–69. Web.

129. Steriade, Mircea, and Robert W. McCarley. *Brain Stem Control of Wakefulness and Sleep.* New York: Plenum, 1990. Print.

130. Marsden, C. D., P. A. Merton, and H. B. Morton. "Servo Action in Human Voluntary Movement." *Nature* 238 no. 5360 (1972): 140–43. Web.

131. Nolte, J. *The Human Brain.* St. Luis Mosby, 1999.

132. Ito⁻, Masao. *Brain and Mind.* Elsevier, 1992. Print.

133. *Diagnostic and Statistical Manual of Mental Disorders.* 5th edition. American Psychiatric Association, 2013.

134. Bateman, A. Fonagy. "Eight-Year Follow-Up of the Patients Treated for Borderline Personality Disorder: Metallization-Based Treatment Versus Treatment as Usual." *Focus* 11 no. 2 (2013): 261–268.

135. Helgoland, M.I. "Kjelsberg Torgersen's Continuous between Emotional and Disruptive Behavior Disorder in Adolescence and Personality Disorder in Adulthood." *Am. J. Psychiatry* 162 (2005): 1926–1947.

136. Linechan, M.M., K. A. Comtois, A. M. Murry, M. Brown, R. J. Gallop, H. L. Heard, K. E. Korslund, D. A. Tutek, S. K. Reynolds, and V. Liridenbiom. "Two-Year Randomized Controlled Trial and Follow Up

of Dialectical Behavior Therapy Versus Therapy by Experts for Suicide Behavior and Borderline Disorder. *Arch. Gen. Psychiatry* 63 no. 7 (2006): 757–766.

137. Ozkan, M., and A. Altindag. "A Co-Morbid Personality Disorder in Subjects with Panic Disorder: Do Personality Disorders Increase Severity?" *Comp. Psychiatry* 46 (2005): 20–26.

138. Schwarze, C., A. Mobascher, B. Pallasch, et al. "Parental Adversity: A Risk Factor in Borderline Personality." *Psychol. Med.* 43 no. 6 (2013): 1279–1291.

139. Svrakic, D.M., and C. R. Cloninger. "Personality Disorder." In *Kaplan and Sadock's Comprehensive Textbook of Psychiatry*, edited by B. J. Sadock and V. A. Sadock. 8th ed. Vol. 2. Philadelphia: Lippincott Williams and Wilkins, 205, 206.

140. Kenneth, R., and M. D. Silk. "Personality Disorder, Part I." *Psychiatric Times* 33 no. 2 (February 2016): 10–15.

141. Zimmerman, M.I., Rothschild, and I. Chelminski. "The Prevalence of DSM IV Personality Disorder in Psychiatric Outpatient." *Am. J. Psychiatry* 162 (2005): 1911–1918.

142. Pincus, A.L., and M. H. Lukowltsky. "Pathological Narcissism and Narcissistic Personality Disorder." *Ann. Rev. Clin. Psychol.* 6 (2010): 421–446.

143. Buscaglia, Leo. *Loving Each Other.* New Jersey: Slack Incorporated, 1984.

144. Buscaglia, Leo F., PhD. *Living, Loving, and Learning.* First Ballantine Book Trade Edition, 1983.

145. Buscaglia, Leo F., PhD. A Fawcett Book, the Ballantine Publishing Group, 1972.

146. Hanson, J. S., and R. W. McCollum. "The Diagnosis and Management of Nausea and Vomiting." *Am. J Gastroenterology* 80 no. 210 (1985).

147. Mitchelson, F. "Pharmacologic Agents Affecting Emesis: Review (Part I)." *Drugs* 43 (1992), 295.

148. Millward, Sadler G.H. et al. *Wrightos Liver and Billiary Disease.* 3rd ed. London: Saunders, 1992.

149. Sherlock, S., and J. Doodley. *Diseases of the Liver and Billiary System.* 9th ed. Oxford: Blackwell, 1993.

150. Beaumont, J.G. *Introduction to Neuropsychology.* Guildford, NY, 2008.

151. Carlson, N. R. *Physiology of Behavior.* Boston: Ally and Bacon, 1999.

152. Okeefe, J., and L. Nadal. *The Hippocampus as a Cognitive Map.* Oxford, 1978.

153. Clarendon, Lopes, F. M. de Silva, and D. E. Arnold. "A Physiology of the Hippocampus and Related Structures." *Annual Review of Physiology* 40 (1978): 185–216.

154. Libet, Benjamin. "Unconscious Cerebral Initiative and the Role of Conscious Will in Voluntary Actions." *Behavioral and Brain Science* 8 (1985): 529–566.

155. Libet B., E. W. Wright, and Gleason. "Readiness Potentials Preceding Unrestricted Spontaneous Preplanned Voluntary Acts." *Electroencephalographic and Clinical Neurophysiology* 54 (1983): 322–325.

156. Libet, Benjamin. *Mind Time: The Temporal Factor in Consciousness.* Harvard University Press, 2004.

157. www.mpg.de/rearch/unconscious-decision-in-the brain Dr-John-Dylan Haynes, Accessed April 14, 2008.

158. www.skillsyoungneed.com/ps/selfmotivation html.

159. Blair, C., and C. C. Raver. "Child Development in the Context of Adversity: Experiential Canalization of Brain and Behavior." *Am. Psychol.* 67 (2012): 309–318.

160. Rizolatti, Giacomo, and Laila Craighero. "The Mirror Neuron System." *Annual Review of Neuroscience* 27 no. 1 (2004): 169–192.

161. Keysers, Christian. "Mirror Neurons." *Current Biology* 19 no. 21 (2010): 97–973.

162. Keysers, Christian. 1-06-23 *The Empathic Brain.* Kindle June 2011 as a kindle E Book.

163. Theories of Emotions."Psychology about.com.Accessed September 13,2013

164. Boufon, M.E. "Learning Theory." In Kaplan and Sadock's *Comprehensive Textbook of Psychiatry.* 9th ed., edited by V. A. Sadock and P. Rulz. Philadelphia: Lippincott William and Wilkins 2009, 647.

165. Whitbourne, S.K., and S. B. Whitbourne. *Plagetis Cognitive Development Theory in Adult Development and Aging.* Biopsychosocial Perspectives. 4th ed. Hoboken: John Wiley & Sons, Inc., 2011, 32.

166. Kolanowski, A.M., D. M. Fick, A. M. Yevechak, N. I. Hill, P. M. Muchall, and J. A. McDwell. "Pay Attention: The Critical Importance of

Assessing Attention in Old Adults with Dementia." *J. Gerontol Nurs.* 38 no. 11 (2012), 23.

167. Fox 2008, 16–17.

168. Scherer, K. K. "What Are Emotions? And How Can They Be Measured?" *Social Science Information* 44 (2005):693–727.

169. Dyer, Wayne W. *The Shift.* California: Hay House Inc., 2010.

170. Dyer, Wayne. *Ten Secrets for Success and Inner Peace.* Hay House Inc., 2001.

171. Ramachandran, V. S. *The Tell-Tale Brain.* W.W. Norton and Company, Inc., 2012.

172. Blom, R.M., C. Hagestein-de Bruijic, R. de Graaf. M. Ten Have, and D. A. Denys. "Obsessions in Normality and Psychopathology." *Depression Anxiety* 28 no. 10 (2011).

173. Macaskill, A. "Differentiating Dispositional Self Forgiveness from other Forgiveness: Associations with Mental Health and Life Satisfaction." *J.SOC. Clin. Psychol.* 31, no. 28 (2012).

174. Sajobitt, T.T., L. M. Lix, I. Clara, J. Walker, L. A. Graff, P. Rawsthorne, N. Millee, L. Rogala, R. Carr, and C. N. Berrstein. "Measures of Relative Importance for Health-Related Quality of Life." *Res.* 21 no. 1 (2012).

175. Vaillant, G.E. "Positive Mental Health: Is There a Cross-Cultural Definition?" *World Psychiatry* 11 no. 93 (2012).

176. Vaillant, G.E. "Spiritual Evolution: A Scientific Defense of Faith." New York Doubleday Broadway, 2008.

177. Lovheim, H. "A New Three-Dimensional Model for Emotions and Monoamine Neurotransmitters." *Med Hypothesis* 78 (2011): 341–8. doi:10 1016/J.Mehy2011.

178. Harmon-Jones, E., K. Vaughn-Scott, S. Mohr, J. Sigelma, and C. Harmon Jones. "The Effect of Manipulated Sympathy and Anger on Left and Right Frontal Lobe Activity." *Emotion* 4 (2004): 95–101. doi.10.1017.

179. Kanner, Leo. (1943) Autistic Disturbances of Affective contact (PDF) Nervous child (1943).

180. Olds, J., and P. Milner. "Positive Reinforcement Produced by Electrical Stimulation of Septal Area and Other Regions of the Rat Brain." *J. Comp. Physiol. Psychol.* 47 (1954): 419–27.

181. Olds, J. "Reward from Brain Stimulation in the Rats." *Science* 122: 878.

182. Draghi-Lorenz, R. "Five-Month-Old Infants Can Be Jealous: Against Cognitive Solipsism." Paper presented, inc.

183. "Symposium Convened for the Biennial International Conference on Infant Studies" (ICIS) 16–19. Brighton, UK, 2000.

184. Hart, S. "Jealousy in Six-Month-Old Infants." *Infancy* 3 (2002): 395–402.

185. Hart, S. "When Infants Lose Exclusive Maternal Attention: It Is Jealousy?" *Infancy* 6 (2004):57–78.

186. Parrott, W. G. "The Emotional Experience of Envy and Jealousy." In *The Psychology of Envy*, edited by P. Salovey. New York: The Guilford press, 1992, 3–29.

187. Parrott, W.G., and R. H. Smith. "Distinguishing the Experiences of Envy and Jealousy." *Journal of Personality and Social Psychology* 64 (1993): 906–920.

188. Darwin, C. *Expression of Emotions in Man and Animals.*

189. Claton, G., and L. Smith. *Jealousy.* New Jersey: Prentice-Hall Inc., 1977.

190. Buunk, B. "Jealousy as Related to Attributions for the Partner's Behavior." *Social Psychology Quarterly* 47 (1984): 107–112.

191. Dehaene-Lambertz. "Ongoing Research at Nicoglab, Neurospin Center." Gif-sur-Yvette, France.

192. Dehaene, Stanislas. *Consciousness and the Brain.* New York: Penguin Group, 2014.

193. Lagercraritz and Changeux, 2009.

194. www.youtube.com, Animal Odd Couple Series.

195. Kovaes, Vogels, and Orban, 1995; Meknik and Haglund, 1999.

196. Locktefeld, James. *Brahman: The Illustrated Encyclopedia of Hinduism* Vol 1. A-M Rosen Publishing.

197. Brodd, Jeffery. *World Religions: A Voyage of Discovery.* Saint Mary's Press, 2009.

198. Bailey, Alice. *The Soul and the Mechanism*, 1973, 82-89 199,*Chattej J.C. The Wisdom of the Vedas.* Quest Books, Theosophical Publishing House, 2012, 56.

200. *Merriam-Webster*, s.v., "consciousness."

201. Van Gulick, Robert. "Consciousness." *Stanford Encyclopedia of Philosophy*, 2004.

202. Farthing, G. *The Psychology of Consciousness.* Prentice Hall, 1992.

203. Popper, Karl R., and John C. Eccles. *The Self and Its Brain*. New York: Springer Verlag, Inc., 1977.

204. Blakeslee, Sandra. "How the Brain Might Work: A New Theory of Consciousness." *New York Times*, March 21, 1995.

205. Andreass, J. L. *Psychophysiology: Human Behavior and Physiological Response*. 5th ed. New Jersey: Lawrence Erlbaum Associates, 2007.

206. Chang, B.S., D. L. Shomer, and E. Niedermyer. "Normal EEG and Sleep Adult and Elderly." In *Electron Cephalography: Basic Principles, Clinical Application, and the Related Field*, edited by E. Neidermeyer. Philadelphia: Lippincott Williams, 2011, 183–214.

207. Barclay, N. L., and A. M. Gregory. "Quantitative Genetic Research on Sleep: A Review of Normal Sleep, Sleep Disturbances, and Associated Emotional, Behavioural, and Health-Related Difficulties." *Sleep Med. Rev.* 17 no. 1 (2013): 29–40.

208. Jenni, O.G. "How Much Sleep Is 'Normal' in Children and Adolescents? Normal Sleep Durations in Children and Adolescents." *JAMA Pediatr.* 167 no. 1 (2013): 91–92.

209. Krieger, M., H. Roth, and T. Dement. *Principles and Practice of Sleep Medicine*. 4th ed. Philadelphia: Saunders, 2005.

210. Haydon, M.M., C. F. Reynolds III, and Y. Dauvilliers. "Excessive Sleep Duration and Quality of Life." *Ann. Neurol.* 73 no. 6 (2013): 785–794.

211. Breger, L. *A Dream of Underlying Fame: How Freud Betrayed His Mentor and Invented Psychoanalysis*. New York: Basic Books, 2009.

212. Freud, S. *The Standard Edition of the Complete Psychological Works of Sigmund Freud*. 24 vols. London: Hogarth Press, 1953–1974.

213. Hess, E. H. "Dilated Eyes and Attractiveness: The Role of Pupil Size in communication," *Scientific American* 233: 110–12.

214. Scheele, D., A. Wille, K. M. Kendrick, B. Stoffel-Wagner, B. Becker, O. Gunturkum, and R. Hurl Mann. "Oxytocin Enhances Reward Responses in Men Viewing the Face of Their Female Partner." *Proceedings of the National Academy of Science* 110 no. 50 (2013) 110, 20308–20313.

215. Fingelkurt, Andrew A., Alexander A. Fingelkurts, and Carlos F. H. Neves. *Consciousness as a Phenomenon in Operational Architectonics of Brain Organization*: Chaos, Solitons and Fractals Press, 2013.V 55 p13-31

216. *Merriam-Webster Dictionary*, s.v., "consciousness."

217. Van-Gulick, Robert. *Consciousness*. Stanford Encyclopedia of Philosophy, 2004.

218. Farthing, G. *The Psychology of Consciousness*. Prentice Hall, 1992.

219. Sacraic, Weiskrantz Barbur, Simmons, William, and Brammer, 1997. See also Morris, Degelder, Weiskrantz, and Dolah, 2001.

220. Sackur, Naccache, Pradat Diehl, Azouvi, Mazevet, Katz Cohen, and Dehaene, 2008; Glinchey-Berroth, M. C., Milberg, Varfaellie, Alaxander, and Kilnduff, 1993.

221. Bahrami, Olsen, Latham, Roepstorff, Rees, and Frith, 210.

222. Marti, Sackur, Sigman, and Dahaene (2010).

223. Baars, Bernard. *A Cognitive Theory of Consciousness.* Cambridge University Press, 1993, 15–18.

224. Block, Ned. "On a Confusion about a Function of Consciousness." In *The Nature of Consciousness,* edited N. Block, O. Flanagan, and G. Guzeldere. Philosophical Debate. MIT Press, 1998, 375–415.

225. "Animal Consciousness Officially Recognized by Leading Panel of Neuroscientists," September 3, 2012 via YouTube.

226. Cambridge Declaration on Consciousness (http://femconference. org) img/Cambridge Declaration on Consciousness.PDF.

227. Koch, *The Quest for Consciousness,* 105–116.

228. "Francis Crick and Christ of Koch: A Framework for Consciousness." (PDF) *Nature Neuroscience* 6 no. 2: 119–126.

229. Graziano, M.S.A., and S. Kastner. "Human Consciousness and Its Relationship to Social Neuroscience: A Novel Hypothesis." *Cog. Neuroscience,* 98-113.

230. Adenauer G. Casali, Olivia Grosseries, Marlo Rosanova, Melanie Boly, Simone Savasso, Karina R. Casali, Silivia Casarotto, Marie-Auelie Bruno, Steve Laureys, Giulio Tononi, and Marcello Massimini. "A Theoretically Based Index of Consciousness Independent of Sensory Processing and Behavior." *Science Translational Medicine* S. 198 (August 2013), 105.

231. Johanson, M., V. Alli, K. Revonsuo A, and J. Wedlund. "Content Analysis of Subjective Experiences in Partial Epileptic Seizures." *Epilepsy and Behavior* 12 (2008): 170–182.

232. Johanson, M., K. Valli, A. Revonsuo, et al. "Alteration in the Contents of Consciousness in Partial Epileptic Seizures." 13 (2008): 366–371.

233. Diefer, Vaitl et al. "Psychobiology of Altered States of Consciousness." *Psychological Bulletin* 131 no. 17 (2005): 98–12.

234. Murphy, M., S. Donovon, and E. Taylor. *The Physical and*

Psychological Effects of Meditation: A Review of Contemporary Research with a Comprehensive Bibliography, 1931–1996. Institute of Noetic Science.

235. Blumenfeld, Hal. "The Neurological Examination of Consciousness." In *The Neurology of Consciousness: Cognitive Neuroscience and Neuropathology,* edited by Steven Laureys, Guiulio Tononi. Academic Press, 2009.

236. Bhattacharya, A. Sutapas. *The Brainstem Brain Wave of Atman Brahman.* New Delhi, India: Gyan Publishing House, 2015.

237. Ogawa, Lee, Kay, and Tank, 1990.

238. Amar, J. "Singh Blood Supply Increases Magnetic Energy of the 'Soul.'"

239. Baker, A.T., R. Jalinous, I. L. Freeston. "Noninvasive Magnetic Stimulation of the Human Motor Cortex. *Lancet* 1 (1985): 1106–7.

240. Roth, B.J., J. M. Saypo, M. Hallet, and L. G. Cohen. "A Theoretical Calculation of the Electric Field Induced in the Cortex during Magnetic Stimulation Electroencephalogram." *Clin. Neuro* 81 (1991): 47–56.

241. Faradar, M. "Effects on the Production of Electricity: Ferom Magnetism (1831)." In *Michael Faraday,* edited by L. P. Williams. New York: Basic Books, 1965, 531.

242. George, M., S. Lisanby, and H. A. Sakeim. "Transcranial Magnetic Stimulation: Application in Neuropsychiatry." *Arch Gen Psychiatry* 56 no. 4 (1999): 300–11.

243. Brake, A.T., I. L. Freeston, and J. A. Jarratt, and R. Jalinous. "Magnetic Stimulation of the Human Nervous System: An Introduction and Basic Principles." In *Magnetic Stimulation in Clinical Neurophysiology,* edited by S. Chokroverty. Boston: Butterworth, S., 1989, 55–72.

244. Hanlon, C.A., M. Canterberry, J. J. Taylor. W. Devries, X. Li. T. R. Brown, et al. "Naloxone Reversible Modulation of Pain Circuitry by Left Prefrontal r TMS." *Neuropsychopharmacology* 38 no. 7 (2013): 1189–97.

245. Wu T., M. Somme, F. Tergau, and W. Paulus. "Lasting Influence of Repetitive Transcranial Magnetic Stimulation on Intracortical Excitability in Human Subjects." *Neuroscience* Let 287 (2000): 37–40.

246. Teneback, C., C. Nahasz, A. M. Speer, M. Molly, L. E. Stallings, K. M. Spicer, et al. "Two Weeks of Daily Left Prefrontal rTMs Changes Prefrontal Cortex and Paralimbic Activity in Depression." *J Neuropsychiatry Clin. Neurosci.* 11 (1999): 426–35.

247. Nahas, Z., M. Lomarev, D. R. Robers, A. Shastri, J. P. Lorberbaum, T. Teneback, et al. "Unilateral Left Prefrontal Transcranial Magnetic

Stimulation (TMS) Produces Intensity Dependent Bilateral Effects as Measured by Interleaved BOLD FMRT." *Biol. Psychiatry* 50 no. 9 (2001): 712–20.

248. Paus, T., M. A. Castro-Alamancos, and M. Petrides. "Cortico-Cortical Connectivity of Human Middorsolateral Frontal Cortex and Its Modulation by Repetitive Transcranial Magnetic Stimulation." *Eur. J. Neuroscience* 14 (2001): 1405–11.

249. Lan and Passingham, 2006.

250. Desmurget Reilly, Richard,Szathmari, Mottolese, and Sirigo, 2009.

251. Tenebaek, C.C., Z. Naha, A. M. Speer, M. Molly, L. E. Stallings, K. M. Spicer, et al. "Two Weeks of Daily Left Prefrontal rTMS Changes Prefrontal Cortex and Paralimbic Activity in Depression." *Neuropsychiatry Clin. Neurosci.* 11 (1999): 426–35.

252. Shajahan, P.M., M. F. Glabus, J. D. Steel, A. B. Doris, K. Anderson, J. A. Jenkins, et al. "Left Dorsolateral Repetitive Transcranial Magnetic Stimulation Affects Cortical Excitability and Functional Connectivity but Does Not Impair Cognition in Major Depression. *Prog. Neuropsychopharmacol Biol. Psychiatry* 36 no. 5 (2002): 945–54.

253. Phelp, James, MD. "Cranial Electrotherapy Stimulation for Bipolar Depression." *Psychiatric Times* (December 2015): P 20, E 20 F.

254. Goodman, Wayne K. "Deep Brain Stimulation Yields Positive Results in Patients with Obsessive Compulsive Disorder." Department of Psychiatry, Mount Sinai Hospital. Winter 2016 Chair's Report, 1–2.

255. Alberstone, C.D., S. L. Skirboll, J. A. Sandra, B. L. Hart, N. G. Baldwin, et al. "Magnetic Source Imaging and Brain Surgery: Presurgical and Intraoperative Planning in 26 Patients." *Journal of Neurosurgery* 92 (2000): 79–90.

256. Smith, S.D., B. R. McLeod, A. R. Liboff, and K. Cooksey. "Calcium Cyclotron Resonance and Diatom Motility." *Bioelectromagnetics* 8 (1987): 215–27.

257. Liboff, A.R. "Electric Field Ion Cyclotron Resonance." *Bioelectromagnetics* 181 no. 1 (1997): 85–7.

258. Perlmutter, J.S., and J. W. Mink. "Deep Brain Stimulation." *Ann Rey Neurosci.* 29 (2006): 230–57.

259. Hynynen, K., and N. McDannold. "MRI-Guided and Monitored Focus Ultrasound Thermal Ablation Method: A Review of Progress." *Int. J. Hyperth.* 20 (2004): 725–37.

260. Mishelevich, D., T. Sato, W. Tyler, and D. Wetmore. "Ultrasound Neuromodulation Treatment of Depression and Bipolar Disorder." US patent No. (20, 120, 283, 50). Washington, DC. US Patent and Trademark Office.

261. www.heartmath.org/reasearch/global-coherencel.

262. McCraty, R., and D. Childre. "Coherence Bridging Personal, Social and Global Health." *Alternat therap. Health Med* 16 no. 4 (2010): 10–24.

263. McCraty, R., M. Afkinson, D. Tomasino, and R. T. Bradly. "The Coherent Heart Brain Interaction: Psychophysiological Coherence and the Emergence of the System-Code Order." *Integr RV* 5 no. 2 (2009): 10–115.

264. Doronin, V.N., V. A. Parfentev, S. Z. Tleulin, R. A. Namvar, V. M. Somsikov, V. I. Drobzhev, et al. "Effects of Variation of the Geomagnetic Field and Solar Activity on Human Physiological Indicators." *Bio Fizka* 43 no. 4 (1998): 647–53.

265. Mikulecky, M. "Solar Activity Revolution and Cultural Prime in the History of Mankind." *Neuroendocrinol Let* 28 no. 6 (2007): 749–56.

266. Burch, J.B., J. S. Reif, and M. G. Yost. "Geomagnetic Disturbances Are Associated with Reduced Nocturnal Excretion of Melatonin Metabolites in Humans." *Neurosci. Let* 266 (1999): 209–12.

267. Cernousss, Vinogradov A., and E. Vlassova. "Geophysical Hazard for Human Health in Circumpolar Auroral Belt: Evidence of Relationship and Electromagnetic Disturbances." *Nat. Hazards* 23 (2001): 121–35.

268. Villoresi, G., N. G. Ptitsyna, M. I. Tiasto, N. Lucci. "Myocardial Infarction and Geomagnetic Disturbances: Analysis of Data on Morbidity and Mortality" [in Russian]. *Biofizika* 43 no. 4 (1998): 623–32.

269. Gorden, C., and M. Berk. "The Effect of Geomagnetic Storms on Suicide." *South African Psychiatric Rev.* 6 (2003): 24–7.

270. Subramanyam, S., P. Narayan, and T. Sirinivasan. "Effect of Magnetic Microstimulations on the Biological Systems—A Bioenvironmental Study." *Int. J. Biomeorol.* 29 no. 3 (1985): 293–305.

271. McCranty, R. "The Energetic Heart Bioelectromagnetic Communication within and between the People." In *EDS Bioelectromagnetic Medicine*, edited by P. J. Rosh, and M. S. Markov. New York: Marcel Dekker, 2004, 541–62.

272. Kemper, K.J., and H. A. Shaltout. "Nonverbal Communication of Compassion: Measuring Psychophysiological Effects." *BMC Compl. Alternat Med* 11 (2011): 132.

273. Persinger, M. "On the Possible Representation of the Electromagnetic Equivalents of All Human Memory within the Earth's Magnetic Field: Implications of Theoretical Biology." *Theor. Biol. Insights* 1 (2008): 3–11.

274. Montagnier, L., J. Aissa, E. Del Guidice, C. Lavelle, A. Tedeschi, and G. Vitiello. "DNA Waves and Water." *J. Phys. Conf. Ser.* 306 (2011): 1–10.

275. Kirsch, D.L., and M. Gilulu. "Cranial Electrotherapy Stimulation in the Treatment of Depression." *Practical Pain Manage.* 7 no. 47 (2007): 33–41.

276. Skou, J.C., and M. Esmann. "The Na, K-ATPase." *J. Bioenerg. Biomember.* 24 (1992): 249–261.

277. Sodi Pllares, D., G. Melrano, A. Bisteni, and J. J. Ponce de Leon. "Deductive and Polyparametric Electrocardiography." Mexico D. F. Inst. National de Cardiol., 1970.

278. www.gavcamera.com.

279. http://www.dictionary.com.

280. Horney, K., MD. Self-Analysis. W. W. Norton & Company, Inc., 1942.

281. Jung, C. G. *Ther. Archetypes and the Collective Unconscious.* Translated by R. F. C. Hull. Princeton University Press, 190.

282. Adams, M. B. "Evolution of Theodosius Dobzhansky: Essay on His Life and Thought in Russia and America." Princeton University Press, 2014.

283. Kanagawa, C., S. Cross, and H. R. Markins. *Who Am I? The Cultural Psychology of the Conceptual Self.* Sage Publication. Personality and Social Psychology, 2001.

284. Somerville, L.H., R. M. Jones, E. J. Ruberry, J. P. Dykes, G. Glover, and B. Casey. "The Medical Prefrontal Cortex and the Emergence of Self-Conscious Emotion in Adolescence." *Psychology Science* 24 no. 8 (2013): 1554–62.

285. Blackmore, S.J. "Development of Social Brain in Adolescents." *JR Soc. Med.* 105 (2012): 111–116.

286. Farina, B., and G. Liotti. "Does a Dissociative Psychopathological Dimension Exist? A Review on Dissociative Processes and Symptoms in Development Trauma Spectrum Disorders." *Clin Neuropsychiatry* 10 no. 1 (2013): 11–18.

287. Markowitsch, H.J. "Psychogenic Amnesia." *Neurogenimage* 20 (2003): s132–s138.

288. Martinex-Taboas, A., M. Dorahy, V. Sar, W. Middleton, and C. Krngar. "Growing Not Dwindling: International Research on the World Wide Phenomenon of Dissociative Disorders." *J. Nerv. Ment. Dis.* 201 no. 4 (2013): 253–354.

289. Thompson, Richard F. *The Brain: A Neuroscience Primer.* 2nd ed. W. H. Freeman and Company, 1993, 6.

290. Kluget et al. "Is God in Our Genes?"

291. Fang, A., and S. G. Hofmann. "Relationship between Social Anxiety Disorder and Body Dysmorphic Disorder." *Clin. Psychol. Rev.* 30 (2010): 1040.

292. Philipp, K.A., A. Pinto, A. S. Hart, M. E. Coles, J. L. Eisen, W. Menard, and S. A. Rasmussen. "A Comparison of Insight in Body Dysmorphic Disorder and Obsessive Compulsive Disorder." *J. Psych. Res.* 46 (2012): 1293.

293. Frost, R.O., D. F. Tolin, G. Stette, K. E. Fitch, and A. Selbo-Bruns. "Excessive Acquisition in Hoarding." *J. Anxiety Disorder* 23 (2009): 632.

294. Grisham, J.R., M. M. Norberg, A. D. William, S. P. Certoma, and R. Kadib. "Categorization and Cognitive Deficits in Compulsive Hoarding." *Behave Res Ther.* 48 (2010): 886.

295. Lervolino, A.C., N. Perrond, M. A. Fullana, M. Gulpponi, L. Cherkas, D. A. Collier, and D. Matrix-cols. "The Prevalence and Heritability of Compulsive Hoarding: A Twin Study." *Am. J. Psychiatry* 116 (2009): 1156.

296. Ronald, W., and M. D. Pres. "Depression: A Five-Minute Seminar for Patients." *Psychiatric Times* 32 no. 3 (March 2016): 28A–28E.

297. Lebano, Lauren. "Novel Therapeutics for Major Depression." *Psych. Congress* 1 no. 2 (Fall/Winter 2015), 40.

298. Tomolo, J. "New Connection Gluctamate and Psychiatry." Psych congress. Summer 2016, 32.

299. Seley, Hans. *The Stress of Life.* Rev. ed. New York: McGraw Hizz, 1978.

300. Corr, C.A., and D. M. Corr. *Death and Dying, Life and Living.* 7th ed. Belmont, CA: Wadsworth, 2013.

301. Learning, M.R., and G. E. Dickinson. *Understanding Death, Dying, and Bereavement.* 7th ed. Stamford, CT: Cengage Learning, 210.

302. Brunk, D. "Earlier Intervention Urged in Prodromal Depression." *Clinical Psychiatry News* (April 2016): 35.

303. Miller, B., MD, PhD, MPH. "Adjunctive Monoclonal Antibody Immunotherapy in Schizophrenia." *Psychiatric Times* (February 2016), 28E.

304. Lonveau, A., I. Smirnov, T. Keyes, et al. "Structural and Functional Features of Central Nervous System Lymphatic Vessels." *Nature* 523 (2015): 337–341.

305. Aspelund, A., S. Antila, S. T. Proulx, et al. "A Dura Lymphatic Vascular System that Drains Brain Interstitial Fluid and Macromolecules." *J. Exp. Med.* 212 (2015): 991–999.

306. Palta, P., J. Samheli, E. R. Miller, et al. "Depression and Oxidative Stress: Results from a Meta-Analysis of Observational Studies." *Psycho Son Med.* 76 no. 1 (2014): 12–19.

307. Ferrari, A.J., F.J. Charlson, R. E. Norman, et al. "Burden of Depressive Disorder by Country, Sex, Age, and Year: Finding from the Global Burden of Disease Study 2010." *Plos Med.* 10 no. 1 (2013): e1001547.

308. Maes, M., P. Galecki, Y. S. Chang, et al. "A Review on the Oxidative and Nitro Stative Stress (OXNS): Pathways in Major Depression and Their Possible Contribution to (Neuro) Degenerative Process in the Illness. *Prog. Neuropsychiopharmacol. Biolpsychiatry* 35 no. 3 (2011): 676–692.

309. Dodd, S., M. Maes, G. Anderson, et al. "Putative Neuro Protective Agents in Neuropsychiatric Disorders." *Prog. Neuropsychopharmacol. Biol. Psychiatry* 42 (2013): 135–145.

310. Jimenz-Fernandez, S., MD, M. Gurpegui, MD, F. Diaz Atienz, MD, L. Perez Costilla, MD, M. Gerstenberg, MD, and C. U. Correll, MD. "Oxidative Stress and Antioxidant Parameters in Patients with Major Depressive Disorder Compared to Healthy Controls before and after Antidepressant Treatment." *J. Clin. Psychiatry* 76 (12 December 2015): 1658–1659.

311. Monn, M. A. "Residents, Interns Report Depression Rate of 28.8%." *J. Clinical Psychiatric News.* (Jan. Nov. 2015).

313. American Foundation for Suicide Prevention: Facts about Physician Depression and Suicide. Updated February 2015.

314. Brower, K.J., MD. "Avoid Burnout with Self-Cave and Wellness Strategies." *Psychiatric Times* 33 no. 4 (April 2016): 9–11.

315. Maslach, C., S. E. Jackson, and M. P. Later. *MBI: The Maslach Burnout Inventory Manual.* Palo Alto: Consulting Psychologists Press, 1996.

316. Kraft, U. "Burn out." *Scientific American Mind* (June/July 2006), 28–33.

317. Thurschwell, P. *Sigmund Freud*. 2nd ed. New York: Routledge, 2009.

318. Freud, S. *The Standard Edition of the Complete Psychological Works of Sigmund Freud*, 24 vols. London: Hogarth Press, 1953–1974.

319. Massey, C. *American Constitutional Law: Power and Liberties*. 2nd ed. Aspen Publishers, 2005, 40.

320. Vaishnavi, S. MD, PhD. "Neural Circuits Approach Could Change Psychiatry for Better." *Clinical Psychiatric News* (May 2016), 23.

321. Mclean, C.P., A. Asnaani, B. T. Litz, and S. G. Hofmann. "Gender Differences in Anxiety Disorder, Prevalence, Course of Illness, Comorbidity, and Burden of Illness." *Psychiatry Res.* 45 (2011): 1027.

322. Stahs, S. *Anxiolytics and Sedatives-Hypnotics, Inc. Essential Psychopharmacology: Neuroscientific Basis and Practical Applications.* Cambridge University Press, 1996, 167–215.

323. McKay, D., and E. A. Storch, eds. *Handbook of Treating Variants and Complications in Anxiety Disorders*. New York: Springer Science and Business Media, 2013.

324. Kalat, J.E. *Biological Psychology*. 2013, 381.

325. *Psychiatr. clin. North Am.* 21 (2001): 75–97.

326. Noel, J.M., and J. L. Gurtis. "The Pharmacological Management of Stress Reaction." In *A Clinical Guide to the Treatment of the Human Stress Response*, edited by G. S. Everly Jr. and J. M. Lating. New York: Springer Science and Business Media, 2013, 2017.

327. Pena, G., S. Dacco, R. Menoth, and D. Caldero. "Antianxiety Medication for the Treatment of Complex Agoraphobia: The Pharmacological Intervention for Behavioral Conditions." *Neuropsychiar Dis. Treat.* 7 (2011): 621.

328. Coelho, C.M., and H. Purkis. "The Origin of Specific Phobia: Influential Theories and Current Perspective." *Rev. Gen. Psychology* 13 (2009): 335.

329. Potina, I.T., E. H. W. Kosteb, P. Philoppote, V. Dethiere, and David Do. "Optimal Attention Focus during Exposure in Specific Phobias: A Meta-Analysis." *Clin Psychol Rev.* 33 (2013), 1172.

330. Karas, P.J. et al. "Deep Brain Stimulus: A Mechanism and Clinical Update." *Neuro Surgery Focus* 35 no. 5 (2013), E1.

331. Benabid A.L., A. Benazzous, and P. Pollack. "Mechanism of Deep Brain Stimulation." *Mov. Disorder* 17 (suppl. 3) (2002): S 73–4.

332. Taghva, A.S. "Deep Brain Stimulation for Treatment Resistant Depression." *World Neurosurg* 80 no.3 (2013): S 27.e 17-s27. E 24.

333. Heller, L., and D. B. Van Hulsteyn. "Brain Stimulation Using Electromagnetic Sources: Theoretical Aspects." *Biophys J* 63 (1992): 129–38.

334. Roth, Y., A. Amir, Y. Levokovitz, and A. Zengen. "Three-Dimensional Distribution of Electric Field Induced in the Brain by Transcranial Magnetic Stimulation Using Figure-8 and Deep H-Coil. *J. Clin. Neurophysiology* (2007): 31–8.

335. Roth Y., A. Zangen, M. Hallet. "Transcranial Magnetic Stimulation of Deep Brain Regions." *Clin. Neurophysiology* (19) 2002: 361–70.

336. Goodman, Wayne, K., Chair, Report, Department of Psychiatry Mount Sinai Hospital. *New York Deep Brain Stimulus Yields Positive Results in Patients with Obsessive-Compulsive Disorder* (16 Winter), 111.

337. Gersper, R., E. Toth, I. Lesserless, and A. Zangen, "Site Specific Antidepressant Effects of Repeated Subcortical Stimulation: Potential Role of Brain-Derived Neurotrophic Factors." *Biol. Psychiatry* 67 (2010): 125–32.

338. Phelps, J., MD. "Cranial Electrotherapy Stimulation and Bipolar Depression: New Data." *Psychiatric Times* (December 2015): 20 E.

339. Tatum, W.O. IV, J. A. Ferreira, S. R. Benbadis, et al. "Vagus Nerve Stimulation for Pharmaco. Resistant Epilepsy. Clinical symptoms with End of Service." *Epilepsy Behav.* 5 (2004): 128–32.

340. Zaba, J. "Controlling Seizures by Changing GABA Receptors Sensitivity." *Epileplesia* 28 (1987), 604.

341. Bassett, C.A. "Becker Regeneration of Electric Potential in Born in Response to Mechanical Stress." *Science* 137 (1962): 1063–4.

342. Chaudhary, S.S., R. K. Mishra, A. Sware, and J. M. Thomas. "Dielectric Properties of Normal and Malignant Human Breast Tissue at Radio Wave Frequencies." *Indian J Biochem. Biophys.* 21 (1984): 76–9.

343. Neuman, E., M. Shaefer-Ridder, Y. Wang, and P. H. Hofschneider. "Gene Transfer in to Mouse Lymphoma Cell by Electroporation in High Electric Field." *EMBO.J* 7 (1982): 841–5.

344. Boggio, P.S., S. P. Rigonatti, R. B. Ribeiro, M. L. Myezknowski, M. A. Nitsche. "A Randomized, Double Blind Clinical Trial on the Efficacy of Cortical Direct Current Stimulation for the Treatment of Major Depression." *Int. J. Neuropharmacol.* 11 no. 2 (2008): 249.

345. Korotkov, K. Ed. *Measuring Energy Field: State of the Art.* Fairlawn: Backbone Publishing, 2004, 1–270.

346. Schroeder, L., Ostranders. *Psychic Discoveries behind the Iron Curtain.* Surrey: Conoda Hancock Books (1977), 124–9.

347. Zhandin, M.N., V. V. Novikov, F. S. Barnes, and N. F. Pegola. "Combined Action of Static and Alternating Magnetic Field on Ionic Current in Aqueous Glutamic Acid Solution." *Bioelectromagnetics* 10 (1998): 41–5.

348. Jhon, Kabata-zinn. *Full Catastrophe Living.* Bantam Books, 2013, 45.

349. Schwitzgebel, Eric. "Belief in Zalta Edward." *Stanford Encyclopedia of Philosophy.* Stanford, CA: The Metaphysics Research Lab, 2006.

350. http://www.religioustolerance.org/Buddhism.htm.

351. http://www.Islam-guide.com/ch3-2 htm.

352. http://www.cofchurist.org/basic belief. Community of Christ.

353. http://www.chabad.org/library/article codo/aid/332555/Jewish/maimonides-13-principlesoffaith.htm.

354. http:/www orthodox-jews.com/Judaism-beliefs-htm#ax224VarchAwl.

355. Taube, Karl, "Ritual Humor in Classic Maya Religion." In *Word and Image in Maya Culture*, edited by William F. Hank and Don S. Rice. Salt Lake City: University of Utah Press, 1989.

356. Vogt, Evan Z. *Tortillas for the Gods: A Symbolic Analysis of Zinacanteco Rituals.* Cambridge: Harvard University Press, 1976.

357. https://Stephenpirie.com/faq/what-is-a-belief-system, 2016.

358. Laugdon, Roben, and Emily Connaughton. *The Neural Basis of Human Belief System.* New York: Psychology Press, Tylor and Francis Group, 2013, 20.

359. Dictionary.com, s.v., "wisdom."

360. *Wisdom.* Oxford University Press.

361. "Character Education: Our Shared Responsibility," Ed, gov.31, May.

362. Harter, Andrew. "C 8." In *Character Strengths and Virtues: A Handbook and Classification*, edited by Christopher Peterson and Martin E. P. Seligman. Oxford University Press, 2004, 181–196.

363. Largesse, B., B. H. Price, and E. D. Murry. "Brain Behavior

Relation." *Encyclopedia of Human Behavior.* 2nd ed., edited by V. S. Ramachandran, MD, PhD. Academic Press, 2012.

364. Shiksha, Vimkut. "Understanding Wisdom." Issue Z (February 1999). http://www Swaraj.org/Shikshant.wmkut.02.html.

365. Ubersax, John S. "Wisdom Lexicon Project: Steps towards the Scientific Study of Sapiens." Online article. 2007. http/John-ubersax.com/Plato/Lexicon.Htm.

366. Lewis, C.T., and C. Short. *Latin Dictionary*, Oxford University Press, 1963.

367. Dhammapada, V., 256, 268–9.

368. Begley, Sharon. "Train Your Mind Change Your Brain." New York: Ballantine Books, 2007.

369. Kabat-Zinn, Jon. *Full Catastrophe.* Living Bantam Books Trade, 2013.

370. Brown, Richard, P., MD, and Patricia L. Gerbarg, MD. *The Healing Power of the Breath*. Boston: Shambhala, 2012.

371. Luders, Eileen, Florian Kuth, Emeran A. Mayer, Arthur W. Toga, Katherine L. Narr, and Christian Gaser. "The Unique Brain Anatomy of Meditation Practitioners: Alteration in Cortical Gyrification." *Frontiers in Human Neuroscience* 6 no. 34 (2012).

372. Critchley, H. D., S. Weins, P. Rotshtein, A. Ohman, and R. J. Dolan. "System Supporting Introspective Awareness." *Nat. Neurosci.* 7 (2004), 189–195. 10-1038/nn1176 [Pub. Med].

373. Hoffman, S.G., P. Grossman, and D. E. Hinton. "Loving-Kindness and Compassion Meditation: Potential for Psychological Intervention." *Clin Psychol* Rev. (2011): 1126–1132. 10.1016/J.Cpr. 2011.07.003 [pub med].

374. Bartley, A.J., D. W. Jones, and D. R. Weinburger. "Genetic Variability of Human Brain Size and Cortical Gyral Pattern." *Brain* 120 no. 2 (1997): 257–269. 10.1093/brain/120.2.257 (PubMed).

375. Kenneth, G. Walton, PhD, Robert H. Schneider, MD, and Sanford Nidich, EdD. "Review of Controlled Research on the Transcendental Meditation Program and Cardiovascular Diseases Risk Factors, Morbidity, and Mortality." *Cardio Rev.* 12 no. 50 (2004): 262–260. http://www.ncbi.nlm.nih.gov/mc/articles/PMC2211376 (HHS public access).

376. Sant Rajinder Singh Ji Maharaj. "Meditation Is Connecting with Our Soul." http/www.sos.org/Meditation connecting-with-our-soul.html.

377. Hozel, B.K., J. Carmody, M. Vangal, S. M. Yerramsetti, T. Gard, and S. W. Lazar. "Mindfulness Practice Leads to Increase in Regional

Brain Grey Matter Density." *Psychiatry Research: Neuroimaging* (2010). dio.10 1016/J.Psych resns.2010.08.006. In *Full Catastrophe Living* (2013).

378. Fab, N.A.S., Z. A. Segal, H. Maberg, J. Bean, D. McKeon, Z. Fatima, and A. K. Anderson. "Attending to the Present: Mindfulness Meditation Reveals Disconnect Neural Modes of Self-Reference. *Social Cognitive and Affective Neuroscience* 2 (2007): 313–322.

379. Hozel, B.K., J. Carmody, K. C. Evans, E. A. Hoge, J. A. Dusek, L. Morgan, R. Pitman, and S. W. Lazar. "Stress Reduction Correlates with Structural Changes in the Amygdala." *Social Cognitive and Affective Neuroscience Advances* 5 no. 1 (2010): 11–17. In *Full Catastrophe Living* (2013).

380. David, R.J., J. Kabat-Zinn, J. Schumacher, M. A. Rosencrantz, D. Muller, S. F. Santoru, R. Urbanowski, A. Harrington, K. Bonus, and J. F. Sheridan. "Alteration in Brain and Immune Functions Produced by Mindfulness Meditation." *Psychosomatic Medicine* 65 (2002): 564–570.

381. Creswell, R., M. R. Irwin, L. J. Burklund, M. N. Lieberman, J. M. G. Arevalo, J. Ma, E. C. Breen, and S. W. Cole. "Mindfulness-Based Stress Reduction Training Reduces Loneliness and Pro-Inflammatory Gene Expression in Older Adults: A Small, Randomized Controlled Trial." *Brain, Behavior, and Immunity* 26 (2012):1095–1101.

382. Khurshid, A. Khurshid, MD, FAASM. "Neuromodulation in Neuropsychiatric Disorders." *Psychiatric Annals* 46, no. 11 (2016).

383. Moscrip, T.D., H. S. Terrance, H. A. Sackheim, and S. H. Lisanby. "Randomized Controlled Trial of the Cognitive Side Effects of Magnetic Seizure Therapy (MST) and Electroconvulsive Shock. *Int J Neuropsychopharmacol* 9 no. 1 (2006): 1–11.

384. http://Wikipedia.org/Wiki/Robindernath, Tagore.

385. http:/www.cnn.com/Interactive/2014/12/shared death, "Beyond Good-Bye," July 2014.

386. Carroll, Bret E. *Spiritualism in Antebellum America*. Religion in North America. Bloomington: Indiana University Press, 248.

387. Braude, Ann. "Radical Spirits: Spiritualism and Women's Rights in Nineteenth-Century America." 2nd Edition. Indiana University Press (2001), 296.

388. Wong, 2009. http://en Wikipedia.org/wiki/Spirituality.

389. *Gavin Flood Brill's Encyclopedia of Hinduism*, edited by Knut Jacobsen 11 (2011). See article on "Wisdom and Knowledge," 881–884.

390. https://www.Lionesroar.com/

Christof-Koch-unites-buddhism-neuroscience-nature-mind. Sam Uttleafair, January 8, 2017, 2.

391. King, Richard. *Indian Philosophy: An Introduction to Hindu and Buddhist Thoughts.* Edinburg University Press, 1999, 69–71.

392. Macleod, Melvin. "Are You Spiritual but Not Religious? Ten Reasons Why Buddhism Will Enrich Your Path." http://www.Lionsroar.com. Accessed January 25, 2017.

393. Buck, Harleah, G.MSN, RN. *Spirituality: Concept Analysis and Model Development.* Lippincott Williams & Wilkin Inc., 2006.

394. Elkin, D. N. *Spiritual Orientation Inventory.* 1988. Available from D. N. Elkin S., PhD, Pepperdine University Center. Published by Smith, Dorothy Woods. January 1, 1994.

395. Roger, M.E. *An Introduction to the Theoretical Basis of Nursing.* Philadelphia: F. A. Davis, 1997.

396. C. J. W. "Spirituality and Personal Maturity." In *Clinical Book of Pastoral Counseling,* edited by R. J. Wickers, R. D. Parson, and D. Capps. Volume 1. Expanded edition. 1993. Mahwah, NJ: Panlist Press, 1993, 37–57.

397. Swami Nityaswarupananda, Swami Vivekananda, School of World Civilization. New Delhi: Ramakrishna Mission, 1967, 25.

398. Joglekar, D.G. *Science and the Spirituality.* Global Religion Vision, Vol. 1 (2001), 111.

399. Otterloo, 2012, 23.

400. Heelas, Paul (ed). *Spirituality in the Modern World within Religious Traditions and Beyond.* Rutledge, 2012.

401. Dalai Lama. *Ethics for the New Millennium.* New York: River Head Books, 1999.

402. Khan, Moosa Murad. Understanding Suicide Bombing through Suicide Research: The Case of Pakistan. *Psychiatric Annals,* 47, no.3 (2017): 145–149.

403. Harris, Sam. *A Guide to Spirituality without Religion.* Simon & Schuster, 2014, 43–49.

404. Daum, Kevin. *The Power of Self-Reflection.* http:// www.Inc.com/ Kevin-daum-/The-power-of-self-reflection.html. Accessed November 21, 2014.

405. Sheldrake, Philip. *A Brief History of Spirituality.* Wiley Blackwell, 2007, 1–2.

406. Burkhardt, Margaret A., and Mary Gail Negai-Jacobson. *Spirituality: Living Our Connectedness.* Delmar Cengage Learning, 14.

407. Cousens, Gabriel, M.D. *Spiritual Nutrition.* Berkeley, CA: North Atlantic Books, 2005, 124–125.

408. Tolle, Eckhart. *The Power of Now.* Namaste Publishing and New World Library, 1999, 147.

409. Chopra, Deepak. *Unlocking the Hidden Dimensions of Your Life.* New York: Three Rivers Press, 2004, 8–10.

410. Feldman, Avi. *The Value of Selflessness.* http://www.meaningfyllife.com/The value-of-selflessness/.

411. Alcoholics Anonymous, World Service Inc. New York, 1991, 564–570.

412. Nicoll, Maurice. *Psychological Commentaries on the Teaching of Gurdjieff at Ouspensky.* Boston and London: Shambla, 1985, p. 142–44.

413. Harding, C.M., and J. H. Zahniser. "Empirical Correction of Seven Myths about Schizophrenia with Medication for Treatment." *Acta Psychiatrica Scandinavica* 90 (1994): 146–149.

414. Koening, H. G., M. E. McCollough, and D. B. Larson. *Handbook of Religion and Health.* New York: Oxford University Press, 2001.

415. Krov, G., R. Kemp, K. Kirov, and A. S. David. "Religion Faith after Psychotic Illness. *Psychopathology* 31 (1998): 234–245.

416. Mistree, K.P. *Zoroastrianism: An Ethic Perspective.* Mumbai: Zoroastrian Studies, 1998.

417. Maqsood, P.W. *Living Islam.* India: Good Word Books, 1998.

418. Haneef, S. *What Everyone Should Know about Islam.* Delhi: Adam Publishing and Distributors, 1994.

419. Novroji, D.M. *The Moral and Ethical Teachings of Zarathustra.* The University of Bombay, 1928.

420. Singh, I.J. *Philosophy of Guru Nank: A Comparative Study.* New Delhi: Ranjit Publishing House, 1997.

421. James, W. *Principles of Psychology.* New York: Holt, 1890.

422. Dawkins, R. (1989) The selfish genes, Oxford: Oxford University Press, 1989.

423. Stuss, D.T. "Self-Awareness and the Frontal Lobe: A Neurophysiological Perspective." In *The Self-Interdisciplinary Approach,* edited by J. Strauss and G. R. Goethals. New York: W. W. Norton, 1991.

424. Damasio, A.R. *The Feelings of What Happens in the Making of the Consciousness.* New York: Harcourt Brace, 1999.

425. Marwaha, B. Sonali. *Colors of Truth: Religion and Emotions.* New Delhi: Concept Publishing Company, 2006.

426. Bach,George,andDeutch,Ronald,Pairing.New York;Avon Book,1970 in (Leo F. BuscagliaPh,D. Loving eachother.The challenge of Human Relationship,Fawacett Columbine New York 1984,p 196.

Printed in the United States
By Bookmasters